The Institute of British Geographers
Special Publications Series

21   The Changing Face of Cities

The Institute of British Geographers
Special Publications Series

EDITORIAL BOARD

Dr M.J. Clark (Secretary)
University of Southampton

Dr R. Flowerdew
University of Lancaster

Dr M. Williams
University of Oxford

Professor N. Wrigley
University of Wales Institute of Science and Technology

18 Rivers: Environment, Process and Form
    Edited by Keith Richards

19 Technical Change and Industrial Policy
    Edited by Keith Chapman and Graham Humphrys

20 Sea-Level Changes
    Edited by Michael J. Tooley and Ian Shennan

21 The Changing Face of Cities: A Study of Development Cycles and Urban Form
    J. W. R. Whitehand

In preparation

Salt Marshes and Coastal Wetlands
Edited by D. R. Stoddart

Wetlands and Wetland Management
Edited by M. Williams

Demographic Patterns in the Past
Edited by R. Smith

Teaching Geography in Higher Education
Alan Jenkins, John R. Gold, Roger Lee, Janice Monk, Judith Riley, Ifan Shepherd, David Unwin

For a complete list see p. 190

The Changing Face of Cities
A Study of Development Cycles and Urban Form

J. W. R. Whitehand

Basil Blackwell

Copyright © Institute of British Geographers 1987

First published 1987

Basil Blackwell Ltd
108 Cowley Road, Oxford, OX4 1JF, UK

Basil Blackwell Inc.
432 Park Avenue South, Suite 1503
New York, NY 10016, USA

All rights reserved. Except for the quotation of short passages for the purposes of criticism and review, no part of this publication may be reproduced, stored in a retrieval system, or transmitted, in any form or by any means, electronic, mechanical, photocopying, recording or otherwise, without the prior permission of the publisher.

Except in the United States of America, this book is sold subject to the condition that it shall not, by way of trade or otherwise, be lent, re-sold, hired out, or otherwise circulated without the publisher's prior consent in any form of binding or cover other than that in which it is published and without a similar condition including this condition being imposed on the subsequent purchaser.

British Library Cataloguing in Publication Data
Whitehand, J.W.R.
   The changing face of cities: a study of
   development cycles and urban form. —
   (The Institute of British Geographers
   special publications series; 21).
   1. City planning
   I. Title
   711'.4   HT166
ISBN 0–631–15459–0

Library of Congress Cataloging in Publication Data
Whitehand, J.W.R.
   The changing face of cities.
   (Special publications series; 21)
   Includes bibliographical references and index.
   1. Cities and towns – Growth. 2. Land use, Urban.
3. City planning. I. Title. II. Series: Special
publications series (Institute of British Geographers);
21.
HT371.W46   1987   307.1'4   87–6588
ISBN 0–631–15459–0

Typeset in 11 on 13 pt Plantin
by OPUS, Oxford
Printed in Great Britain by Page Bros (Norwich) Ltd

To my mother
and to the memory
of my father

Contents

Preface	ix
1 Background to urban morphology	**1**
Justification for urban morphology	2
Approaches to urban morphology	2
The present approach	9
2 Fluctuations in urban development	**11**
Explanations for building cycles	12
Fluctuations in land-use composition	16
Explanations for the changing composition of urban development	26
3 Land values and land use	**30**
Theories of the land market	30
Empirical patterns of land values	33
Empirical patterns of land use	34
Land values and the course of urban development	36
A theory of urban development	39
The model tested	45
Intensity of development	51
Complications to the model	59
4 Innovation and planning	**60**
Innovation and constructional activity	61
Innovation, land use and land value	66
Planning	70
Innovation adoption and economic explanations	74

5	Fringe belts	76
	Fringe-belt formation	78
	Fringe-belt modification	83
	Other developments of the fringe-belt concept	93
6	Residential growth and change	95
	Cycles and residential development	95
	Landownership and residential development	99
	Internal change	104
	Inter-urban and international variations	107
7	Commercial cores	112
	Redevelopment	113
	A case study	115
	Amount and character of secular change	127
	Fluctuations	130
	Innovations	132
	Inter-urban variations	133
8	Conclusion	138
	The perspective	138
	Main findings	140
	Managing change	144
Notes		148
Bibliography		169
Index		184
Related titles: list of IBG Special Publications		190

Preface

In 1981 the Institute of British Geographers brought out a Special Publication entitled *The Urban Landscape: historical development and management*. In it attention was confined to the work of M. R. G. Conzen, the doyen of British urban morphologists. It was apparent by the end of the 1970s, when that volume was conceived, that urban morphology was undergoing a minor renaissance that derived an important part of its inspiration from Conzen's work. However, although the number of papers being published was rising and various advances were being made, there remained the need to synthesize this new work in monograph form. In the mid-1980s, after a further half-decade of active research, it is clear that the task of integrating the new findings far exceeds the capacity of a single volume. This volume therefore concentrates largely on one aspect that has been near the forefront of research over the past 15 years, the cyclical perspective on the changing form of cities. A further prominent concern, the roles of the agents responsible for urban landscape change, will be the subject of another volume.

The present volume draws on the contents of a number of papers that I have published in journals and collections of essays. Bibliographic references to these are provided in footnotes, but I should like to thank the following for permission to reproduce and adapt copyright material: the Editor, *Transactions of the Institute of British Geographers* for figures 3.7–3.13 (from *Transactions*, 56 (1972), pp. 39–55); the Editor, *Area* for figures 5.5–5.9 (from *Area*, 4 (1972), pp. 215–22); the Editor, *Journal of Historical Geography* and Academic Press for figures 3.15–3.21 and tables 3.1–3.2 (from the *Journal*, 1 (1975), pp. 211–24); the Editor, *Geografiska Annaler* Series B for figures 7.1–7.5 and tables 7.1–7.2 (from *Geografiska Annaler* 60B (1978) pp. 79–96); the Editor, *Erdkunde* for figures 2.5–2.13 (from *Erdkunde*, 35 (1981), pp. 129–40); John Wiley &

x *Preface*

Sons Ltd for figure 5.3 (from *Suburban Growth*, edited by J. H. Johnson, 1974, pp. 31–52); and Dr M. Pacione and Croom Helm Ltd for figure 1.1 (from *Historical Geography: progress and prospect*, edited by M. Pacione, 1987). I should also like to thank Professor Michael P. Conzen for permission to reproduce as figure 5.4 a diagram from his unpublished paper presented to the 19th Annual Meeting of the Association of American Geographers, West Lakes Division, 1968.

During the years of research of which this volume is a product I have accumulated a debt of gratitude to far more people than it would be practicable to acknowledge here. I am particularly indebted to fellow members of the Urban Morphology Research Group at the University of Birmingham. Four of them – Dr T. R. Slater, Dr P. J. Larkham, Dr M. Freeman and Mr N. D. Pompa – read and commented on a draft of the manuscript. A fifth, Mrs S. M. Whitehand, assisted in innumerable ways during the course of the research upon which it was based. Professor M. R. G. Conzen provided a major intellectual stimulus, particularly in the formative stages of the research, Mr R. G. Ford has been a tireless adviser on knotty problems, and Mr R. C. Swift has ensured the smooth running of a variety of technical services. The illustrations were prepared for publication by Mr T. G. Grogan and Mrs J. L. Dowling, the photography was by Mr G. P. Dowling, and the word processing was shared by Miss L. E. Ford, Miss Z. Wills and Mrs M. Smith. Mr E. Sullivan, Mrs M. S. Sullivan and Miss C. M. Whitehand helped in various ways, especially in the final stages of preparing the manuscript. Last, but not least, I should like to acknowledge the financial support of the Economic and Social Research Council (formerly the Social Science Research Council), which provided grants and/or studentships to members of the Urban Morphology Research Group covering much of the period of some 15 or more years during which the bulk of the research described here was undertaken.

J. W. R. Whitehand
University of Birmingham

1
Background to urban morphology

As an organized body of knowledge, urban morphology has existed for nearly a century. It was an integral part of urban geography from the inception of that subject,[1] and in the German-speaking countries it has remained an important aspect.[2] In the English-speaking world urban morphology, like urban geography, has a shorter history, dating essentially from the inter-war years. Furthermore, outside central Europe its position has been peripheral to the mainstream of geography for long periods, especially in the United States. This is reflected in the rarity of large-scale integrating studies, that by Vance being one of the few in the English language.[3]

Between the mid-1960s and the mid-1970s urban morphology appeared only rarely on the geographical research agenda of English-speaking countries. This reflected first a preoccupation with the analysis of quantitative data, which were generally hard to come by in urban morphology, secondly a shift of attention to sociological and political questions, and thirdly an increased concern with scales of analysis at which the structure of individual settlements was less important. In all these preoccupations an element of 'placelessness' was apparent. Geographers were losing contact with their roots and frequently contributing as much to other disciplines as to their own. A reaction to this tendency is now evident.[4] At such a time urban morphologists, concerned as they are above all with the character of places as revealed in the landscape, should put their house in order. This volume is an attempt to do this.

We begin in this chapter by considering first the economic, social and cultural importance of the physical form of cities, secondly by outlining different approaches that have been adopted in urban morphology, giving special attention to the German morphogenetic tradition, and thirdly by introducing the approach that will be developed in this volume.

JUSTIFICATION FOR URBAN MORPHOLOGY

Urban areas are the environment of the large majority of the population of economically advanced countries. Production and maintenance of the physical fabric of that environment, especially the buildings, roads and services, absorbs a large amount of the wealth of the Western world.[5] In most Western countries housebuilding alone absorbs some 20–5 per cent of gross fixed investment.[6] It also has major ramifications for other aspects of the economy. But the importance of the physical form of towns and cities derives at least as much from its social and cultural significance as from its economic role. This relates to a large degree to the role that the physical fabric performs as the visually dominant part of the urban environment, the urban landscape, or townscape.

M. R. G. Conzen draws attention to three aspects of the importance of the physical fabric viewed as townscape.[7] First, it has practical utility at the most basic level in providing orientation: our mental map and therefore the efficiency with which we function spatially is dependent on our recognition of the identity of localities. Secondly, it has intellectual value by helping both individual and society to orientate in time: a townscape, especially a well-established one, provides a strong visual experience of the history of an area, helping the individual to place himself within a wider evolving society, stimulating historical comparison and thus providing a more informed basis for decision making. Thirdly, the townscape has aesthetic value: for example, in the visual impact of, and orientation provided by, dominant features, such as churches and castles, and in the stimulus to the imagination provided by variations in street width and orientation. These three attributes are interrelated, and emotional and aesthetic experiences are particularly tightly entwined with, though not necessarily dependent on, appreciation of historical and geographical significance. As far as the creation and maintenance of townscapes are concerned, social and cultural aspects are rarely independent of economic factors. Nevertheless, the approaches that researchers have adopted have varied widely in the attention that has been paid to these various aspects.

APPROACHES TO URBAN MORPHOLOGY

If attention is confined to urban morphology within the discipline of geography, as distinct from other fields, such as urban design,[8] the majority of research has come from three regions of the world – central

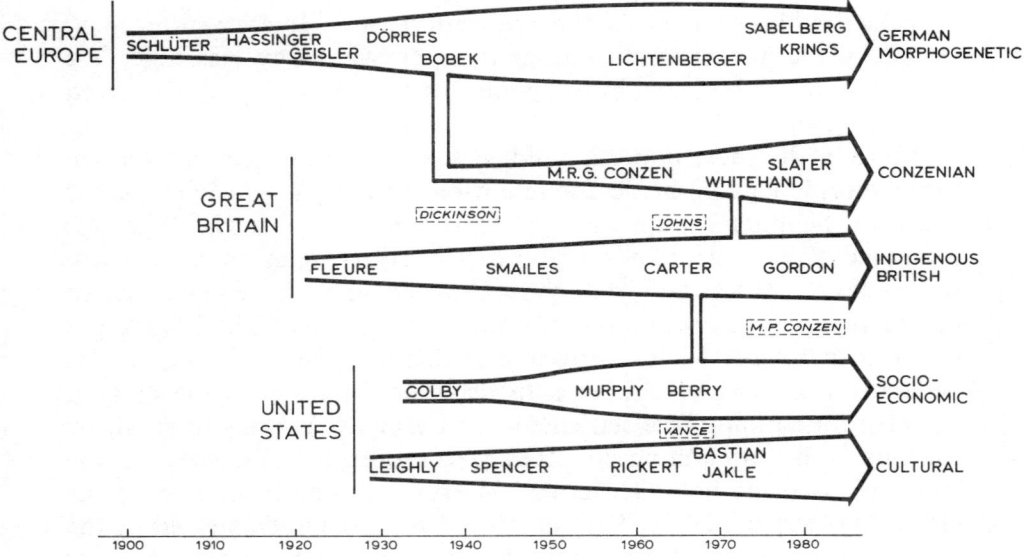

Figure 1.1 Major traditions in urban morphology: a schematic genealogy, showing a sample of authors

Europe (the home of the German morphogenetic tradition), Great Britain, and North America (principally the United States). The amount of work from outside these areas, though by no means negligible in absolute terms, is comparatively small. In France, despite the early work of Blanchard,[9] the long tradition of research on the form of rural settlements, and the importance of urban geography as a whole, urban morphology is a relatively minor interest.[10]

The central European tradition must take pride of place in any consideration of the development of the major lines of thought. It is not only important in itself but has given rise to a separate line of development in Britain (figure 1.1). Of the three main geographical areas, central Europe is the only one in which research has had sufficient unity for it to be appropriate to speak of a single 'school'. It is possible to trace an essentially unbroken lineage back at least to the end of the nineteenth century. At that time Schlüter postulated a morphology of the cultural landscape as the counterpart in cultural geography of the rapidly developing field of geomorphology.[11] Within urban geography he regarded the physical forms and appearance of the town, the 'urban landscape' (*Stadtlandschaft*), as the main object of research. The marked morphological emphasis that Schlüter imparted to human geography in general and urban geography in particular became increasingly evident over the first three decades of the twentieth century. It was reinforced by studies of the historic architectural styles of Vienna by Hassinger,[12] a type of work which later, in the publications of Schaefer, was referred to as 'art geography'.[13]

Probably the most important single source of influence on German urban morphology in the decade following the First World War was the work of Schlüter's pupil Geisler. His work on Danzig (Gdańsk) examined aspects of urban form in much greater detail than had been done before.[14] It was followed by his *Die deutsche Stadt*, which included comprehensive classifications of the sites, town plans and building types of German towns.[15] This proved particularly influential, but it also generated controversy, which was fuelled four years later by the study of the plan formation of the settlements of Germany, urban and rural, by Martiny.[16] By attempting to produce comprehensive surveys of the whole of Germany both Geisler and Martiny exposed themselves to the criticism of superficiality. They allowed themselves to be pushed by the enormous scope of their projects into essentially morphographic classification, often relying on the depiction of settlement plans on topographical maps, without uncovering the origins and development of the plans they were describing. This, combined with a failure to use large-scale topographical plans, which are essential for the study of plot patterns, led to the overlooking of the period compositeness of town plans. Genetically distinct parts of plans became confused. Profuse nomenclatures were produced that were not adequately grounded in the historical development of settlements.

One reason for this deficiency was the fact that research by architects on the history of town planning and research by urban historians was little known to German-speaking urban geographers at the time. A second reason was the fact that urban geographers themselves had not yet produced a sufficiently coherent body of knowledge about the social and economic organization of towns to make possible a more penetrating urban morphology.

Major advances came in the middle inter-war years as a result of two developments. The first was the recognition by urban geographers of the work of urban historians, such as Meier and Rörig, and of architects who were interested in the history of town planning, such as Klaiber and Siedler.[17] The second development was the wider recognition of the illogicality of concentrating attention on forms in the urban landscape at the expense of the forces creating them. This was partly the result of the work of Bobek,[18] and a little later of Christaller.[19] Their work ultimately had the effect of shifting the focus of attention in German urban geography from form to function. Within urban morphology the importance of relating forms to their socio-economic context and historical development became widely acknowledged. For example, in his study of eight medieval towns in a monograph published in 1941, Scharlau refers to the relevant literature in urban history, analyses the genesis of town plans, and uses cadastral plans showing streets, plots and the block-plans of buildings.[20]

Post-war urban morphology in central Europe is a direct descendant of the German morphogenetic tradition of the inter-war years. One key feature is the integrated treatment of individual cities – less frequently several cities or parts of cities – including the interweaving of non-morphological aspects. Another key feature is the extensive use of graphical and cartographical representations of facts and concepts. Such work is seen at its best in two major studies of Vienna, one by Bobek and Lichtenberger, and the other by Lichtenberger.[21]

This type of morphological analysis has continued in central Europe in the 1980s, for example, in the work of Krings and Sabelberg.[22] But the German morphogenetic tradition is also important for a branch that developed from it in the 1930s. This branch took root in Britain and its development in the post-war period has been such that it deserves consideration in its own right.

The scholar responsible for this offshoot in Britain was M. R. G. Conzen (figure 1.1). A student in the Geographical Institute in the University of Berlin during the late 1920s and early 1930s, Conzen was influenced by such scholars as Louis, who later became internationally renowned as a geomorphologist, and Bobek. Emigrating to Britain in 1933, he worked first as a town planner, before returning to geography. This period in planning had a long-term influence, stimulating an attempt to devise a framework for the organization of planning science[23] and much later revealing itself in attempts to construct a theory of townscape management. But Conzen's main contributions were to urban morphogenetics rather than town planning. In 1949 he published, in association with a paper on settlements in north-east England, a map of settlement types over the whole of the region, showing symbolically the complete range of urban and rural settlement forms.[24] In conception and style this map shows unambiguously the influence of the German morphogenetic tradition. This is also true of his contribution to *A Survey of Whitby*, published in 1958.[25] This was not only a unique record of the building types and land and building utilization of a whole town but a demonstration of how a detailed elucidation of a town's physical development can form the basis for conservation of the urban landscape.

Conzen's major work and arguably still the most important single contribution to urban morphology in the English language was *Alnwick, Northumberland: a study in town-plan analysis*, first published in 1960.[26] The achievements of this study can be summarized under five heads: first, the development of a framework of principles for urban morphology; secondly, the adoption for the first time in the geographical literature in the English language of a thoroughgoing evolutionary approach; thirdly, the recognition of individual plots as being the fundamental units of analysis; fourthly, the use of detailed cartographical analysis, employing large-scale plans in conjunction with field survey and documentary evidence; and fifthly, the conceptualization of developments in the townscape. Conzen also recognized the now widely accepted threefold division of the townscape into town plan, building forms and land use. The town plan was itself subdivided for analytical purposes into streets and their arrangement in a street system, plots and their aggregation in street-blocks, and buildings, or more precisely their block-plans.

In discussing his approach in the Alnwick study Conzen wrote: 'An evolutionary approach, tracing existing forms back to the underlying formative processes and interpreting them accordingly, would seem to provide the rational method of analysis.'[27] The 'retrogressive' method of working back from present-day forms was rejected because a proper understanding of processes cannot be attained from the analysis of relics. This is so even in the case of the town plan, which produces a more complete collection of residual features than the building fabric or the land-use pattern. Those parts of the townscape that have been removed are as important to a theory of townscape development as those that have survived. Thus the morphographic approach of classifying present-day survivals was rejected, although for the urban archaeologist these may be all that is available. Instead evolutionary patterns were assembled by utilizing such historical sources as rentals, building plans submitted in connection with applications to build, and large-scale printed and manuscript plans, in association with detailed plot-by-plot and building-by-building field surveys that included the recording of detailed topographical information on large-scale Ordnance Survey plans. The continuation of this approach is clearly seen in the town-plan analyses of Slater.[28]

Conzen's conceptualizations of aspects of the development of the town plan have a variety of derivations. Occasionally a concept, or a term used to describe it, can be related fairly directly to earlier German studies. This is the case with the term 'urban fallow', used to describe the temporary urban wasteland caused by socio-economic changes leading to building clearance. This was derived from Hartke's *Sozialbrache* or social fallow, a term applied, by analogy to the fallow in agricultural rotation, to rural field or vineyard land lying partly or wholly waste while the owner works elsewhere.[29] But the burgage cycle, relating to the progressive building over of the principal plots within medieval towns and their ultimate clearance prior to redevelopment, was a new concept. Nevertheless, such a developmental concept is consistent with the German research tradition in which Conzen grew up, and it is a little paradoxical that Möller, a German urban morphologist,[30] should in her review of *Alnwick*[31] see in the use of the word 'cycle' a suggestion of recurrence and therefore the influence of a supposedly 'simplifying biologistic approach characteristic of Anglo-Saxon settlement geography'. Conzen, well aware of the non-recurrence of the burgage cycle, though he envisaged the possibility of many redevelopment cycles, employed the word 'cycle' in the more general sense of 'a round, course or period through which anything runs to its completion'.[32]

Conzen's work has led to the development of a Conzenian school in Britain.[33] But there is also an essentially indigenous strand in British urban morphology (figure 1.1). This derived an important part of its initial impetus from Fleure, who in the early 1920s provided perceptive, descriptive generalizations about the form of European towns.[34] Most of the subsequent work in this tradition has been undertaken since the Second World War. It has been influenced by the writing of Smailes.[35] He emphasized the characterization of present townscapes in broad terms, recommending rapid reconnaissance surveys rather than building-by-building surveys. History was important for what it contributed to the present rather than in its own right. Eloquently espoused by Smailes, this perspective co-existed with the detailed developmental analyses undertaken by Conzen during much of the 1950s and 1960s. It was succeeded briefly at the end of the 1960s and in the first half of the 1970s by quantitative, mainly morphographic, analyses, such as those of Davies and Johnston,[36] in which historical geography remained subordinate or absent. Carter was almost alone among British-born urban geographers at this time in giving a major place to historical geography in its own right.[37]

Both the indigenous strand within British urban morphology and the Conzenian school were subjected to influence from America during the 1960s and 1970s. American urban morphology had itself been characterized by two distinctive strands (figure 1.1), at least from the middle inter-war years: a cultural geography strand having much in common with rural settlement geography and the Berkeley school,[38] and a somewhat eclectic socio-economic perspective, emphasizing land-use studies.[39] It was the second of these that had by far the greater impact on British urban morphology. Having by the 1950s adopted the concentric zone model of sociologist Burgess[40] and the sector model of land economist Hoyt[41] and created their own multiple-nuclei model,[42] the followers of this branch of American urban geography exported their ideas widely to other English-speaking countries in the 1960s. Their perspective was morphological only in its concern with land-use patterns: town plan and building form were generally treated as land-use containers, if considered at all. Perhaps its most important effect on British urban morphology was to generate interest in the theoretical explanations of neo-classical economics. This was reflected in attempts to explore the relationship between urban-rent theory and the historical development of land-use patterns.[43]

The cultural geography strand in America has always been comparatively weak within urban geography. It has arguably provided the only true urban morphology within America. Starting with Leighly,[44] a line can be traced through the work of Spencer[45] to that of Rickert, Bastian and Jakle.[46] The main concern of this research has been with architectural styles, but links with the long, continuing line of central European research on this aspect have been minimal.

The approaches to urban morphology that have been discussed all reflect to some extent influences received directly or indirectly from outside of geography. Two influences deserve mention for their contextual importance rather than their influence on a specific approach: first, studies, primarily by urban historians, of the historical development of individual towns; and secondly, the resurgence of interest in the 1970s, among a variety of social scientists, in capitalism viewed in terms of the economic interests of different classes in society.

The influence of urban history on geographical urban morphology has not on the whole taken the form of an explicit transfer of ideas and methods. More significant has been the moderating effect that urban history has had on the influence of other disciplines. In their concern with explaining particular events rather than searching for general forces at work, historians of urban development, especially those with a strong interest in the landscape, have acted as a counterbalance to the social scientist's (especially the economist's) concern with theory. While economic theory has mainly influenced urban morphology through its influence on North American urban geography, the influence of urban history has been more direct. Dyos's study of the development of the London suburb of Camberwell in the nineteenth century[47] has been especially important in generating interest in the individuals responsible for particular urban developments. Less widely consulted by geographers, but impressive in their scope and detail, are the volumes produced by the Greater London Council's Survey of London. These document specific parts of London, describing, for example, the internal and external appearance of buildings, the roles of people associated with them, and the events with which they were connected.[48]

By comparison with the general influence of urban history, the second influence is more limited and more recent. Research on the workings of capitalism and, more paritcularly, on the relations between the different types of economic interest involved in the development, use and exchange of property, deserves greater attention from urban morphologists than it has hitherto received. Barras, for example, recognizes four types of capital – commercial, financial, landed and construction – going into the development process.[49] Viewing development in this way has implications for understanding the urban landscape. For example, instead of thinking of a building in terms of the use it performs (for instance as a shop or an office), which is a perspective familiar to urban morphologists, attention is directed to the financial return it provides to the various parties involved in creating, managing and using buildings. Some owners, for example, conceive of buildings primarily as investments, whereas others view them primarily as the containers and symbols of their businesses. This difference of perspective is likely to lead to differences in the design of buildings and the timing of their construction, which an examination of buildings purely in terms of their use is liable to overlook.

THE PRESENT APPROACH

The approach adopted in this volume is to a considerable degree within the Conzenian tradition, but a number of other perspectives are utilized to varying extent. The main departure from Conzen's work is in the way in which explanations are developed. The Conzenian tradition is concerned with conceptualizing developments in the urban landscape in terms of an integrated historical context. The stress is on synthesis. In this volume there is greater concern with analysis and with the specification and testing of relationships underlying urban landscape development. Whereas the roles of economic fluctuations, innovation, and the economics of location are largely implicit in Conzen's work, here they are made more explicit. The incorporation of elements of urban-rent theory introduces ideas from the different intellectual environment of American land economists. The deductive constructs involved are absent, at least in an explicit form, from the urban morphogenetic tradition. Similarly, in articulating the role of economic fluctuations and innovation, considerable use is made of the findings of economic historians, although in relation to ideas about innovation diffusion a theoretical basis essentially indigenous to geography is utilized.

The aim of the ensuing chapters is to piece together, largely by drawing upon more specific studies undertaken since the mid-1960s, the major elements in a theory of urban form. The main empirical flesh on the theoretical skeleton is provided by Western cities. The starting point is an examination of fluctuations in urban development. These fluctuations are related to land-value theory to create a schema of urban growth and internal change in which the creation and modification of elements in the urban landscape is linked to pressures on land over time and space. To this construct ideas about innovation and planning are added. The last half of the book consists principally of an examination of major constituent parts of the urban area – the urban fringe, residential areas and the commercial core – in relation to the theoretical schema. In conclusion, the implications of these relationships and the resulting physical forms are considered in relation to the problem of creating a satisfactory basis for the future management of the urban landscape.

2
Fluctuations in urban development

One of the most notable aspects of urban development is its uneven pace. Largely because of its economic implications, this aroused interests during the inter-war years, mainly in the United States.[1] Subsequently there has been a great deal of research on both sides of the Atlantic on fluctuations in economic activity, especially their cyclical character. Time series, both national and local, have been compiled for many different aspects of economies, including those bearing directly on the physical form of urban development. Most attention has been devoted to the nature, timing and explanation of cycles, rather than their implications for the physical character of urban areas. However, for the urban morphologist a great deal of interest attaches to the potential insights they offer into how urban landscapes have developed.

The most readily available single measure of the pace of development is the changing rate of constructional activity. Time series of this activity have been compiled at varying scales and for different purposes. Both short- and long-term fluctuations are evident as far back as records exist. The different measures of constructional activity that have been used – for example, building permits, brick consumption, floor space, and building value – make exact temporal and spatial comparisons difficult. However, the great magnitude of the fluctuations, especially long-term oscillations with a wavelength of some 15 to 20 years, is beyond question. Time series for Stockholm, Montreal and Paris (figure 2.1), England and Wales (figure 2.2), and the United States and Great Britain (figure 2.3) demonstrate this point at different scales over a variety of time spans during the last 200 years. Gottlieb provides many other examples.[2]

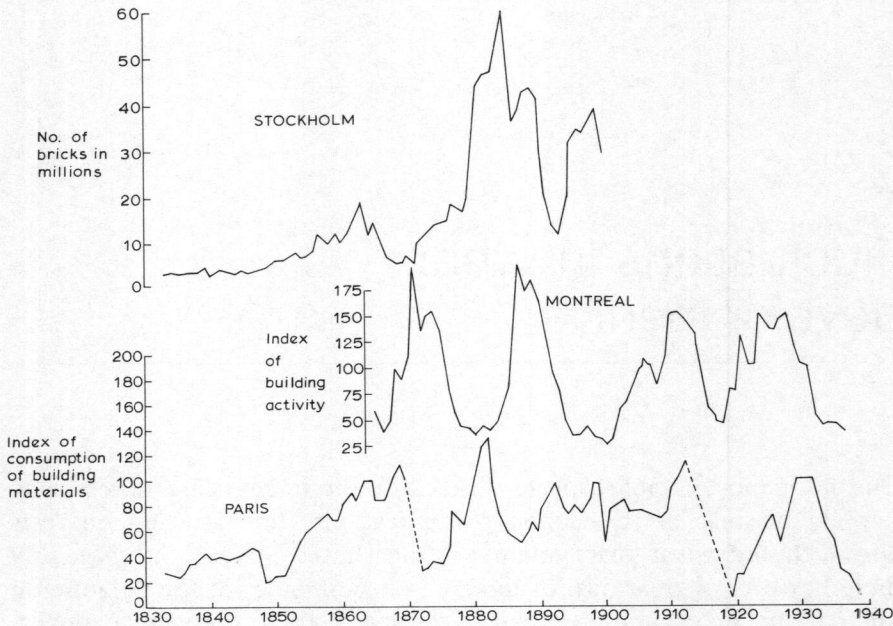

Figure 2.1 Building activity in Stockholm, Montreal and Paris
Sources: Stockholm – Hammarström, 1979, fig. 5. Montreal – Warren and Pearson, 1937, fig. 37. Paris – Flaus, 1949, p. 187.

EXPLANATIONS FOR BUILDING CYCLES

Much ink has been spilled on the cyclical nature of these and numerous other, mainly economic, time series. Although our principal concern is with the repercussions of these fluctuations in the urban landscape, it is desirable to consider briefly the main explanations for them that have been advanced. Broadly speaking, as far as the nineteenth century is concerned there are two schools of thought: one stressing interaction between New World and Old World, the other giving most attention to intra-national factors.

First, there are explanations that stress the significance of the undoubted fact that cycles in the New World, most importantly in the United States, were to a considerable extent the inverse of those in Great Britain. According to Thomas, building cycles, in the Anglo-Saxon world at least, were mainly a reflection of the interaction between a

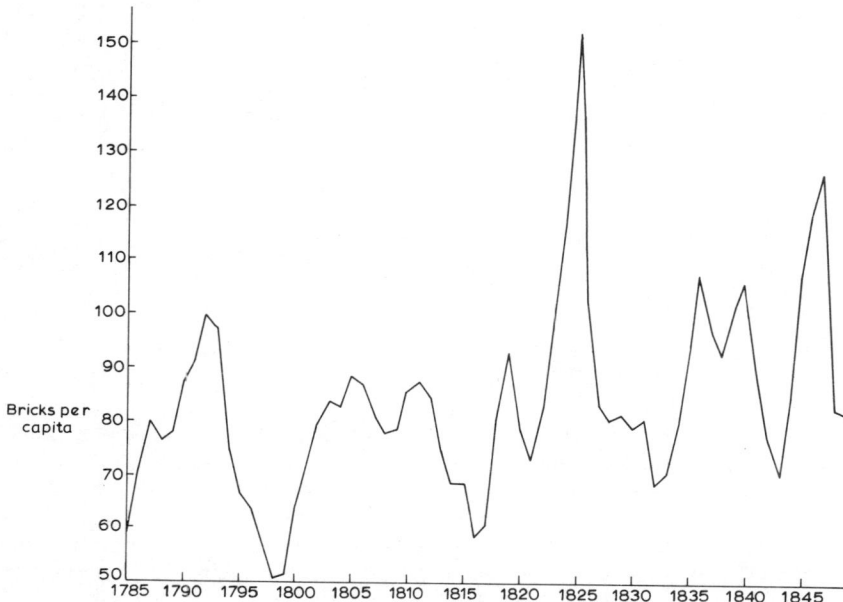

Figure 2.2 Bricks produced per capita in England and Wales, 1785–1849
Source: Warren and Pearson, 1937, fig. 26.

highly industrialized creditor country and underdeveloped debtor countries that were undergoing a process of new settlement.[3] Rapid industrialization in America and other countries of new settlement was associated with shifts of capital and migrants from Europe. This was the boom phase of the migration-lending cycle for New World debtor countries as they developed their infrastructure. This limited the capacity for Great Britain to have her own upsurge in capital formation. However, eventually the production of food and raw materials, made possible by the investment boom in the New World, produced a return flow of imports into Europe and a resurgence of capital formation in the home country. A fresh wave of investment in the New World, as further settlement took place, caused a repetition of the sequence.

Secondly, there is the view that the important influences were domestic rather than international. Abramovitz, for example, regards long-term fluctuations in unemployment within the United States as being crucial.[4] Habakkuk concludes that in Great Britain long swings in housebuilding were essentially a reflection of trade cycles,[5] and Saul argues that the fate of the building industry in Great Britain was largely

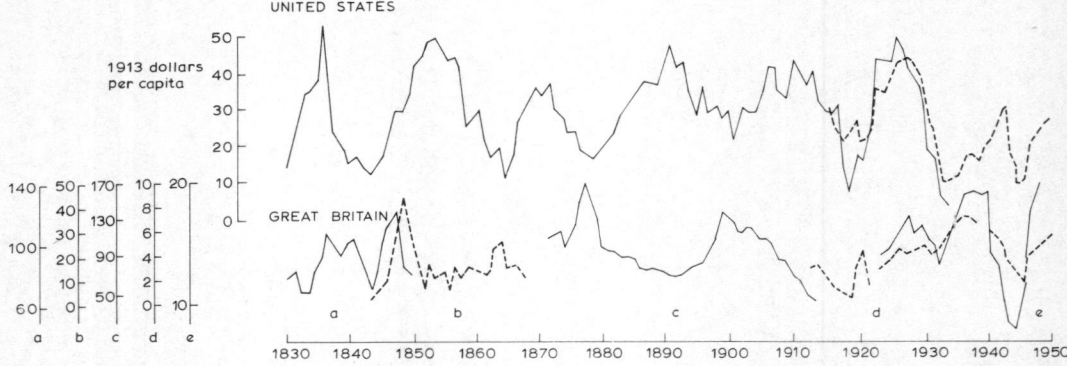

Figure 2.3 Building activity per capita in the United States and Great Britain. British building scales: (a) bricks taxed per capita in England and Wales, 1830–49; (b) railway miles opened per million of population in the United Kingdom, 1843–68; (c) building per capita in Great Britain (Lewis's weighted index), 1870–1913; (d) volume of building per capita in Great Britain based on estimated cost of plans approved and Board of Trade index, 1911–50; (e) building employment per 1000 of population in the United Kingdom, 1923–47. *Source*: Thomas, 1973, fig. 37.

determined internally by the state of demand and the nature of the operation of the trade itself.[6]

Whatever the relative weights to be attached to intra-national and international factors, it would clearly be wrong to envisage whole countries as homogeneous in terms of the timing and amplitude of building fluctuations. Although in both the United States and Great Britain there was a tendency for cycles in different cities approximately to correlate, some cities were ahead of the national cycle and others were behind it. Some places were sufficiently out of step to have an inverse relation to the national cycle, at least over several decades. The towns of the South Wales coalfield from the 1890s to the First World War are an example (figure 2.4). The explanation in this instance would appear to be that at the time the prosperity of the South Wales coal industry was more strongly connected with the health of export industries and the development of certain overseas economies than with demand within Great Britain. These export industries and overseas economies were booming during periods of falling construction at home.[7] But it was not only a matter of regions differing; towns within the same region sometimes differed. In the Lancashire cotton manufacturing area in the early 1880s the towns that first changed to mule yarns were relatively

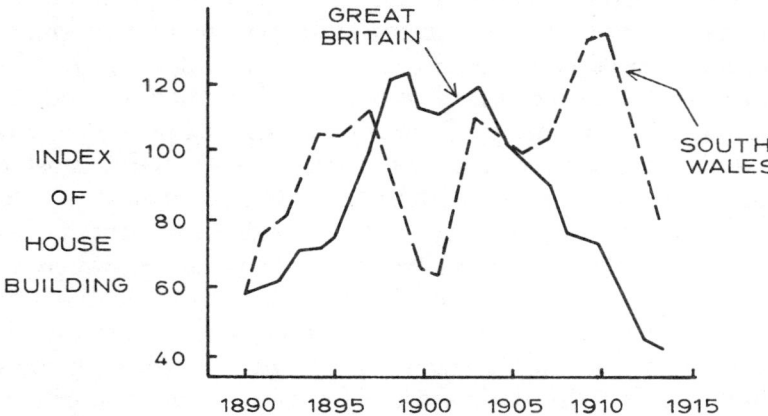

Figure 2.4 Housebuilding activity in Great Britain and the South Wales coalfield, 1890–1913
Source: Lewis, 1965, p. 317.

prosperous compared with those still dependent on the old-fashioned throstle yarns.[8] Thus housebuilding was booming in Oldham while it was at a low level in nearby Rochdale.[9] One of the most notable examples of a major city being out of phase with its national building cycle is London between the 1850s and the 1890s. Since London has no dominant industry to whose fortunes fluctuations in building can be ascribed, other explanations must apply. One of these is transport development,[10] a factor that will be considered in a wider context in chapter 4.

As far as more recent long swings in building are concerned, at least some of the forces at work have changed. Thomas suggests that events since the Second World War can be regarded as the nineteenth-century story in reverse, with the United States becoming the principal source of finance, though not, of course, of migrants.[11] Such changes make it inappropriate to search for a theory of 'the building cycle'. We can, nevertheless, with advantage view the nineteenth and twentieth centuries, and perhaps earlier periods, in terms of Lewis's theory of building cycles in the plural. In this theory alternative possibilities are allowed to operate. It is in some ways an eclectic perspective, incorporating not only elements of the explanations just considered, but other elements too.[12]

Lewis's theory is concerned with housebuilding, quantitatively the most important sort of building activity in the long term. In it population and credit are assigned key roles. In simplified terms, an increase in population (caused by a rise in birth rate and/or a change in the balance of immigration and emigration) increases the demand for housing, which is more likely to become effective if associated with a 'shock' of some kind that raises real incomes at a time when credit is plentiful. The ensuing boom in building, partly because of the long period of gestation in the building industry, tends to continue even when most other economic activities undergo a short-term decline; indeed, a buoyant building industry may, under certain conditions, benefit from a redirection of investment associated with a downturn elsewhere in the economy.[13] Thus a boom in housebuilding frequently has the momentum to bridge the slump between two general business booms, leading in the long term to only a moderate positive correlation between housebuilding and the trade cycle. However, a severe credit crisis, brought on partly by the strain that building imposes on the credit situation, has an impact on incomes that greatly reduces the prospect of letting or selling new houses. Furthermore, in such difficult times there is likely to be increased emigration, which makes the excess of houses over effective demand more marked. Even if there is no credit crisis, a downturn in building eventually occurs owing to the accumulation of a stock of houses well in excess of effective demand. The decline in housebuilding that follows has an effect on employment, incomes and population as birth and marriage rates fall and emigration increases. 'Economic cycles impinge, once again, on population cycles, which in turn affect the economy.'[14]

FLUCTUATIONS IN LAND-USE COMPOSITION

Most studies of building cycles have been concerned either with aggregate building or, more commonly, with housebuilding, which often comprises more than one-half of the total.[15] These studies enable inferences to be drawn about the pace of urban development at different scales. For an understanding of the composition of the landscape, however, it is essential to disaggregate building into various categories and also to consider the various types of urban land use in which building is either not involved or plays a minor role. This presents considerable problems of data compilation and comparability. Data on some types of development are broadly comparable to those already considered, comprising amounts of construction measured by value or by number of buildings/dwellings. Others consist of number of developments (parks, golf courses, and so on) and land transactions. Rarely is information available in areal measures. Nevertheless, by recourse to a variety of sources it is possible to compile data for spans of time of varying lengths between the mid nineteenth and mid twentieth centuries that permit generalizations to be made about the composition of both building activity and other types of urban development.

Most Western countries gather information from which it is possible in principle to assemble data on various types of building activity, at least from the end of the nineteenth century. The most important sources of this information are building applications submitted to local authorities for the purposes of building regulation. These vary widely in the information they provide, the extent of their survival, and the degree to which attempts have been made to organize records and compile different types of data. Information is presented here at the national scale for the United States, Great Britain, Australia and Italy, and at the city scale for a selection of British cities: a selection determined largely by the accessibility of published data.[16]

Data at the national scale for the United States, the United Kingdom and Australia, although in each case assembled on a different basis, all suggest that non-residential construction has been subject to less pronounced fluctuations than residential construction.[17] This is reflected in considerable variations over time in the relative importance of non-residential and residential construction (figure 2.5). Viewed in terms of cycles in housebuilding, the general pattern in all three countries is for the relative amounts of non-residential building to be small during housebuilding booms and large during housebuilding slumps. For example, in the United States non-residential building (excluding public works and utilities) comprised only 35 per cent of all new floor space created in the high housebuilding years of 1939 and 1959 but 66 per cent and 72 per cent in the slump years of 1920 and 1945.[18]

If non-residential construction is disaggregated, it is apparent that the fluctuations were of greater magnitude in commercial and industrial building than in public/institutional building and on the whole it was public/institutional building that was responsible for the greater stability of the non-residential sector. For example, the ratio of the highest to the lowest annual scores recorded was substantially lower in public/institutional building than in any other category of building in Australia and the United States, the two countries for which the available data allow comparisons.[19] All the major sub-categories of non-residential

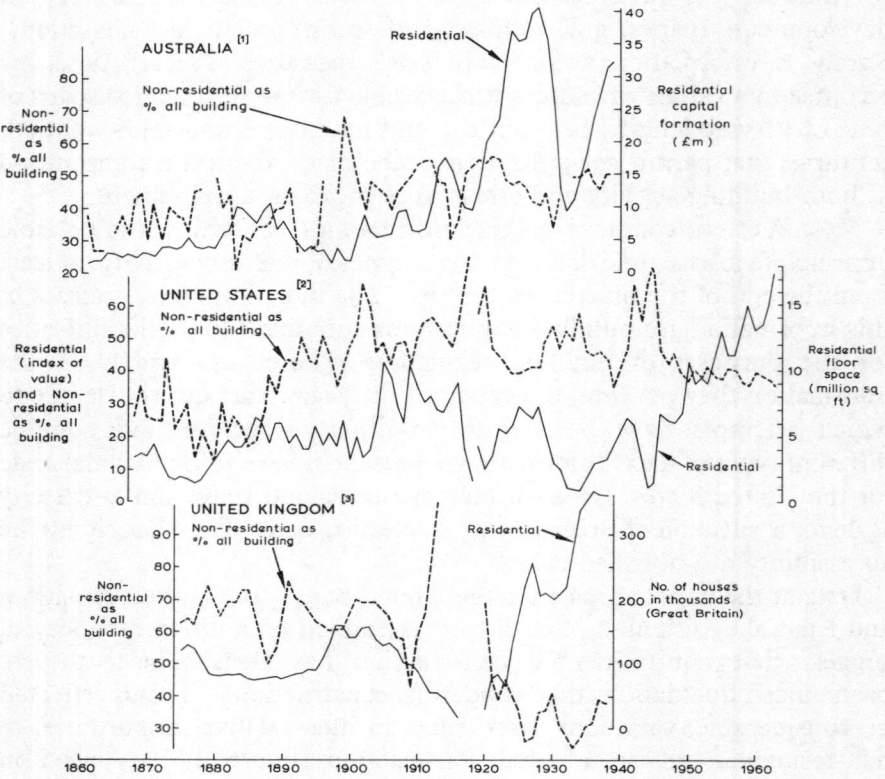

Figure 2.5 Non-residential building as a percentage of all building. The percentages are based on gross capital formation for Australia, value or floor-space for the United States, and net domestic capital formation or gross domestic capital formation for the United Kingdom

Sources: Australia – Butlin, 1959, tables II and IV. United States (1868–1919) – Long, 1940, appendix B, section 2. United States (1919–63) – Lipsey and Preston, 1966, pp. 20–1. United Kingdom – Feinstein, 1972, table 48; Richardson and Aldcroft, 1968, p. 67; Mitchell and Deane, 1962, p. 239.

1 'All building' comprises the following components of capital formation: residential (including public housing), industrial, commercial, and public buildings.

2 Data for 1919–63 are floor-space whereas those for 1868–1918 are Long's index of value. For 1919–55, data for certain states were not available and the figures for floor-space in these years have therefore been weighted (in proportion to the number of states for which data were available) to make them comparable with those for 1956–63 which are for 48 states. Long's index is based on an increasing number of cities over time – before 1899 less than 12 cities are involved and the index is of doubtful reliability.

3 Non-residential building as a percentage of all building is based on net domestic capital formation for 1875–1913 and gross domestic capital formation for 1920–38. Non-residential building includes civil engineering works during the period 1875–1913.

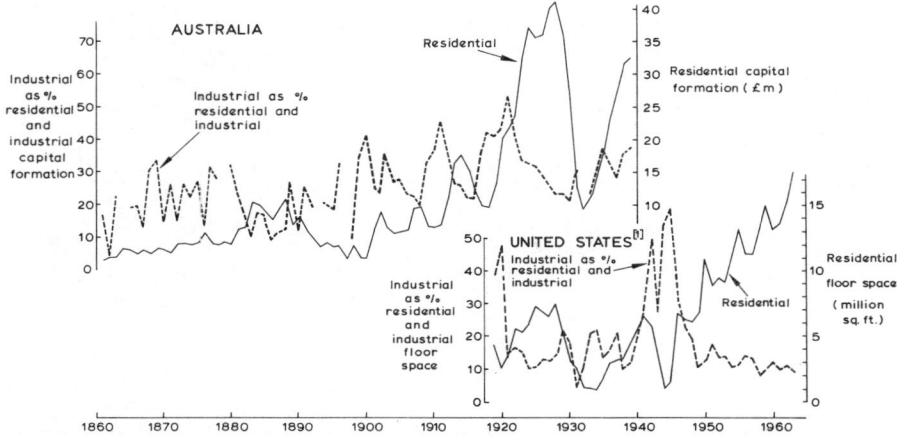

Figure 2.6 Industrial building as a percentage of residential and industrial building combined

Sources: Australia – see fig. 2.5. United States – Lipsey and Preston, 1966, pp. 20–1.
 1 For 1919–55, data for certain states were not available and the figures for floor-space in these years have therefore been weighted (in proportion to the number of states for which data were available) to make them comparable with those for 1956–63, which are for 48 states.

construction held up better than residential construction during housebuilding slumps (figures 2.6–8) and, with the exception of Australia in the early 1930s, in each case of a prolonged slump in housebuilding there was a marked rise in public/institutional building as a proportion of residential and public/institutional building combined (figure 2.8). On the whole such rises were associated with absolute falls in the amount of public/institutional building, although cases of actual increases in this type of construction during housebuilding slumps were by no means unknown, as has been revealed in Scotland in the early 1880s and early 1900s[20] and in Germany during the 15 years before 1914.[21]

Since building densities vary considerably, building activity, whether measured by floor space, value, or number of buildings, is an incomplete measure of urban development. Some developments, such as parks and sports grounds, involve little or no building yet occupy extensive areas of land. National data on such developments are time-consuming to compile but those available strongly suggest a pattern distinctive from that of housebuilding. An investigation of the creation of golf courses and rugby union clubs in England and Wales since the middle of the

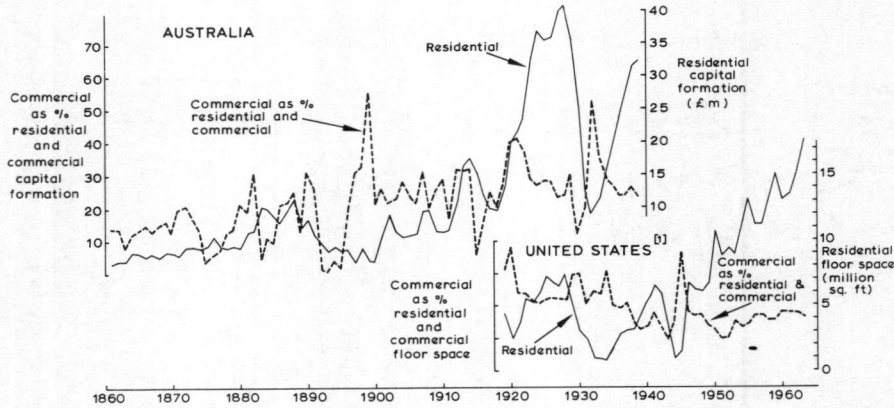

Figure 2.7 Commercial building as a percentage of residential and commercial building combined. *Sources*: Australia – see figure 2.5. United States – see figure 2.6.
 1 See figure 2.6, note 1.

nineteenth century has revealed major fluctuations[22] but of different timing from those in housebuilding (figure 2.9). In the case of golf courses, if the periods of the two world wars are excluded, the main fluctuations were counter to those in housebuilding, with the main peaks in golf course creation occurring during housebuilding troughs. In the case of the foundation of rugby union clubs, there was little or no correlation with housebuilding fluctuations.

These findings, added to those on different types of building activity, suggest that at the national level there have been major differences in the composition of urban development between housebuilding booms and slumps. It is necessary now to examine these differences at the more local scales at which they have taken on significance for the arrangement of land uses on the ground.

At the sub-national scale data are again fragmentary but broadly consistent with the findings pieced together at the national level. Gottlieb has drawn attention to the regular changes in the proportions of private (taxable) and public (exempt) building in the state of Ohio between 1853 and 1912, and to the tendency for there to have been an inverse relationship between public building and residential construction.[23] Of the data for individual British cities, those for Glasgow for the period from 1871 to 1936 are probably still the best available. These reveal that neither institutional and public building nor commercial and industrial building had much relationship to housebuilding, which was subject to longer swings than other types of building.[24] An impression of

Fluctuations in urban development 21

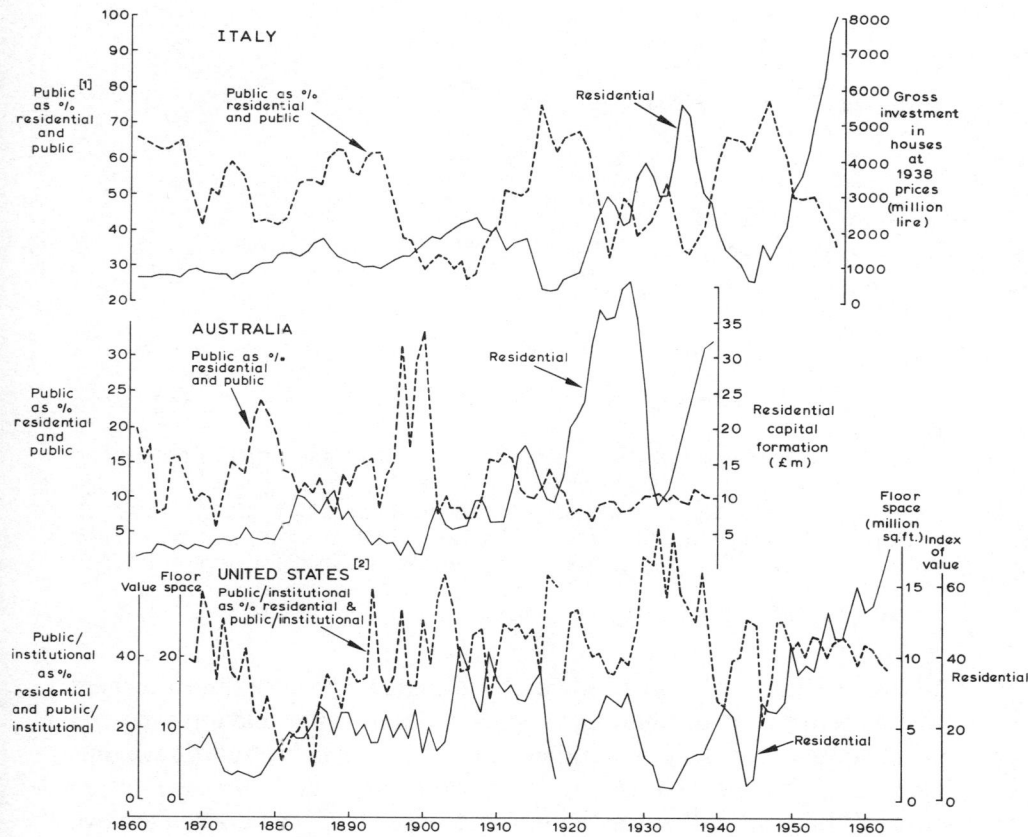

Figure 2.8 Public/institutional building as a percentage of residential and public/institutional building combined. The percentages are based on gross investment in the case of Italy, gross capital formation in the case of Australia, and value or floor-space in the case of the United States. *Sources*: Italy – *Annali di Statistica*, series 8, vol. 9, 1957, pp. 266–7. Australia and the United States – see figure 2.5.

1 These are 'public works', whereas 'public buildings' have been used in the graphs for Australia and the United States. 2 See figure 2.5, note 2. 3 Public and institutional 1868–1918; public 1913–63.

the effect of this on changes over time in the functional composition of urban development is given by Cairncross: the value of plans for houses and shops comprised well over one-half of the value of all plans in housebuilding booms but fell to less than one-fifth during housebuilding slumps.[25] Long-period data for Bradford, Hull and Liverpool reveal marked fluctuations in the proportions of residential and non-residential

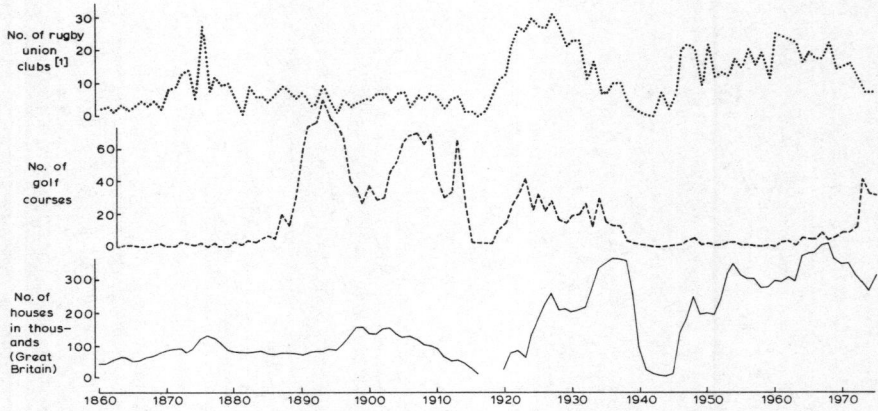

Figure 2.9 Number of golf courses and rugby union clubs established in England and Wales
Sources: Golf courses and rugby union clubs – *The Golfing Annual* 1888/9–1909/10, vols 1–21; *The Golfer's Handbook* 1902–77, vols 1–74; *Rugby Football Union Handbook* 1976. Housebuilding – Mitchell and Deane, 1962, p. 239; Department of the Environment, 1971, p. 7; 1975, p. 23; 1978, p. 24.
  1 Only those still existing in 1975 are included.

building. In Bradford, non-residential building ranged between 10 per cent and 100 per cent of all buildings approved, high values having occurred during housebuilding slumps and low values during housebuilding booms (figure 2.10). This largely reflected the massive long swings in housebuilding rather than any long-term inverse relation between the two types of building – before the First World War long swings in non-residential building were hardly perceptible.[26] Similar tendencies were apparent in both Hull and Liverpool (figure 2.10), and comparison of Openshaw's graphs of residential and non-residential building in South Shields between 1854 and 1939 suggests that in that town too there were major fluctuations in the composition of new development, reflecting larger long-term fluctuations in housebuilding than in non-residential buildings.[27]

Developments in which building was generally an incidental feature (such as parks and sports grounds), though often individually of large extent, were numerically sufficiently few within any one city to require extra caution in generalizing about their incidence. Information has, however, been compiled on the acquisition of sites for public parks and recreation grounds in eight British cities and plotted against housebuilding

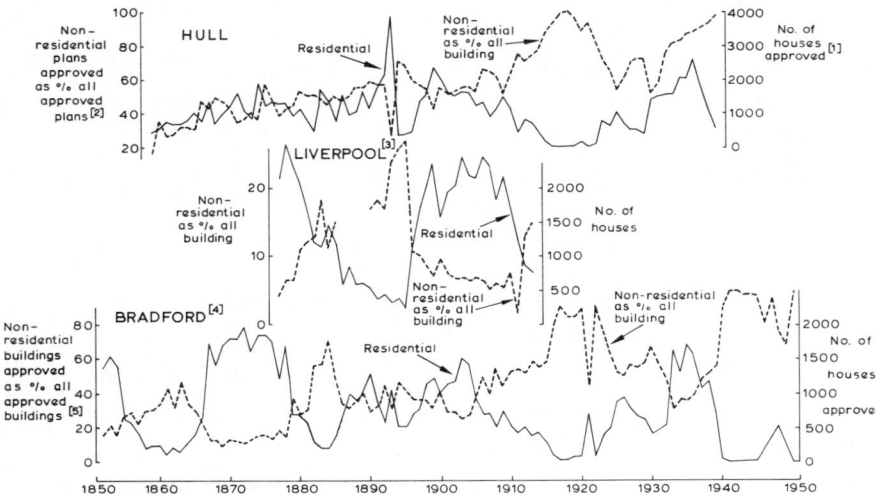

Figure 2.10 Non-residential building as a percentage of all building in three cities. The non-residential percentages for the different cities are not directly comparable since 'miscellaneous' buildings are included in Bradford, but not in Hull and Liverpool, and the percentages are based on number of plans in Hull but on number of buildings and houses in the other two cities. Local-authority dwellings, which only became a significant part of building towards the end of the period for which data are graphed, are excluded

Source: Lewis, 1965, pp. 322–5, 335–40, 342–52.

1   The number of houses plotted for 1893 does not include 3514 houses listed as 'not to be built', 99% of which were lapsed plans.

2   Data for non-residential building in 1902, 1909 and 1911 are incomplete.

3   The administrative area of Liverpool, to which the data refer, was considerably extended in 1895 and to a lesser extent in 1902, 1905 and 1913.

4   There were substantial changes to the boundaries of the administrative area to which the data refer in 1873, 1882, 1899, 1930 and 1937.

5   Dwellings associated with shops have been included in the non-residential category. There are occasional omissions in the data for non-residential building but it is unlikely that these are significant.

activity (figure 2.11). The creation of parks and recreation grounds – whether measured by number or area – appears to have continued unabated during slumps in housebuilding, resulting in substantial variations over time in the relative amounts of land developed for parks/recreation grounds and housing.

The data presented so far provide a context within which changes in the land-use composition of urban development in particular areas may be viewed. There remains the need, however, to move a further step

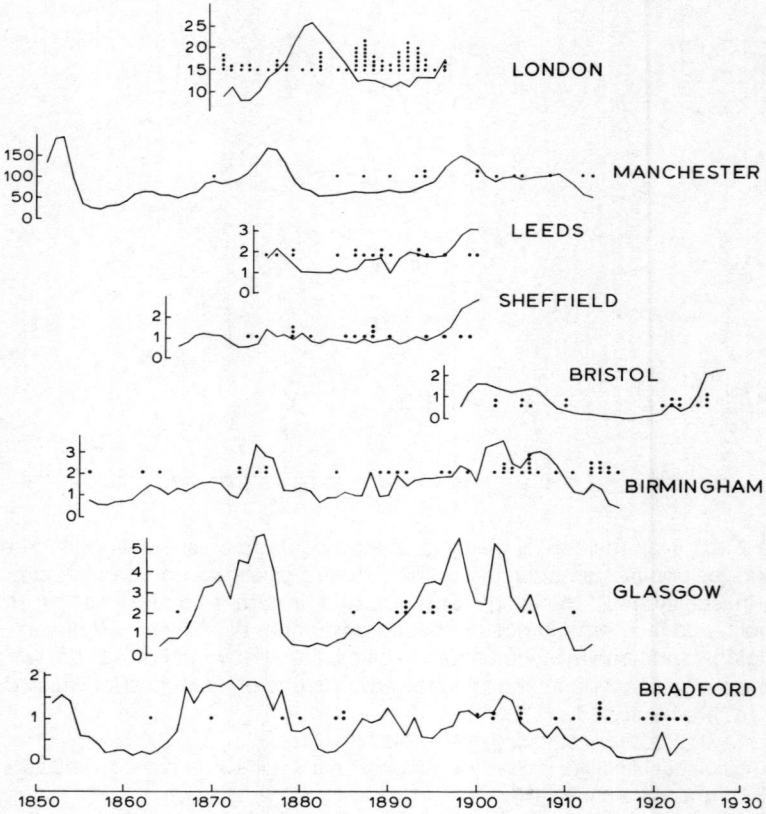

Figure 2.11 The establishment of parks and public open spaces in eight cities. Each dot represents a site. The curves show houses built (in thousands) in Birmingham after 1900, London, Leeds, Sheffield and Bristol; houses approved (in thousands) in Birmingham before 1900, Glasgow and Bradford; and a housebuilding index (1901–10 = 100) for the conurbation in the case of Manchester.

Sources: London – Hunter, 1897, pp. 405–14; Spensley, 1918, p. 210. Manchester – City of Manchester Recreational Services Department, n.d.; Lewis, 1965, pp. 314–15. Leeds – Branston, 1972, p. 61, table 1; Lewis, 1965, p. 309. Sheffield – Lee, 1974, pp. 12–13; Aspinall, 1977, fig. 3. Bristol – information on parks and open spaces supplied by the City of Bristol Engineer's Department and on housebuilding by the City of Bristol Planning Department. Birmingham – Lewis, 1965, p. 308; Langford, 1879, p. 36; City of Birmingham, 1951, p. 67; Dent, 1916, pp. 60–9. Glasgow – Lewis, 1965, p. 308; Corporation of the City of Glasgow, 1914, pp. 162–81. Bradford – Lewis, 1965, pp. 323–5; Bentley, 1926, pp. 13–93.

Note: Dates are those of acquisition except for the case of a minority of sites in Bradford which are those of public opening. Sites included are generally those lying within the city boundaries (boundaries of the Metropolitan Police District in the case of London) at the time of their acquisition, together with those city-owned sites outside that were not acquired by the incorporation of neighbouring local authorities. In the case of a few of the sites shown (notably

Fluctuations in urban development 25

down the areal scale to consider the transactions in land that accompanied the types of changes in land-use composition that have been detected. If a large number of sites are to be analysed, the consideration of such transactions may for practical reasons be as close as it is feasible to get to the decisions about the way in which land was developed.

The ease with which land transactions can be employed in a systematic analysis varies considerably from country to country. In England such records are sporadic, but Scotland possesses in its Register of Sasines a comprehensive and centrally located record of all land transactions over an extended period and this has been used as a source of data for the study of a small area. One such study does not provide a basis for generalization but it indicates the sort of analysis which if reproduced elsewhere would help to establish links between highly aggregated time series such as those just described and historical descriptions that view particular localities (often individual estates) in isolation.

The extraction of data from the Register of Sasines is greatly facilitated if large blocks of land in single ownership prior to urban development are selected and the chronological sequence of disposal of this land to urban users and developers is traced by means of Search Sheets. Three such blocks of land were selected within 2 km of the edge of the built-up area of Glasgow as it was in 1900 (figure 2.12). They comprised those parts of the estates of Garscube, Kelvinside and Killermont within the administrative boundary of the city of Glasgow in 1970 when the data were extracted.[28] In almost all cases the intended urban use of the land was either explicit in the Search Sheets or could be inferred from the description of the purchaser/fuear or was known from other sources. A small number of doubtful cases were omitted. Intended uses, the large majority of which subsequently came into existence, could virtually all be grouped into one of three broad categories – housing, institutions[29] and industry (including transport and storage). The most important

---

the London commons) use as an open space precedes acquisition by a city council. There are doubts concerning the precise year of acquisition of a small minority of the London commons, and commons are excluded in Bristol. In addition to public parks and major open spaces, recreation grounds are included in London, Manchester, Sheffield, Bristol and Bradford. Extensions to sites are included in London, Sheffield, Bristol and Birmingham but not elsewhere. Transfers to parks departments of sites originally controlled by other city departments are excluded. Overall, with the proviso that the bases for assigning public open spaces to different categories may have differed between cities, the data are, as far as is known, largely complete with the one exception of Manchester, for which dates were available for only a minority of sites in the source used.

category measured by number of transactions was housing, but by area of land it was institutions, industry being the least important by both criteria. The area of land involved in the transactions relating to each category of use is plotted by 5-year periods for 1900 to 1969 in figure 2.13. The magnitude of the fluctuations in the acquisition of land for institutional and industrial uses was accounted for by a few large sites and it should be noted that only 222 transactions were involved in the whole analysis. The most striking aspect was the peaks in the acquisition of land for non-residential purposes when little land was being acquired by housebuilders, notably the acquisition of land for institutional purposes immediately after the two world wars. The changes over time were greater than those identified for developments at the national or city levels. In accounting for this both the large impact of a few decisions in a limited area and the distinction between land acquisition and development should be borne in mind. Another factor was the location of this small area. By the beginning of the twentieth century most of it was relatively accessible to parts of Glasgow already in urban use. In contrast the national data, and often those for individual cities, included sites well outside the built-up area. As will be shown later, the admixture of land uses created varied over time according to the accessibility of sites. An inverse relation between housing development and the development of land for non-intensive uses, such as by many types of institution, may have been characteristic of relatively accessible areas, even though over a wider area the fluctuations in the two types of development may have been unrelated or even positively correlated.

EXPLANATIONS FOR THE CHANGING COMPOSITION OF URBAN DEVELOPMENT

The prime aim of this chapter has been to give an account of the changing composition of urban development. The data presented have various shortcomings, not least the fact that they are only for those countries and cities for which an extensive, but by no means exhaustive, search has produced usable information. This should not obscure the fact, however, that major regularities in the changing character of urban development have been revealed over diverse areas and at a wide variety of scales. The theories of building cycles already summarized provide an obvious starting point in the search for explanations of fluctuations in the land-use composition of urban developments of the type that have been

Fluctuations in urban development 27

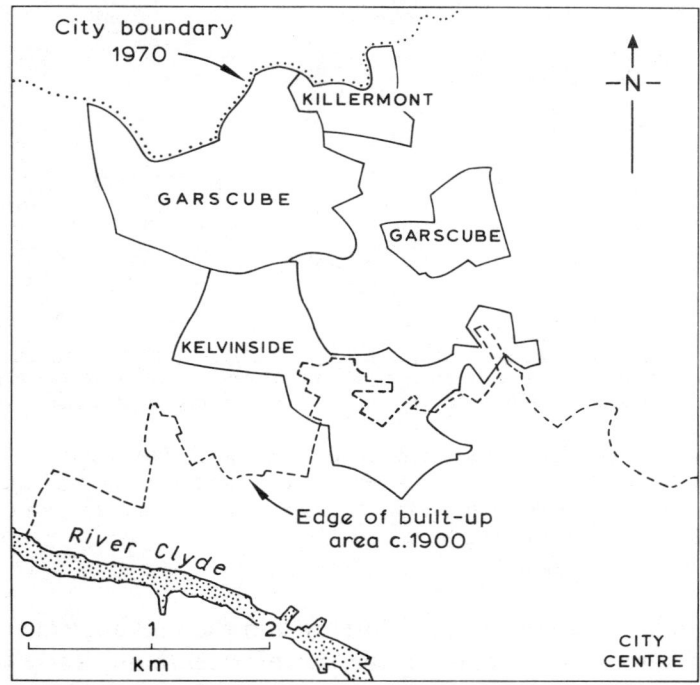

Figure 2.12 The location of three estates in north-west Glasgow
Sources: Garscube estate – unpublished map at Garscube Estates Office, Glasgow. Killermont estate – unpublished plans in the possession of Kerr, Macleod and Macfarlan, C.A., Glasgow. Kelvinside estate – unpublished map in the possession of Montgomerie Fleming, Fyfe, Maclean and Co., Glasgow. The principal basis for delineating the edge of the built-up area *c.*1900 was the map in Post Office, 1899.

identified. But these fluctuations would not seem to be explicable primarily in terms of the direct influence of demographic changes and the geographical switching of capital investment. It is true that allowance must be made for the fact that different population thresholds exist for different types of land-use development and that locally at least this might give rise to variations in the phasing of development for different land uses. However, at a national scale a more attractive hypothesis is that in addition to geographical shifts of capital from Great Britain to the New World and vice versa there were intra-national shifts of capital between different types of development: for instance, between industrial and residential building and between both these types of building and developments for educational, health and recreational purposes.[30] There

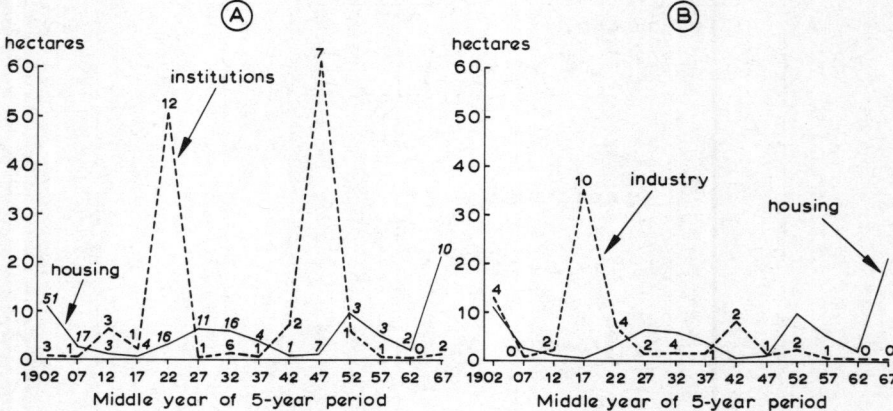

Figure 2.13 Area of land acquired for urban land use on three estates in north-west Glasgow. The figures on the graphs indicate the number of transactions. A. Land acquired for use by institutions and for housebuilding. B. Land acquired for use by industry and for housebuilding.
Source: Register of Sasines, Register House, Edinburgh.

are examples of corresponding shifts within the building trade. During building slumps in Scotland in the late nineteenth and early twentieth centuries it was not uncommon for speculative housebuilders to become subcontracted to undertake part of an industrial or public project, or to revert to their specialist trades – for example, as masons, joiners, or plumbers.[31]

These theories of the switching of capital, whether geographical or between different types of investment, offer only partial explanations. The different ways in which various types of development were brought into being, especially as regards their financial basis, are also important. Systematic data on the funding of urban development are largely lacking but it is possible to piece together a fairly consistent picture from the variety of studies that touch on the subject. A striking contrast between different types of development was the different degrees of uncertainty that were involved in the provision and marketing of buildings. At one extreme was speculative housebuilding, frequently undertaken on an insecure financial basis by speculative builders who possessed minimal capital, relied heavily on loans, and produced for a market full of uncertainties.[32] At the other extreme were contractual works, notably public buildings, constructed for specific clients on a relatively secure financial basis, such as accrued company profits, endowments invested in high-grade securities, and income from taxation.[33] The uncertainties in the financial basis of housing provision were added to when it came to obtaining a return on the finished product by the greater role of non-pecuniary factors and ignorance among private house buyers, which tended to engender overspending in booms and undue timidity in slumps.[34] Speculative overbuilding was a major factor in the severity of the fluctuations in housebuilding,[35] whereas in commercial and industrial building it was less common and in public building it was virtually absent.[36]

This explanation is by no means complete. Two further factors are relevant. First, since land for building purposes, especially for dwellings, occupied such a large proportion of urban areas, major fluctuations in building activity were an important element in the operation of the land market. Changes in land values would be likely to have a bearing on intensities and types of land use: the tendency for fluctuations in housebuilding and golf course creation to be inversely related may partly reflect the increased opportunities for land-extensive uses to acquire sites during periods of reduced demand for land by housebuilders. Secondly, over a long span of time a variety of innovations are adopted that affect urban development, some of them involving the bringing into existence of new types of land use. The roles of these factors are complex and have a significance for the urban landscape that extends beyond the subject of the present chapter. Their significance for fluctuations in the land-use composition of urban development will, however, be returned to after land values and innovation have been considered in their own right in the next two chapters.

3
Land values and land use

Like building activity, land values have a long history of academic enquiry. However, their implications for the physical configuration of the city, especially land-use patterns, have been more widely considered than those of building activity. Much of the early work on urban land values was undertaken in the German-speaking countries,[1] perhaps largely because data were more readily available.[2] But apart from the early work by von Thünen on agricultural land,[3] contributions from central Europe have been much less influential in modern writing than those from America. The work of Hurd and Haig in particular ensured a continuing role for land values in a variety of research on cities, especially by economists, regional scientists and geographers.[4] But views on the nature and importance of this role have varied widely.

THEORIES OF THE LAND MARKET

Although Marshall devotes a small part of his *Principles of Economics* to urban land values,[5] Hurd was the first to produce a major treatise devoted exclusively to this topic. For Hurd land value depended on 'nearness'.[6] If we add to this the notion, attributed to von Thünen, that land use and land value are 'mutually determining',[7] we have two major elements in the more elaborate theories developed much later by economists such as Alonso[8] and Evans.[9] In the words of Alonso, 'land uses determine land values', and 'land values distribute land uses'.[10] However, questions about this standpoint had been raised much earlier. In 1925, in his bibliographic contribution to *The City* by human ecologists Park, Burgess and McKenzie, Wirth wrote that 'land values are the chief determining influence in the segregation of local areas and in the determination of the uses to which an area is to be put'.[11] To this

Haig replied in 1926: 'But is it not the uses which determine the land values rather than *vice versa*?'[12] The viewing of the relationship between land use and land values as reciprocal rather than one-way was subsequently endorsed by other human ecologists.[13]

Haig's questioning of the reciprocity of land value and land use has both antecedents and subsequent support. As early as 1885 the view that 'density determines value' appeared in *The Building News*.[14] This is consistent with the Ricardian view that land value depends on the profitability of land use. According to this view, when profits rise builders bid up the price of land and vice versa: land prices are a residual consequence of the level of house prices relative to construction costs.[15] Much the same view was expressed by Turvey: 'high rents . . . make dense building profitable and make sites valuable; it is misleading to reverse this and say that high site values cause building to take place at a high density.'[16]

The contrary view that land value determines the type and intensity of land use is, however, widely assumed to have validity.[17] It receives support in Harvey's argument that monopoly rents enter into the costs of production and thereby determine land use.[18] But how often have landowners been in positions in which they could extract monopoly rents? Harvey is of the opinion that this condition is prevalent in contemporary metropolitan centres and was the norm in older commercial and administrative centres, such as London, in the eighteenth and nineteenth centuries.[19] More recent work, however, has cast considerable doubt on the extent to which landowners in capitalist cities are able to exercise anything approaching a monopoly. Evans will only go as far as to concede that in some circumstances the peculiarity of a site or the control of a large amount of land in a single urban area by a single owner might lead to monopoly rents.[20] Springett's study of one such landowner in nineteenth-century Huddersfield suggests that such caution is justified,[21] as does Ball's revelation of the time lag between development profitability and residential land prices in Great Britain between 1970 and 1981.[22] The fact of the matter is that the evidence for the direction of causation between land values and land use is far short of allowing a conclusion one way or the other. The strengths of the directional components must surely vary over both space and time. Thus the Thünian view that land use and land value are mutually determined appears to be no less tenable than it was in the early nineteenth century.

Clearly, a further variety of elements enter into land value. Some of these must await our consideration of innovation and planing in chapter

4. It is necessary for the purposes of the present chapter, however, to refer briefly to some elementary characteristics of models of the von Thünen type that bear upon our line of argument.

The essence of the application of Thünian analysis to urban areas is that the land-use pattern reflects the relative advantage that land users derive from substituting rent for transport costs from the city centre and vice versa.[23] Such reasoning is conventionally applied to profit-making uses involved in competitive bidding for sites. It may be extended to include non-profit-making uses, which have in a large part to justify their locations in similar terms. The allocation of land uses to sites by owners of large areas of land, especially local authorities in recent times and major estate owners in the eighteenth and nineteenth centuries, may be viewed in much the same way. Even if a formal market mechanism is absent *within* an area of single landownership, the allocation of land uses to sites is likely to take account of the extent of transport costs, however measured, relative to the amounts of land occupied. It is probably rare for land uses to be allocated to sites in a way markedly at variance with the dictates of the market operating in neighbouring areas without some consideration of the rent thereby forgone or the transport costs thereby incurred.

In the most widely accepted theory of the urban land market, differing trade-offs between rent and the transport costs associated with different land uses yield bid–rent curves that decline outward from the city centre. The steepest gradients are associated with land uses with high transport costs relative to site area, such as many types of retailing, and the shallowest gradients are associated with land uses with low transport costs relative to site area, such as golf courses. The resulting land-value surface, declining from centre to periphery, and the associated concentric pattern of land use is one of the best-known generalizations in urban geography. However, while the plausibility of these regularities is widely acknowledged, various objections have been put forward to the mechanism purporting to underlie them. One concerns the basic assumption in models of the von Thünen type that 'distance from the city centre incurs a "penalty" in the form of transportation or communication costs'.[24] Harvey, for example, points out that a land-value surface peaking at the centre, and therefore consistent with this assumption, would result from the fact that, because there is only one centre and a whole continuum of periphery, monopoly rents tend to be most easily established at or near the centre.[25] Thus the problem is the familiar one of apportioning weights to different causes that are liable

Land values and land use 33

to result in similar patterns. It is doubtful, however, whether there are many capitalist cities in which monopoly rent assumes the dominance that Harvey claims.

There are a variety of other factors of which the Thünian theory of land values takes no account. Essentially non-economic factors, including governmental interventions, will be dealt with in later chapters. Here it should be noted that other imperfections in the land market, such as the poor knowledge of the market by buyers and sellers and the legal complexities of the ownership and occupation of land, have been widely acknowledged.[26] As far as theory construction is concerned, these have tended to be employed as explanations for the departure of reality from received economic theory rather than themselves forming components in a theory. An assessment of whether this is justified must await the sifting of more empirical evidence, some of which will be done in the remainder of this chapter.

EMPIRICAL PATTERNS OF LAND VALUES

Reliable land-value data are hard to obtain. The paucity of sales of undeveloped land within the urban area constitutes an especial problem. Even when suitable sale prices are available, achieving direct comparability of prices over time and space is difficult. For some areas and periods only ground rents, as distinct from freehold prices, are available.

Despite the problems, the evidence of land-value patterns conforming to those predicted by models of the von Thünen type is strong. Studies of a variety of cross-sections in time and of a variety of parts of the world point virtually without exception to the existence of peaks in land values in commercial cores, followed within short distances by sharp declines in an outward direction and thereafter gentler declines, interrupted by subsidiary peaks. In Winchester as early as 1148 land values in High Street, the central trading area, were some five times higher than those in the next most valuable street and twenty-two times higher than those of the least valuable streets within the town walls.[27] *The Builder* in 1871 provides a similar picture of declining values outward from the commercial heartland of the City of London[28] and Lichtenberger depicts much the same pattern in her map of land-price categories in the Old Town of Vienna in 1900.[29] Still the most convincing study for the nineteenth century and early twentieth century, however, is Hoyt's reconstruction of land values in Chicago, in which he mapped land values for the whole city for several cross-sections in time and left no room for doubt that the Central Business District (CBD) was the land-value peak of the city and that the suburbs were the low-lying plains that rose gently towards the CBD save for interruptions by outlying hills.[30] Corroborations of this general pattern, though in some cases based on residential land values only, are found, for example, in Philadelphia in 1950–2,[31] the London and Birmingham areas in 1960–2,[32] Paris in 1962–3,[33] Marseilles in 1963,[34] Bonn in 1969/70 and 1974/5,[35] central Brisbane in 1973,[36] and St Louis in 1966–7.[37] Studies using land values assessed for tax purposes, for example in Los Angeles County[38] and Washington DC[39] suggest a similar pattern. Summarizing a large number of other studies,[40] as well as drawing on Clark's earlier compilation,[41] Evans concludes that the evidence for an inverse relation between land value and distance from the city centre is overwhelming. It is apparent too that the existence of this relationship is by no means confined to Western cities. For example, Hawley's study of Okayama in 1940 and 1952, using assessed valuations for tax purposes,[42] and Benevelo's map of the price of building land in Tehran in 1960–1[43] reveal an essentially similar pattern.

EMPIRICAL PATTERNS OF LAND USE

The study of land use is less fraught with conceptual and measurement problems than the study of land values. Furthermore, the number of studies that have been undertaken is larger. Again, at a general level there is a resemblance between observed patterns and those generated by models of the von Thünen type. In medieval Winchester there was evidence of a decline in land-use intensity with distance from the commercial core,[44] and Lichtenberger's reconstruction of the Old Town of Vienna in 1566 shows that centrally located burghers' houses of three or more storeys were succeeded outward by burghers' houses of one or two storeys, and finally at the urban fringe there were the houses of the nobility, religious houses, charities, and a variety of other low-intensity land uses.[45]

For the industrial era the evidence of land-use patterns in American and British cities is widespread, though often uncoordinated and made up of observations of uncertain representativeness. Examination of nineteenth-century Ordnance Survey large-scale maps and plans reveals that the contact zone between the edge of the built-up area and the countryside frequently included land-extensive urban or quasi-urban land uses, such as large houses in ornamental parks, public open spaces and utilities, brickfields and various other uses that were forerunners of more intensive development. While systematic analyses of this period are uncommon, the accounts of urban historians sometimes convey a sense of the temporal and spatial order of the urban fringe, with the main laying out of streets and plots preceded by a less intensive development of individual villas.[46] From a different perspective Cowan analyses systematically the location of hospitals in London and reveals how in the mid nineteenth century they formed a wide circular band around the city. Furthermore, he found a strong correlation between 'cemeteries, burial grounds, gasworks and other indications of low land values, and the location of hospitals'.[47] The converse pattern of high-intensity land use in the CBD was most manifest in America.[48]

In modern times evidence of the association between intensity of development and location is abundant. Not only do land values diminish with distance from the centre of London but so do the densities at which new residential sites are developed.[49] Based on a questionnaire survey of 245 local authorities, Lever revealed major variations in 1968 in the densities at which new residential development took place according to both settlement size and whether greenfield sites (presumably mostly at the urban fringe) or redeveloped (more centrally located) sites were used. Residential densities were highest in major cities, notably London, and on redeveloped sites.[50] For a similar point in time Berry examined the interrelationship between land prices and land-use intensities in Melbourne. He discovered that at higher land prices the intensity of use increased.[51] Although data of comparable quality are seldom available for non-Western cities, Pannell concludes from his study of the Taiwanese city of T'ai-chung that patterns of land value and intensity of use follow the Western pattern, though the scale is more compressed.[52]

The foregoing evidence leaves little doubt that, in terms of centre–periphery variations, patterns of land values and land use broadly accord with Thünian precepts. But the picture that has been presented is essentially static. It is in marked contrast to the evidence of urban growth presented in chapter 2. Spatial associations of land values, land use and intensity of use have been described for cross-sections of time, usually determined by the availability of data, and it has been shown that these are for the most part consistent with a static theory. But little is known of how land values functioned in bringing land uses into existence. The dynamic of change remains obscure. Our cross-sections in time are snapshots, whereas what is required is a moving picture. In industrial countries at least, most cities have undergone growth and internal change for as long as there are reliable records. The urban fringe of the first quarter of the nineteenth century is more often than not within the inner city of the last quarter of the twentieth century. If land values have the central role that evidence adduced so far would suggest, they must be considered over time as well as over space. It is also necessary to consider what relation land values have to the cyclical character of growth already discerned in our examination of urban development over time.

LAND VALUES AND THE COURSE OF URBAN DEVELOPMENT

In view of the problems of data and measurement already discussed it is not surprising that there is a paucity of data on changes in land values over time, especially for the long spans of time necessary if comparisons are to be made with long swings in building activity. Indexes of land rents based on assessments of the value of land in its existing use, such as those of Singer[53] and Rodger,[54] must be treated with caution since in many cases the market (or exchange) value of land reflects a more profitable prospective use. Over a long period, however, studies of long-term changes in land values have slowly accumulated that, taken together, provide a valuable body of evidence. With few exceptions they refer to individual cities or parts of cities. The data for England (figure 3.1) are particularly problematic because of the small number of prices upon which the medians for certain periods are based and there are gaps in several of the time series for individual cities. Despite the uneven quality of the information and the variations in the measures used, if we consider together figures 3.1 to 3.3 and Daly's information for Sydney,[55] then there is a reasonable basis for commenting on the incidence of the main changes in land values in England and in major cities in four other Western countries. The most striking feature is the marked long-term fluctuations. The timing of these fluctuations varies between places, to the extent of being counter-cyclical in a few cases. All the series reveal a single boom between the two world wars. This occurs first in Chicago (in the mid-1920s) and last in England (in the late 1930s). The peaks in Sydney, Paris, the Brussels region and the four German cities occur between those two dates, with some clustering around, and more particularly just before, 1930. Again, all the series suggest that a slump

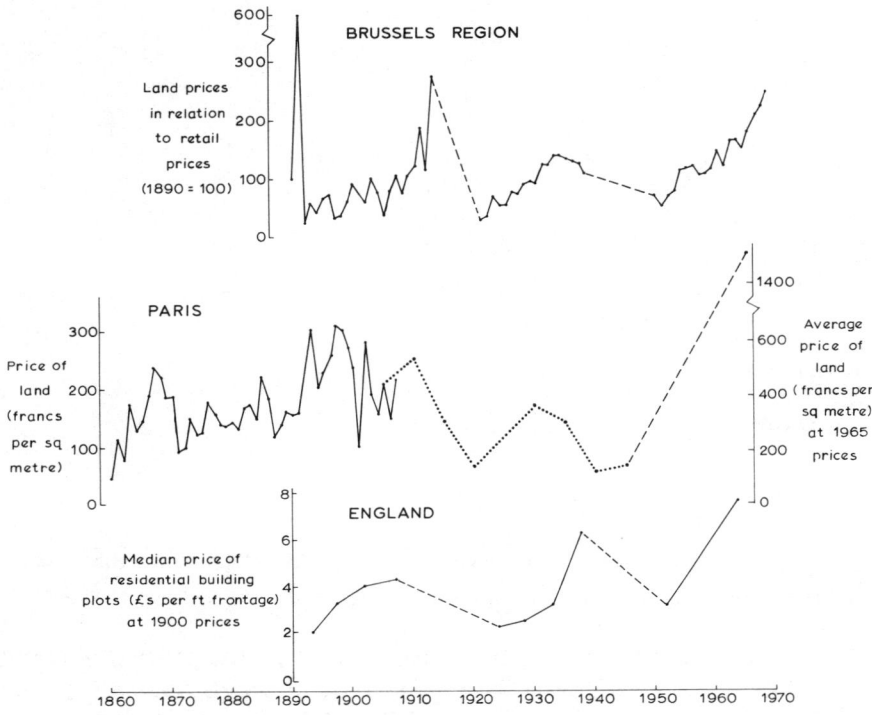

Figure 3.1 Land prices in the Brussels region, Paris, and England
Sources: Brussels region – Hallett, 1979, fig. 7. Paris – Halbwachs, 1909, table B, col. 5; Granelle, 1970, p. 161. England – Vallis, 1972, p. 1017.

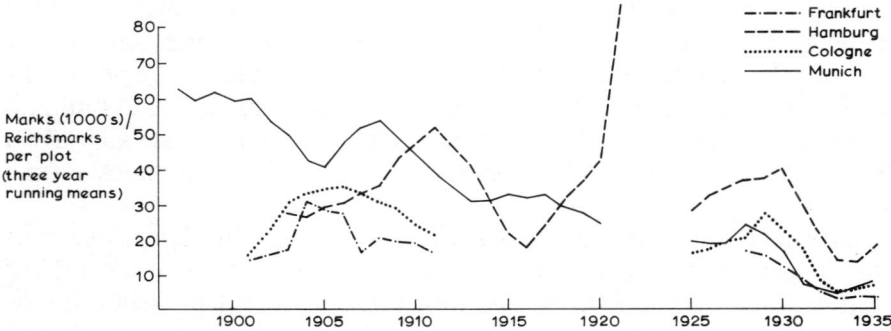

Figure 3.2 Land prices in four west German cities
Source: Polensky, 1974, fig. 1.

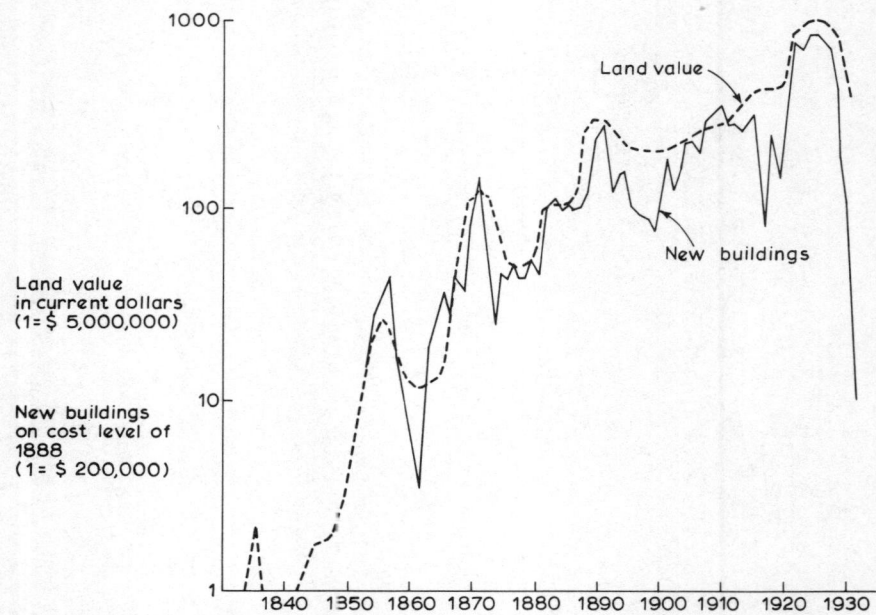

Figure 3.3 Land values and building activity in Chicago. *Source*: Hoyt, 1933, p. 406.

in land values occurred during the 1910s. However, the preceding boom occurred just before the First World War in the Brussels region, Chicago and Hamburg, but between about 1900 and 1910 in the other cities. Thus during the 15 years preceding the First World War there were major differences of timing both between German cities and between cities in different countries.

To the evidence for marked long-term fluctuations in land values during the late nineteenth and the twentieth century should be added evidence for earlier periods. Polensky has revealed that such fluctuations occurred in the eighteenth century in Munich, well before the beginning of the industrial era.[56] Though less well documented than building cycles, land-value cycles appear to be as endemic to the process of urban development. This raises the question as to the relationship between the two types of cycles.

Since land for building purposes (especially for dwellings) occupies such a large proportion of urban areas, it would seem reasonable to suppose that fluctuations in building activity have had major implications for the land market. A relationship between building activity and land values has long been acknowledged.[57] Unfortunately, the number of cases in which comparable data have been compiled for land values

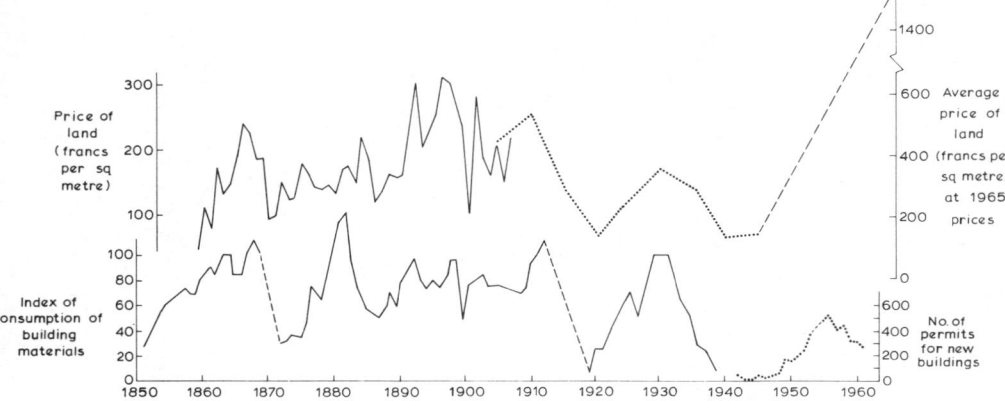

Figure 3.4 Land prices and building activity in Paris
Sources: Halbwachs, 1909, table B, col. 5; Granelle, 1970, p. 161; Flaus, 1949, p. 187; Sutcliffe, 1970, p. 348.

and building activity over long periods has grown only slowly. In order to provide data with which to examine the relationship between the two variables it is necessary to draw on studies that have appeared over a long period and to bring together previously uncorrelated time series. Still the best comparative data are Hoyt's for Chicago between 1833 and 1933 (figure 3.3). These strongly suggest that in general land values rose during building booms and fell during building slumps. Data for Paris between the mid nineteenth century and the mid twentieth century (figure 3.4), for Hamburg between the late nineteenth century and the mid-1930s (figure 3.5), and for England between 1892 and 1969 (figure 3.6) reveal a similar relationship. Information for shorter periods, such as for freehold ground rents in London at 5-year intervals between 1892 and 1912,[58] and a large number of disparate observations, particularly concerning the condition of the land market during pronounced booms and slumps in building, are also broadly in accord.[59] This relationship would seem to be important to an understanding of the way in which the urban landscape is brought into being, and it is to this that attention will now be devoted.

A THEORY OF URBAN DEVELOPMENT

There are considerable variations in the amounts of capital that different land users apply per unit area of the sites they develop. For example, the

40 J. W. R. Whitehand

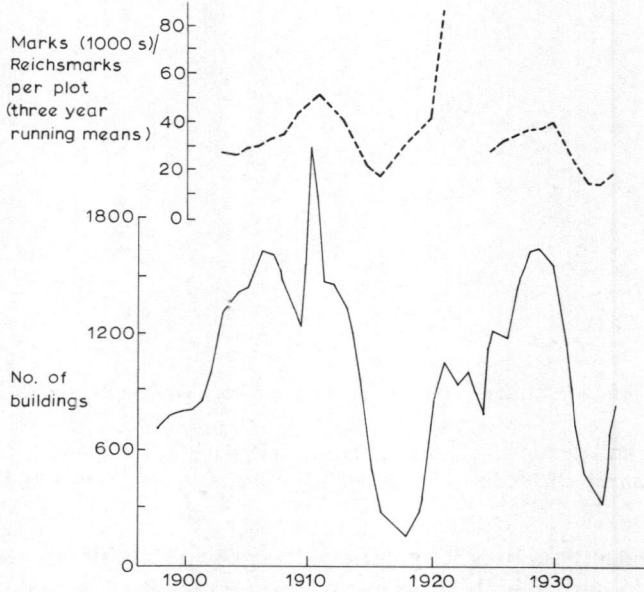

Figure 3.5 Land prices and building activity in Hamburg
Sources: Polensky, 1974, fig. 1; Warren and Pearson, 1937, fig. 30.

conversion of land to housing normally involves a much larger investment of capital than the utilization of land as playing fields. Broadly speaking, shops and offices use land more intensively than housing, which itself varies considerably in intensity between working-class and middle-class areas. Developments for institutional purposes (educational, medical, military, central and local government, research, recreational, and religious) often include large areas that are not built over and tend on average to be land-extensive. Variations in land values over time and space have different implications for different land uses. The implications over space may be viewed as an extension of the Thünian trade-off between rent and transport costs. A major factor underlying the nature of that trade-off for particular land users is the intensity at which they develop their sites. Since building costs vary little over space, at least within a particular urban area, but the spatial variation in land values is considerable, it is reasonable to assume that users applying relatively small amounts of capital per unit of land are more likely to be located on cheaper, less accessible sites. This argument is consistent with theoretical and empirical studies of the spatial

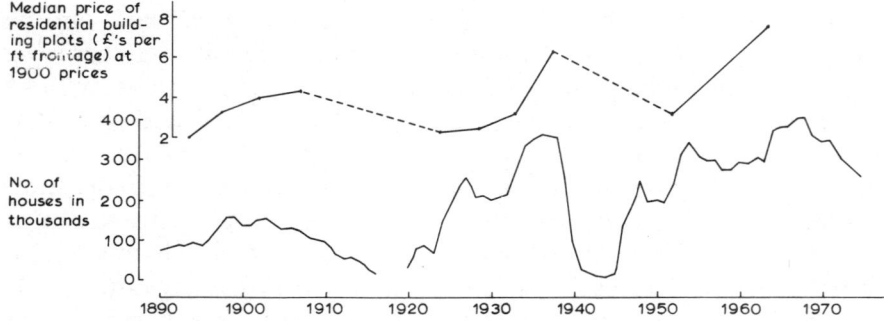

Figure 3.6 Land prices and housebuilding in Great Britain. Number of houses are annual totals for Great Britain. Land prices are for periods of 3–12 years' duration for England and Wales
Sources: Vallis, 1972, p. 1017; Mitchell and Deane, 1962, p. 239; Department of the Environment, 1971, p. 7.

relationship between land values on the one hand and building density and other measures of intensity of use on the other.[60]

The implications over time of this line of reasoning have been accorded comparatively little attention. They depend to some extent on the variability of building costs over time. Data on building costs differ markedly according to the criteria used,[61] and investigations of their long-term relationship with land values are lacking. However, in the light of the high correlation between land values and building activity it is significant that Newman found little connection between building activity and building costs in the United States between 1875 and 1933.[62] Similarly, on the basis of American data for 1914–41, Muth found no correlation between construction costs and the rate of construction of new housing, and concluded that on empirical grounds it was reasonable to assume that non-land costs remained constant.[63] Though Maiwald demonstrated substantial fluctuations in building costs in the United Kingdom during the period 1845–1938,[64] comparison with Lewis's index of housebuilding for the period 1856–1913[65] reveals only a slight positive correlation ($r = +0.25$, $\alpha > 0.05$). Furthermore, Gottlieb detected only the slightest suggestion of cyclical movements in the indexes of building costs for London, the United States and Germany.[66] On balance, although the evidence relates to disparate areas and periods, it suggests that fluctuations in land values have not been accompanied by commensurate fluctuations in building costs.

It follows from this that an argument similar to that concerning the spatial relation between land value and intensity of use can be developed about these two variables over time. Much as users applying relatively small amounts of capital per unit of land are more likely to be located spatially on land of lower value, so they are more likely, other things being equal, to acquire land during periods of lower land values. Slumps in land values are the temporal analogue of less accessible sites. In addition it should be recalled that the nature of the provision of finance for development is such that the type of development that normally takes up a greater part of the urban area than any other single category of land use, namely housebuilding for the mass market, is not only one of the more intensive uses of land but particularly susceptible to a shortage of funds during a period of financial stringency. Indeed, this would appear to be a major factor underlying the fall in land values. It would seem that certain more land-extensive types of development are not only less disadvantaged in their provision of funds during an economic slump, but they have more to gain from the associated fall in the price of land.

These arguments about space and time can be put together in what amounts to a dynamic urban rent theory.[67] In Thünian terms this can be expressed graphically in the form of bid-rent curves. Figure 3.7 assumes the simplest case of two distinct land uses, one land-extensive and the other land-intensive. Because for the land-extensive use accessibility is a low priority relative to the large area of land required, less advantage will be gained from developing sites close to sources of employment and existing residential areas and services. In contrast, accessibility for the land-intensive use is a high priority relative to the area of land required. This condition will be reflected in the rents or prices that the two uses are prepared to pay for sites at varying distances from the city centre. The land-intensive use (a) is prepared to pay high rents for accessible sites but relatively low rents for sites further away. The land-extensive use (b) has less to gain from an accessible site but less to lose from a remote one. Its bid-rent curve therefore has a gentler slope. The overall levels of the two curves and whether or where they cross will reflect the state of the market for the two land uses. Figure 3.7A represents an active period in the development of sites for use (a), which forms an inner zone, relegating use (b) to less accessible, cheaper sites. Figure 3.7B represents a slump in the development of sites for use (a), enabling the land-extensive use (b) to acquire accessible sites which under the boom conditions

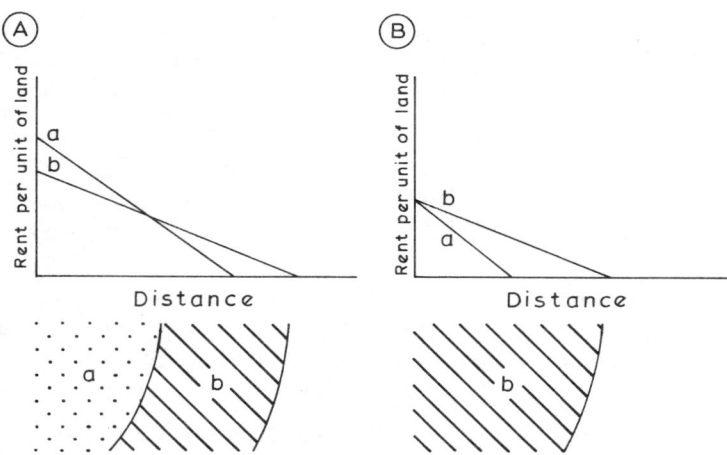

Figure 3.7 Relationship between bid rents for land-intensive use (a) and land-extensive use (b) and distance from the city centre: (A) during a housebuilding boom, (B) during a housebuilding slump

prevailing previously would have been acquired for land-intensive use. The curve of the land-intensive use has slid further down the rent axis than the curve of the land-extensive use.

The bid-rent curves shown in figure 3.7 are averages of the individually unique curves of all the users in each land-use category; and their positions relative to one another are merely two of the many that can be envisaged, depending on the magnitude of the boom or slump.

What do these relationships mean in terms of developments in the landscape? Let us envisage the process by which rural land is taken up for urban use. Industrial land use apart, the two main categories of land-use development at the urban fringe are for housing and, if broadly defined, institutions. Taking these two land uses as representative of land-intensive and land-extensive uses, it is possible to derive from a diagram such as figure 3.7 the expected variations in the relative amounts of development for the two uses with increasing distance from the edge of the built-up area. Figure 3.8 shows these for both housing-boom and housing-slump periods. It has been drawn on the assumption that the ratio of new institutional development to new housing is related to the differences between the rents or prices that the two uses are prepared to offer for sites.

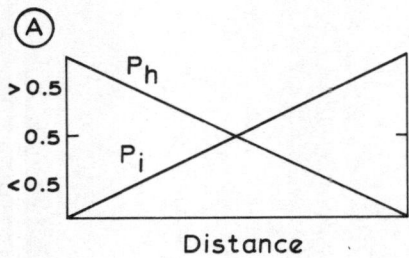 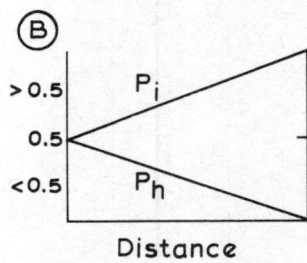

Figure 3.8 Hypothetical variations in the proportion of new housing development and new institutional development with distance from the edge of the built-up area: (A) during a housebuilding boom, (B) during a housebuilding slump

These postulated outcomes have implications for the land-use composition of extensions to the urban area. Housebuilding booms will be characterized by the development for new housing construction of sites adjacent to the built-up area. Few institutions will be able to compete for these sites and any new institutional development is likely to take place on more distant sites which are as yet insufficiently attractive to the housebuilder. In contrast, housebuilding slumps will be characterized by a contraction in the demand for sites by housebuilders and there will be a greater probability of development of the more accessible sites by institutions.

Because housebuilding booms and slumps tend to be of many years' duration the postulated proportions of housing and institutions are, in a large city, likely to be reflected in considerable numbers of actual developments. However, neither in a boom nor in a slump will the edge of the built-up area be static. Therefore, institutions originally located at some distance from the edge of the built-up area, on what were sub-marginal sites for the housebuilder, may be surrounded by new residential development by the end of a housebuilding boom. A zone of housing will have been added to the built-up area, but scattered beyond it and sometimes lying within it will be the sites of institutions. During a housebuilding slump institutions will tend to develop accessible sites which, added to what were outlying institutional sites developed during the previous boom, will form a zone with a strongly institutional character. Repeated cycles of booms and slumps are likely to result in a series of alternating zones characterized by different proportions of institutions and housing.

THE MODEL TESTED

It is difficult to establish whether the actual process of site acquisition by housebuilders and institutions conforms to this model. It is virtually impossible to establish the rents or prices that potential users are prepared to offer for sites even if land is publicly auctioned. What we can do is see whether the locations of actual institutions and housing areas are such that they could be explained by our postulated mechanism. This entails examining in detail a local area, and it is convenient for this purpose to return to the part of Glasgow considered in chapter 2. In order to test the model effectively, however, it is necessary to examine the whole north-west quadrant of the city (figure 3.9), of which the three estates previously considered are only a part. It would be extremely time-consuming to extract data on land transactions for such a large area and on this occasion more readily available data on actual land development will be used.[68]

North-west Glasgow is well suited to testing our two-use model since the area is dominated by housing and institutions. The complications afforded by other land uses, which in this case comprised only 15 per cent of new development at the urban fringe, are thereby minimized. A further advantage of the area is that housebuilding in Glasgow between the mid nineteenth century and the mid twentieth century underwent pronounced booms and slumps (figure 3.10) which in their incidence were broadly in keeping with those for Great Britain as a whole. For the purposes of the test, data were compiled for two booms (1840–58 and 1894–1908) and two slumps (1878–93 and 1909–23). Information was also assembled for a fifth period (1959–77) which comprised both a slump and a boom. Figure 3.11 shows for the five periods the actual variations in the proportion of new institutional development and new housing in relation to distance from the edge of the built-up area. It also shows schematic curves which assume a linear increase in the ratio of institutional development to housing development with increasing distance from the edge of the built-up area. They are in effect regression lines, any deviation from which may be regarded as unexplained by the model.

In general the shape of the ratio curves conformed to the expected pattern, but part of the value of the comparison is in highlighting the limitations of the model. For example, during the predominantly boom period of 1840–58 the ability of institutions to develop sites close to the

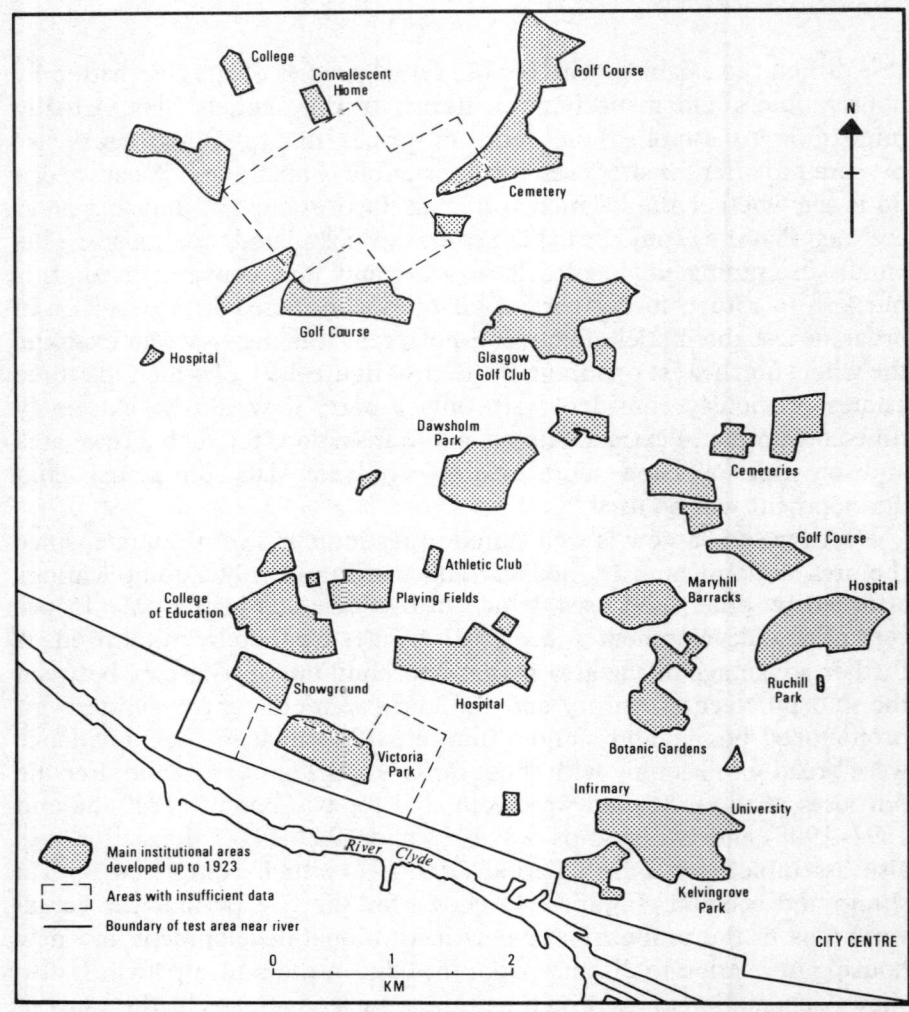

Figure 3.9 Simplified map of the Glasgow test area, showing the main institutional areas

built-up area was greater than expected. This can be explained partly by the influence exercised by the Corporation of Glasgow: on social grounds they developed as open spaces land that corporation documents reveal should on economic grounds have been developed for housing. In

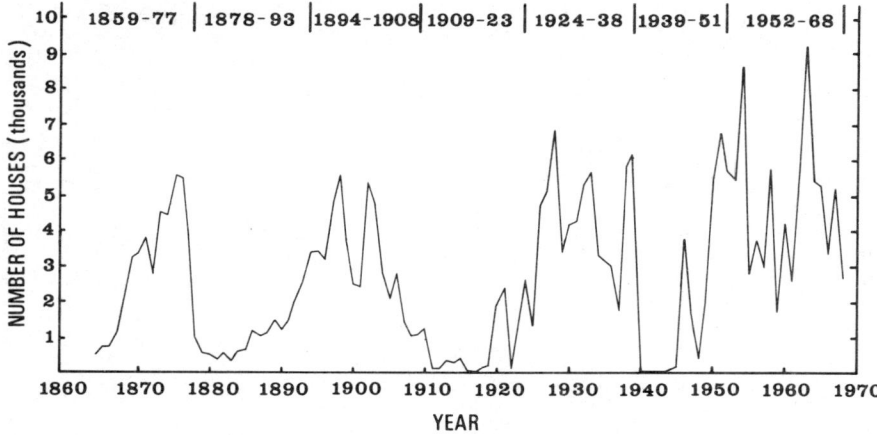

Figure 3.10 Number of houses authorized to be built in Glasgow, 1864–1968

1878–93 the housing proportion actually increased slightly at approximately 4.5 km – a trend not explicable in terms of the postulated bid-rent curves. In other respects the curve conformed to the expected pattern for a slump and, except at the immediate edge of the built-up area, institutional development was predominant.

In figure 3.12 new development in each period is expressed as a percentage of the land available for development in each distance zone. Here the concentration of development on the immediate edge of the built-up area during housebuilding slumps and its more widely dispersed character during housebuilding booms is apparent. The composite character of the 1859–77 period is particularly evident in the intermediate character of its institutional curve. The marked reduction in housing development during slumps, compared with sustained or even increased institutional development is consistent with the postulated changes in the relative abilities of housebuilders and institutions to compete for sites.

In figure 3.13 the curves of the percentage of available land converted to the two uses during the five periods are superimposed to show whether in combination these developmental sequences created an overall pattern consistent with our model. In general, areas in which the land was fully developed for urban purposes, or nearly so, the landscape had taken up a form approximating to that hypothesized. But it is significant that there were three instead of the expected two periods contributing to the inner institutional zone. Thus the postulated

48 J. W. R. Whitehand

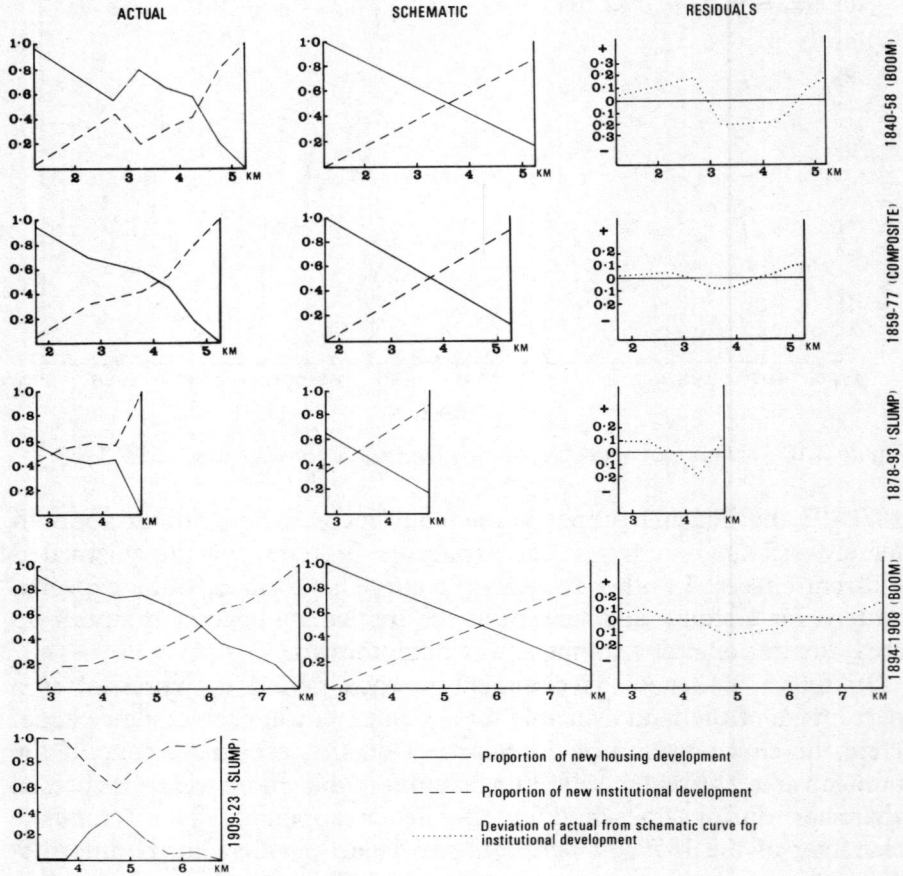

Figure 3.11 Actual and schematic proportion of new housing development and new institutional development in north-west Glasgow during five time periods related to distance from the city centre. The actual proportions are the running means of three distance zones of 0.5 km width

synchronism between building-cycle phase and land-use development may be considerably distorted in the real world. Furthermore, the fact that some of the deviations remained in the same locations in successive periods, rather than moving outward as development moved outward, suggests a systematic inadequacy in the model. The model assumes that each locational decision is independent of preceding decisions, whereas in reality once a particular use has been located, it will tend to attract or

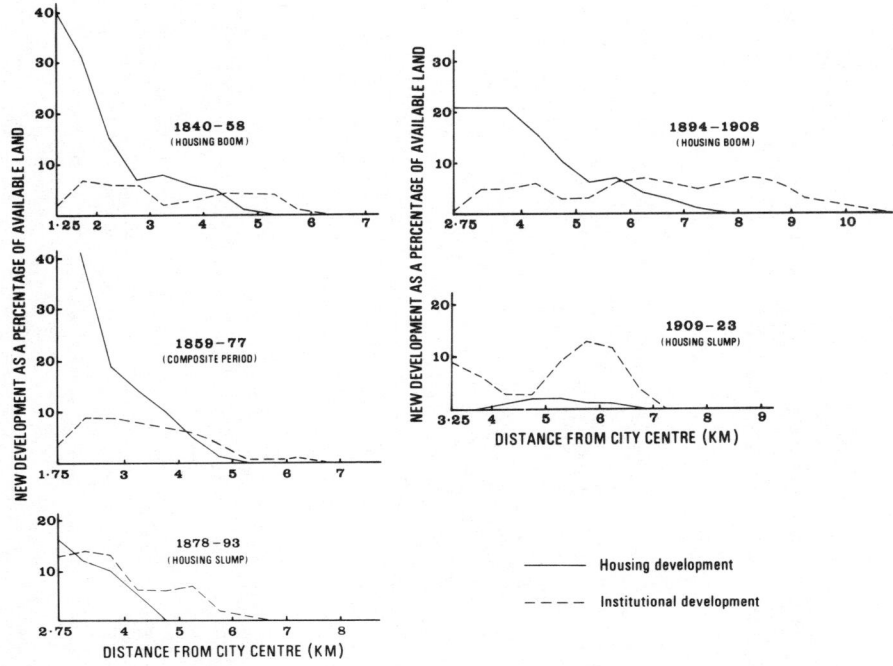

Figure 3.12 New housing development and new institutional development (as percentages of available land) in north-west Glasgow during five time periods related to distance from the city centre. The percentages are the running means of three distance zones of 0.5 km width

repel potential occupiers of nearby sites. The high incidence of institutional development at the 3 km distance in 1909–23 was almost entirely the result of new or ancillary developments occurring adjacent to existing institutions – an evidently important process not allowed for in the model. Permanent residuals at fixed distances might also be associated with the presence of physical features, administrative boundaries and other antecedent features arranged roughly parallel to the distance zones. Nevertheless, although the actual land-use pattern was constrained by such factors, the cyclical forces we are postulating appear to be of underlying importance.

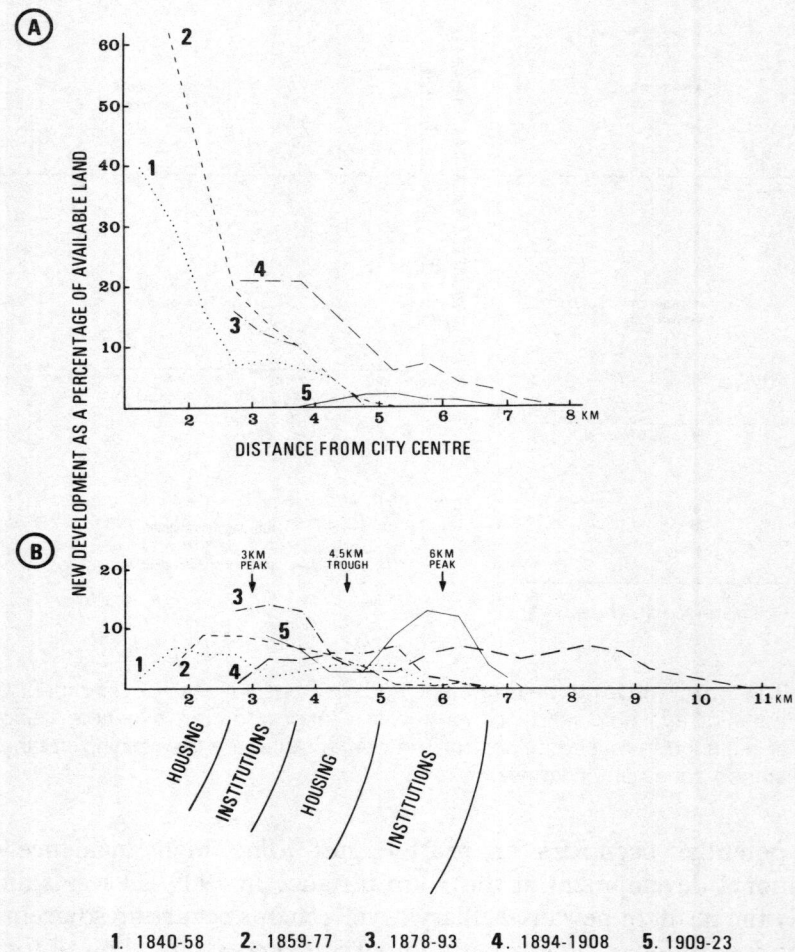

Figure 3.13 New development in north-west Glasgow as a percentage of available land for five periods superimposed: (A) housing development, (B) institutional development (including the approximate positions of the landscape zones emerging in 1923)

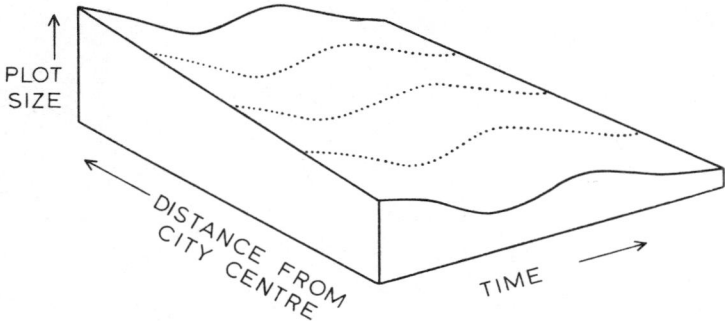

Figure 3.14 Hypothetical variations in the size of new plots developed in relation to time and distance from the city centre

INTENSITY OF DEVELOPMENT

If a theory is to justify acceptance it requires a number of different tests in a variety of conditions. Furthermore, hypotheses derived from the main argument need to be explored. So far attention has been largely confined to the implications of our argument for land-use patterns, but the same reasoning can be applied to intensity of land use, as measured by floor-space concentration or, to use the planner's term, plot ratio. Owing to the nature of the available data, here the highly correlated variable of size of building plot will be explored.

In relation to size of plot, some of the consequences of the theory for extensions to urban areas are summarized diagrammatically in figure 3.14. During any period of time the average size of new plots developed increases with distance from the city centre. Within any distance zone the secular trend is a diminution in the size of new plots developed but this is interrupted by rises during housebuilding slumps and falls during housebuilding booms. Within a given area a slump of intensity similar to a previous slump is likely to be associated with smaller plots than its predecessor, owing to the fact that during the intervening boom the area would have become more centrally located relative to the urban area as a whole, resulting in a greater demand for sites, higher land values and a more intensive use of land. Despite the simplicity of this model, the economic reasoning on which it is based would seem to be sufficiently central to the development process to justify testing it.

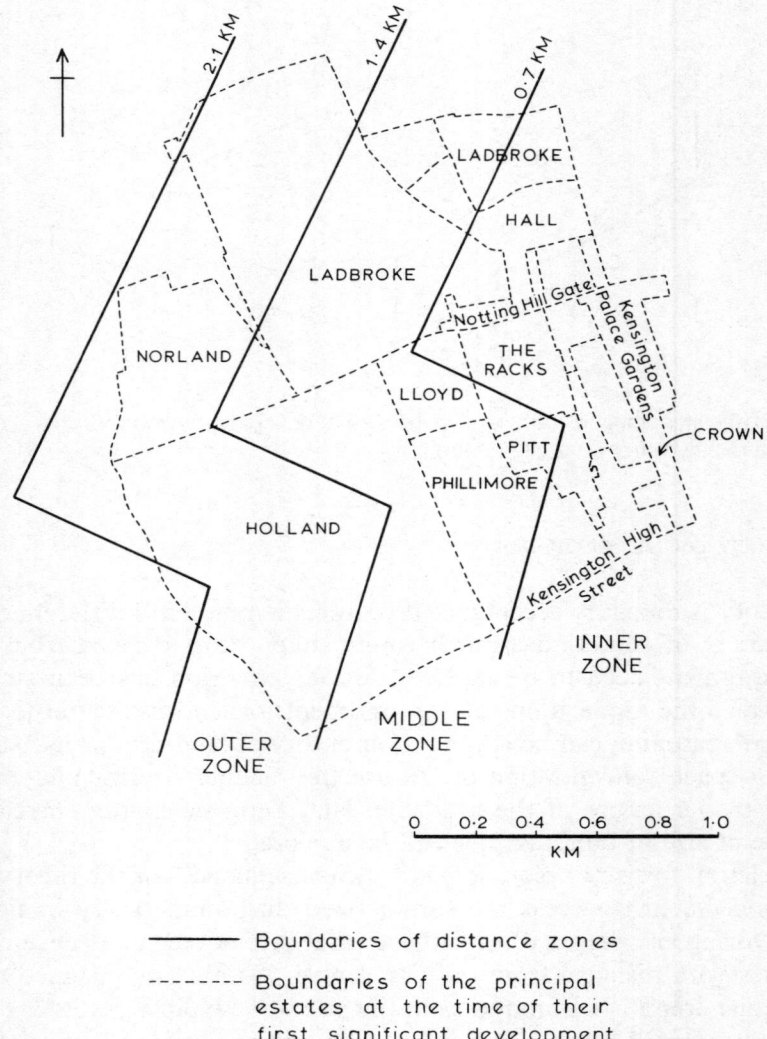

Figure 3.15 Test area in northern Kensington, showing the principal estates and the boundaries of the distance zones. The estate boundaries are taken from Greater London Council, 1973, end map

A rare set of records on building construction and leases that may be used for this purpose has been compiled for the London suburb of northern Kensington.[69] It includes, for an area of approximately 4 km², the location and date of initial urban development of over 2500 plots

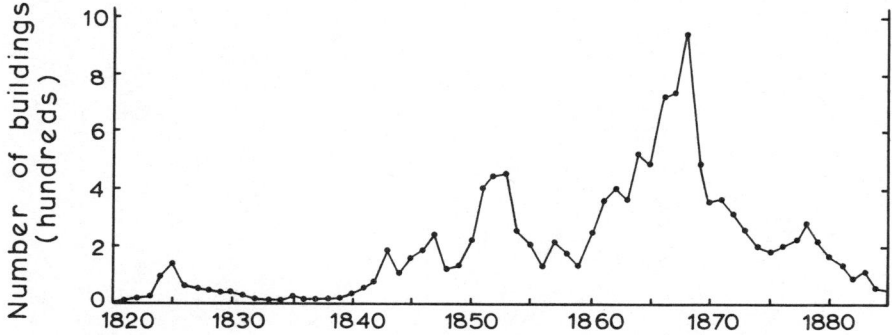

Figure 3.16 Number of buildings constructed in northern Kensington, 1820–85
Source: Greater London Council, 1973, p. 6.

(approximately one-half of the plots developed in that area during the middle part of the nineteenth century). The area (figure 3.15) was largely developed as a middle-class residential extension of the West End of London during the period 1826–69. During this time it underwent two building slumps and two building booms (figure 3.16). For a sample of 44 plots or groups of plots, selected to match as far as possible the sizes and spatial distribution of plots in the area, there was, as expected, a high negative correlation between size of plot and floor-space concentration, the relationship being markedly curvilinear (figure 3.17).

Figure 3.18 affords a general comparison between the model and developments in the test area. The actual variations in the size of new plots developed over time broadly conform to the hypothesized pattern. Within each of the distance zones the median plot size (used in preference to the mean because of the highly skewed distributions) is higher in slumps than in booms and there is a general trend for median plot sizes to decline over time. In contrast, the variations in the size of new plots developed in relation to distance do not conform to those hypothesized. Instead of increasing to a peak in the outer zone, median plot sizes tend to be highest in the middle zone and in the outer zone fall to approximately the level of the inner zone.

Our hypothesis concerning variations in the size of new plots developed over time is examined more precisely in figure 3.19. The predictions concerning both the secular trend and the characteristics of slumps and booms require that the plot sizes in each slump should differ significantly from those in the subsequent boom. This is confirmed by table 3.1. An impression of the overall character of each of the frequency distributions is provided by figure 3.20, which shows the cumulative

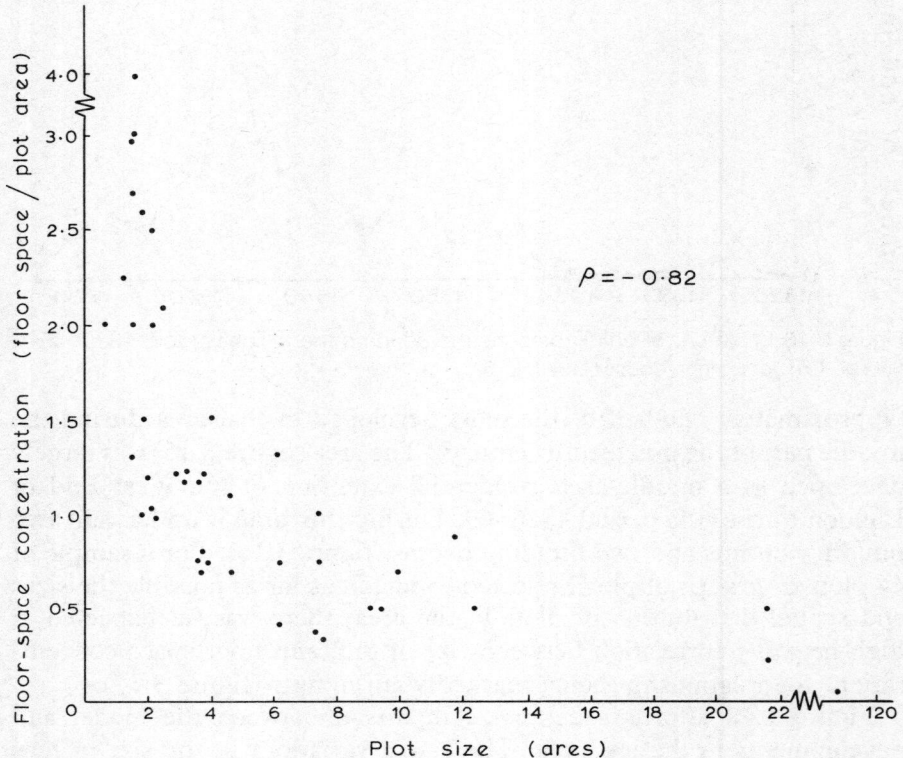

Figure 3.17 Relationship between plot size and floor-space concentration in northern Kensington

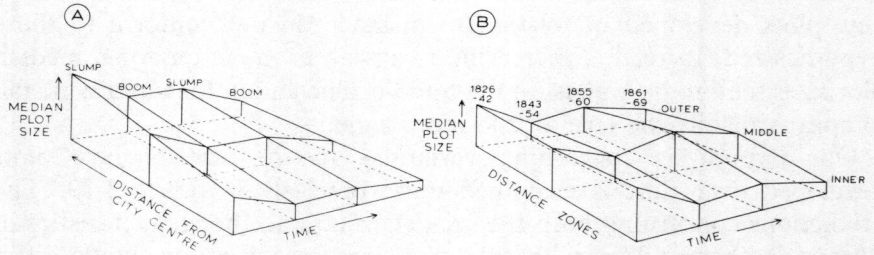

Figure 3.18 Approximate variations in the size of new plots developed in relation to time and distance from the city centre: (A) hypothetical, (B) northern Kensington. To aid legibility building booms and slumps are shown as equidistant on the time scale

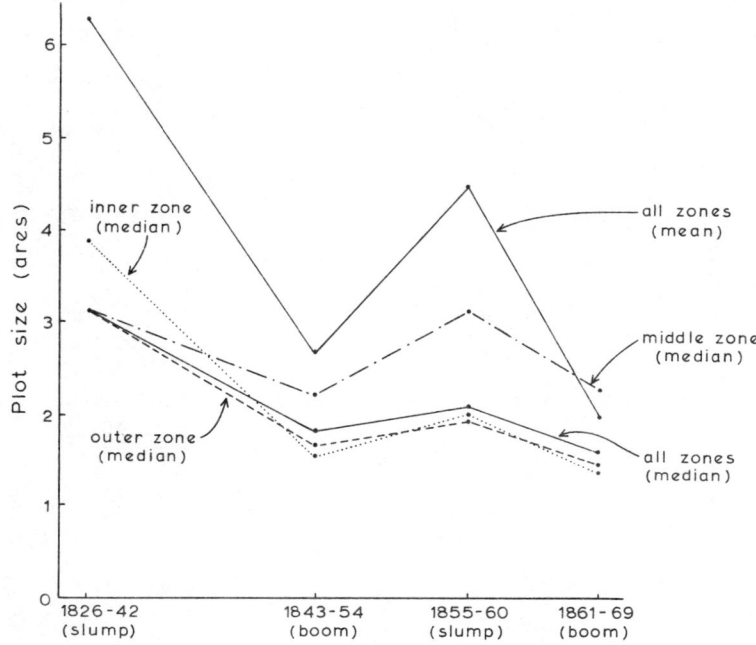

Figure 3.19 Mean and median sizes of new plots developed in northern Kensington in relation to time

percentage of plots in each size category for each zone during each period. With the minor exception of the first of the slump–boom pairings in the middle zone, each slump curve is entirely to the right of the curve for the following boom. In all cases there are some slump plots that are so much larger than the average that it is impracticable to use an arithmetic scale to show the complete cumulative percentage curves on the diagram and an arbitrary cut-off point has been adopted.

This test does not enable that part of the difference in plot size accounted for by a secular trend to be separated from the part attributable to the change from a slump to a boom. Although there would appear to be no satisfactory method of separating these two influences, it is possible to compare the 1843–54 boom with the subsequent slump and determine whether the change to slump conditions is associated with the development of significantly larger plots in spite of an opposing secular trend. Table 3.2 confirms that this is so.

Table 3.1 Comparison of the sizes of new plots developed in each slump with those developed in the following boom

| | | Slumps | | | | | | Booms | | | | Mann–Whitney test | |
| | | | Plot size (ares) | | | | | Plot size (ares) | | | | | |
Zone	Period	No. of plots	median	mean	S.D.	Period	No. of plots	median	mean	S.D.	U	z
Inner	1826–42	44	3.91	8.79	19.73	1843–54	305	1.56	2.94	4.20	2901	6.09*
Inner	1855–60	201	2.03	2.63	5.10	1861–69	121	1.39	1.90	0.86	8297	4.78*
Middle	1826–42	181	3.13	4.03	10.10	1843–54	495	2.21	2.94	4.78	35915	3.95*
Middle	1855–60	59	3.13	4.28	5.62	1861–69	131	2.28	3.12	4.15	2246	4.61*
Outer	1826–42	49	3.13	12.30	20.84	1843–54	440	1.68	2.20	2.97	6106	4.98*
Outer	1855–60	206	1.97	6.30	17.48	1861–69	320	1.44	1.57	1.25	12833	11.83*

*$\alpha < 0.001$

Table 3.2 Comparison of the sizes of new plots developed in the boom of 1843–54 with those developed in the slump of 1855–60

| | Boom (1843–54) | | | | Slump (1855–60) | | | | Mann–Whitney test | |
| | | Plot size (ares) | | | | Plot size (ares) | | | | |
Zone	No. of plots	median	mean	S.D.	No. of plots	median	mean	S.D.	U	z
Inner	305	1.56	2.94	4.20	201	2.03	2.63	5.10	25783	3.03*
Middle	495	2.21	2.94	4.78	59	3.13	4.28	5.62	9514	4.38**
Outer	440	1.68	2.20	2.97	206	1.97	6.30	17.48	30362	6.77**

*$\alpha < 0.01$
**$\alpha < 0.001$

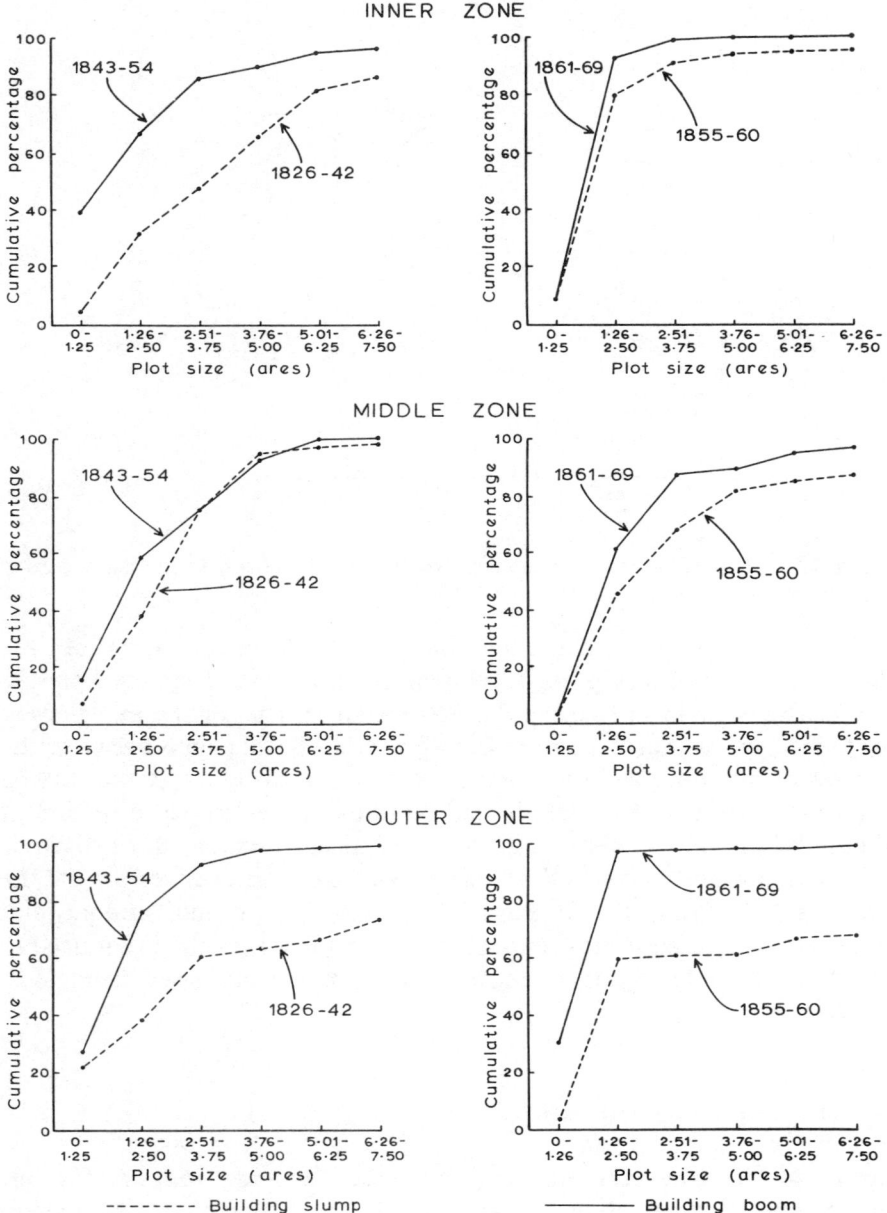

Figure 3.20 Cumulative percentage of plots developed in each size category during each period in each distance zone in northern Kensington. The curve for each building slump is paired with that for the following boom

58 J. W. R. Whitehand

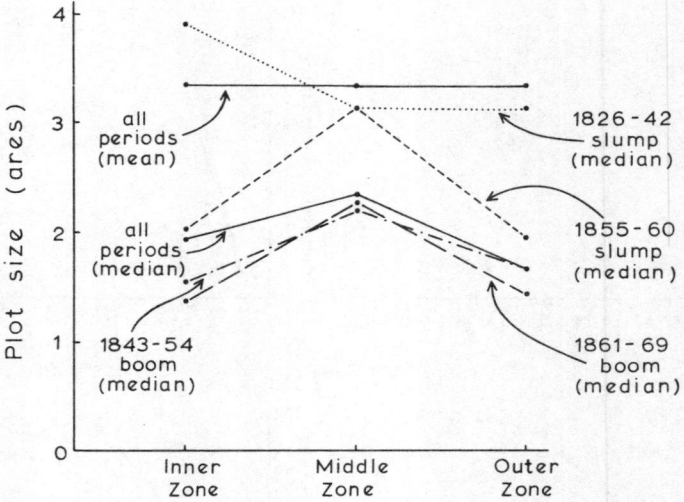

Figure 3.21 Mean and median sizes of new plots developed in each distance zone in northern Kensington

The lack of support for the hypothesis that during any period of time the average size of new plots developed increases with distance from the city centre is plain in figure 3.21. A substantial part of the explanation for this may be that it is an effect of scale. The distance between the centres of the inner and outer zones is only 1.4 km in a city that by the end of the study period already had a radius in a westward direction of about 8 km. Hoyt demonstrated in Chicago major short-distance variations in land values subsumed in, but sometimes reversals of, the overall decline from the city centre.[70] If, as we have been assuming, plot sizes exhibit related trends, an area considerably larger than that used in the present study might be required to separate city-scale from local trends.

COMPLICATIONS TO THE MODEL

Both the Glasgow and Kensington studies provide support for our theory. But the revealed deviations from the models reinforce the need to bear in mind that other factors may in individual circumstances outweigh or obscure the economic relationships that underlie the theory. First, even if the interests of those responsible for urban development are primarily economic, the nature of those interests may differ according to individual circumstances. The fact that in northern Kensington the four estates possessing enough plots to justify a separate analysis had secular and cyclical variations in plot sizes consistent with the theory should not blind us to such individual circumstances.[71] Slater, for example, has demonstrated the significance of the family life cycle for the decision making of landowners.[72] Secondly, decisions about landscape change are frequently interdependent. In Glasgow there were clear cases of institutions favouring sites adjacent to one another. Conversely in Kensington it seems probable that the location of a brickfield in the north-west part of the study area and the insalubrious character of areas beyond it were factors discouraging the construction of high-class housing in the vicinity. These are just a few examples of elements in decision making that our theory ignores and which will be explored in later chapters.

Three other matters arising out of the tests should be noted. First, they were undertaken within what were at the time essentially single-nucleus cities during periods of fairly compact outward growth: the implications of the theory for urban areas in which development was diffuse or polynuclear in character remain to be explored. Secondly, the theory has been examined so far only in relation to the development of the urban fringe. The important matter of the changes that take place when developments become embedded within the built-up area will be discussed in chapter 5. Thirdly, and of more immediate concern, it is necessary to consider long-term changes in the nature of society that inevitably affect the way in which urban forms are brought into existence. Innovation and planning are germane to this and will be the subjects of the next chapter.

4
Innovation and Planning

It is difficult to envisage a realistic theory of the long-term development of cities that does not take account of the course of innovation. The numerous innovations that have had an impact on urban forms during the industrial era may for convenience be grouped into four broad types: first, those directly relating to construction (for example, concerned with building materials and legislation); secondly, functional innovations, such as new methods of manufacturing and trading; thirdly, transport innovations, which are a particular kind of functional innovation important enough to distinguish in their own right; finally, perhaps one may recognize as a separate category innovations in town planning. All of these are, of course, interrelated and closely connected with the development of social attitudes.

Although innovational activity is difficult to quantify, there is some basis for the view that it fluctuates over time.[1] Furthermore, there is evidence that for some individual innovations the curve of the number of adopters over time approximates to a normal probability distribution.[2] These two factors make it plausible that the adoption of innovations in general fluctuates over time. Unfortunately much of the evidence for this is impressionistic. In Great Britain it is possible to recognize periods of relative quiescence in the adoption of innovations with a direct influence on the urban landscape (for example, in the 1880s, 1910s and 1940s) separating periods characterized by the relatively rapid adoption of innovations. For instance, the 'Edwardian' period of the late 1890s and early 1900s was characterized by peak rates of adoption of the tunnel-back house,[3] art nouveau,[4] and the electric tram,[5] to take three contrasting innovations. Corresponding peaks in the inter-war period were those of the universal plan,[6] Stockbrokers' Tudor[7] and the motor bus.[8] The association between certain innovations would sometimes appear to be a fairly direct relationship; for instance, between certain town-planning innovations and innovations in building. But the connection in other cases (for instance, between innovations in retailing and those in constructional materials for housing) is likely to be indirect. The explanation most probably lies in the connecting links between a great variety of types of innovation and the general state of the economy. If this is so, the periodicities involved suggest that the connection should be sought in long swings in the economy (cycles of approximately 20 years' duration) rather than in the short-term business cycle (3–4 years). Arguably the most important of such long swings for the urban landscape are building cycles, already the subject of considerable discussion in chapters 2 and 3. An obvious next step, therefore, is to consider what relation, if any, there is between innovation and variations in the level of constructional activity.

INNOVATION AND CONSTRUCTIONAL ACTIVITY

Connections between various types of innovation and constructional activity have been suggested in several studies. Particularly relevant in the present context is the relation between the adoption of transport innovations and fluctuations in general building activity in the United States (figure 4.1). Isard concludes that the six building cycles that occurred in the United States between the late 1820s and the early 1930s reflected such a relationship.[9] The first building boom coincided with a boom in canal construction. The following three occurred at the same time as three major outbursts of railroad construction. The fifth was associated with electric-railway development, and the sixth with a boom in motor-car registrations. Also relevant is the strong association in the same country between inventive activity in the building industry (measured by the number of building patents) and fluctuations in residential, commercial and industrial building combined (figure 4.2).[10] In a more detailed study of an individual British city, Forster has demonstrated how innovations embodied in building legislation interact with housebuilding cycles.[11] He postulates a model in which housebuilding increases and building styles diversify with the impending adoption of more stringent regulations concerning minimum housing standards. After the new legislation comes into force, housebuilding diminishes and building styles become more homogeneous.

In arguments concerning the direction of causation between innovation and building the view that favours a causal role for innovations

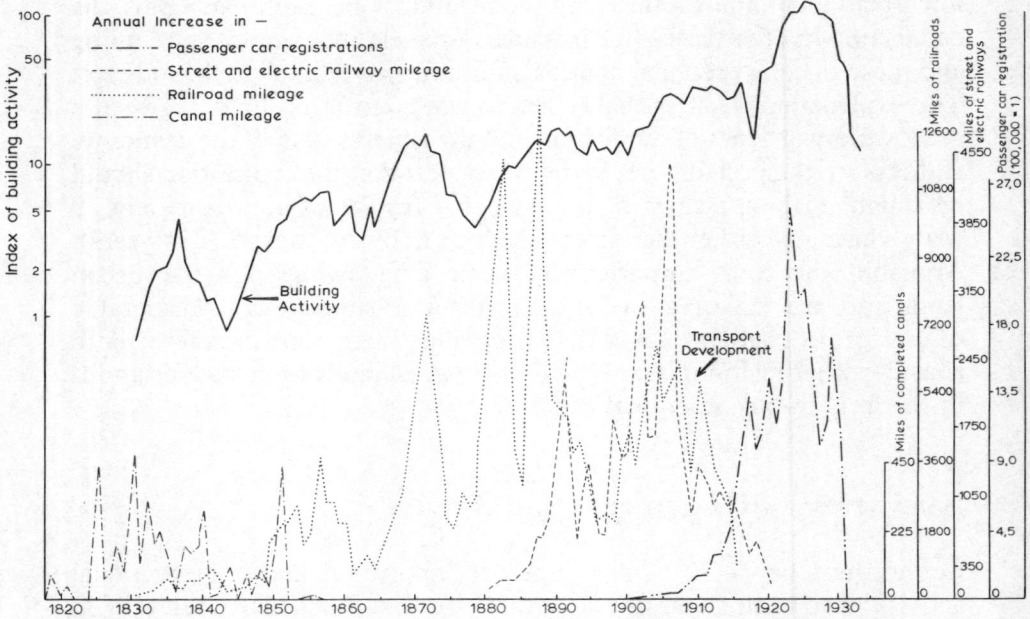

Figure 4.1 Transport development and building activity in the United States
Source: Isard, 1942, Quarterly Journal of Economics, 57, p. 100.

appears on the whole more plausible, at least in the case of certain types of innovation. Especially if they are of a functional kind (for instance, in manufacturing and service industries) innovations tend to generate higher incomes and employment opportunities. This in turn fosters population growth, both by affecting the balance of immigration and emigration and by encouraging the formation of families and the birth of children. This increases the demand for residential accommodation and other types of building. Given the availability of credit, a boom in constructional activity ensues. Closer inspection of the three examples just considered, however, suggests a less tidy relationship. Whereas transport development appears to synchronize with or lead building activity (figure 4.1), building patents lag behind building activity in two out of six building booms (figure 4.2). Furthermore, it would be oversimplifying to regard legislation as playing an entirely causal role in Forster's conception of the interaction of by-laws and building cycles.

Whatever the direction of causation between innovation and building activity, one aspect of the relationship is particularly relevant to the form taken by the urban landscape. This is the extent of the correspondence between the adoption curves of individual innovations and cycles in

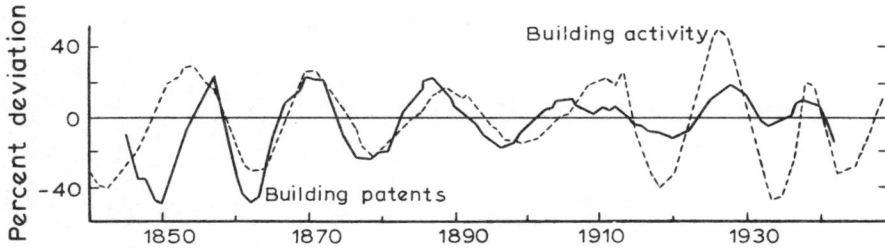

Figure 4.2 Building activity and building patents in the United States, 1840–1950: deviations of 7-year from 17-year moving averages. Patents are counted according to year of granting up to 1873 but according to year of application after 1873.
Source: Schmookler, 1966, p. 132.

construction. Although the approximation of innovation adoption curves to a normal probability distribution is an acknowledged regularity, few innovations with a direct bearing on the urban landscape have been systematically studied. Some transport innovations, such as the electric tram in Great Britain, have largely been adopted within a single building boom, whereas others, such as the railroad in the United States, have undergone booms and slumps in adoption corresponding to several building cycles. Measurement problems are considerable, particularly as innovations change in the course of their adoption and thereby raise questions about the definition of a particular innovation. The spread of Marks & Spencer retail outlets in Great Britain serves as an illustration, though it is a less complicated case than many. It largely took place during two building booms – those of the 'Edwardian' period and the 1930s – but looked at more closely that part of the adoption curve associated with each boom represents a distinct innovation (figure 4.3): the bazaar in the period of approximately 15 years preceding the First World War and the variety store from the late 1920s to the end of the 1930s.[12] In contrast, another major retailing innovation, the department store, was adopted rapidly in comparatively unchanged form during both the Edwardian and inter-war periods.[13] In another field, building technology, although Victorian sash windows with plate glass seem to have largely superseded small-pane Georgian sash windows in England within the middle two decades of the nineteenth century, cavity walls, of which examples existed well before the end of the nineteenth century,[14] only finally achieved virtually complete country-wide adoption after the Second World War. Although evidence is of variable quality and often impressionistic, it seems probable that adoption curves have generally been much more variable in length than building cycles.

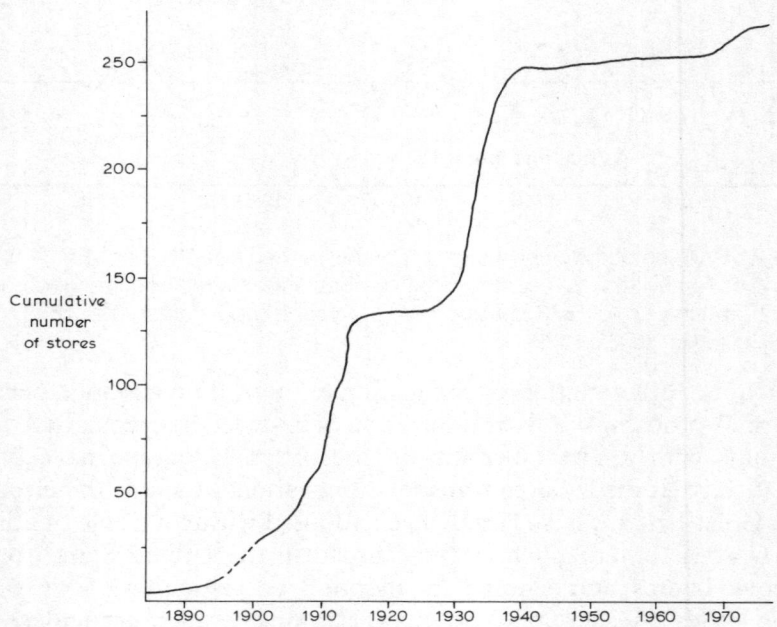

Figure 4.3 Cumulative number of Marks & Spencer shops opened in Great Britain, 1884–1976
Source: Cooper, 1977, p. 10.

These inferences suggest the need for circumspection in our attitude towards models of urban growth in which each building cycle is associated with a distinctive growth annulus in terms of its material forms. Adams constructs such a model of cities in the American Midwest, in which each building cycle is characterized by particular architectural styles.[15] This is consistent with an association between innovation and constructional activity, but the negligible representation in the landscape of innovations occurring during slumps in constructional activity and their supersession by the time that constructional activity is renewed could also be part of the explanation. Whatever the relative strengths of these influences, the proposed synchronism between a building cycle and the adoption of particular innovations falls well short of perfection in reality. It remains, nevertheless, a significant link in the relationship between the extent and the character of the material forms created in the landscape.

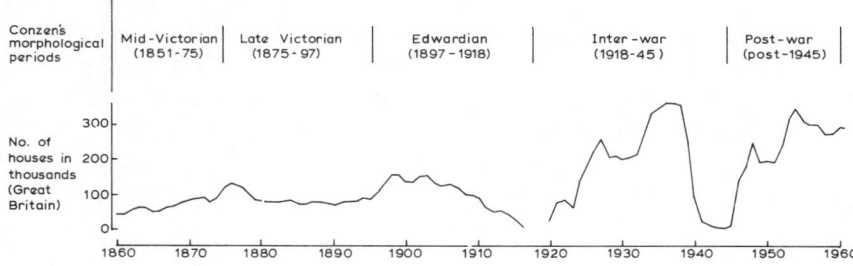

Figure 4.4 Conzen's morphological periods of Alnwick and housebuilding cycles in Great Britain. The years of the First and Second World Wars, omitted by Conzen, have been included in the Edwardian and inter-war periods respectively
Source: Conzen, 1960, p. 8; Mitchell and Deane, 1962, p. 239; Department of the Environment, 1971, p. 7.

If each building cycle is to some degree characterized by a particular cluster of innovations, the question arises as to the relationship between cycles and morphological periods. Defined by Conzen broadly speaking as time spans in which distinctive material forms are created in the cultural landscape, morphological periods have an important place in urban morphogenetic research. Their basis in the English market town of Alnwick has been summarized by Conzen in his classic study.[16] The defining characteristics vary from one period to another.[17] Events of major social, economic and cultural significance, tend to separate different morphological periods. These events may have a pronounced effect over large areas within a short time, as in the case of the two world wars. But other distinguishing features of morphological periods may be more difficult to date precisely, as in the case of the introduction of new building fashions. Some may occur at different times in different places, the advent of the railway being a major nineteenth-century example. In practice there is a considerable resemblance between Conzen's morphological periods of Alnwick and British housebuilding cycles, at least from the 1870s onward (figure 4.4). For earlier periods the incompleteness of information makes comparisons more difficult.

For the moment it seems justified to treat building cycles and morphological periods as interrelated but not necessarily synonymous. This view is based on limited, purely empirical evidence. There is a danger in the case of both building cycles and morphological periods of exaggerating their unity, thereby obscuring the complexity of the underlying social and economic processes to which anomalies in the empirical record may provide clues. A significant problem already mentioned is the fact that several individual innovations clearly had adoption curves spanning several building cycles. An additional problem is the fact that the assumed synchronism at the national level between a building cycle and the adoption of a particular cluster of innovations is subject to various qualifications when large numbers of widely distributed towns of different sizes and with different economic bases are examined.

For the diffusion of many innovations, ranging from those concerning architectural detail to those of major functional significance, observation suggests that both neighbourhood and hierarchical effects existed. In contrast, in the case of fluctuations in building activity, although the available data are limited, there is at present no firm evidence for the existence of such effects. For instance, if on the basis of Lewis's data[18] British towns of more than and less than 75,000 population in 1891 are examined for the peak year of their Edwardian housebuilding boom, this does not appear to occur significantly earlier in the larger towns. Although these data are too sporadic to satisfactorily test for a neighbourhood effect and those compiled by Thomas on a regional basis refer to units that are too large both in time and space to justify such an analysis,[19] it would seem that time lags as long as those in innovation diffusion did not occur. This is consistent with the widely held, but poorly documented, view that, in Great Britain at least, innovations that characterized the metropolis during one building cycle were often still being adopted in small and distant places in a subsequent cycle, though the extent of the time lag tended to diminish as communications improved.[20] However, a thorough examination of the relationship between regional variations in building cycles and the spread of innovations in urban form has yet to be undertaken.

INNOVATION, LAND USE AND LAND VALUE

Innovation affects the urban landscape in two ways. The first effect is direct in that many innovations require accommodation in the landscape: they are themselves directly observable topographical features, ranging from 'penny bazaars' to supermarkets and from golf courses to squash clubs. The second effect tends to be less directly observable in the landscape but may have wider consequences. This is the influence that certain innovations, for example in communications and town planning, have on the form taken by a host of developments in the landscape that are not directly connected with those innovations, such as the effect of the motor car on accessibility or of green belts on areas beyond their boundaries.

The only aspect of the first type of effect that need detain us here is the distinction between the creation of a long-term staple land use, such as housing, and the introduction of more specialized land-use innovations – for example, associated with different types of recreation. Whereas variations in the size of population increments may well influence housebuilding fluctuations, the adoption of an innovation in the early or middle stages of its diffusion is likely to be more influenced by population size than by population change. Thus, in the case of the space-consuming recreational innovations of the mid nineteenth century considered in chapter 2, it might have been expected that nationally the creation of public parks, golf courses and rugby union clubs would have been less volatile than housebuilding, at least until these land uses became widespread. The fact that of the three, only public park creation seems to have had a more even incidence than housebuilding does not invalidate this argument, though it is a reminder that other factors may be more important. The nature and incidence of legislation, already discussed in relation to housing, is just one example.[21]

The second type of effect is more complex and because of its importance requires more consideration. The innovations involved are numerous and diverse. Attention will be confined to major examples in transport, construction and planning. Each in different ways can transform the potentialities of an urban area.

Innovations in the way in which people, commodities and information are conveyed are of major significance. In the American Midwest Adams distinguishes four periods characterized by different modes of intra-urban transport – the walking/horse-car era, the electric streetcar period, the era of the recreational automobile, and the freeway auto era.[22] Allowing for differences of timing, both within and between countries, this sequence has widespread applicability. Each introduction of a new mode of transport increased accessibility, although the streetcar necessarily channelled this more narrowly than the automobile.

The theoretical implications of increases in accessibility have been developed in several studies. There is general agreement among economists that *ceteris paribus* transport improvements lead to a

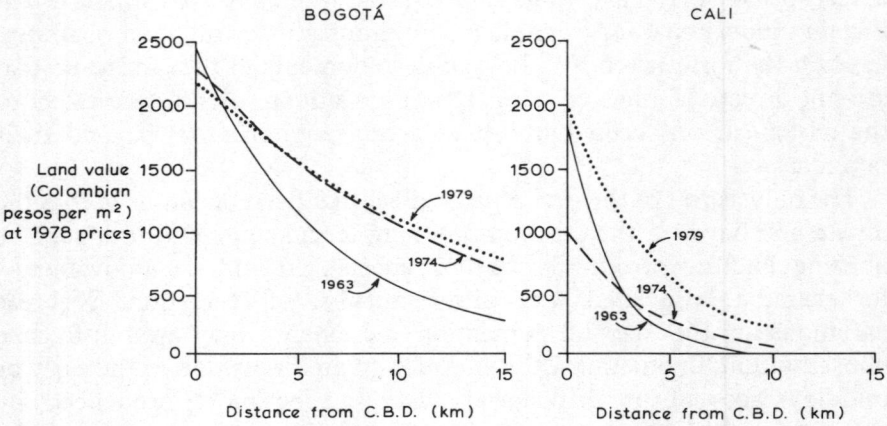

Figure 4.5 Relationship between land value and distance from the CBD in Bogotá and Cali, 1963–79, according to Mohan and Villamizar
Source: Mohan and Villamizar, 1982, pp. 232, 234.

reduction in the land-value gradient between city centre and urban fringe.[23] The empirical evidence, though fragmentary, is on the whole consistent with this view. For the nineteenth century Granelle's data are particularly valuable. These suggest that between 1830 and 1900 land values grew most rapidly in absolute terms in the city centre but in relative terms sites farther out tended to have larger increases.[24] However, within the Old Town of Vienna the main commercial streets underwent larger increases than more peripheral streets, both in absolute and relative terms, during the last 40 years of the nineteenth century,[25] although in this case the area studied comprised little more than the city centre.

Data for the twentieth century, the period during which urban transport has undergone the most profound developments, provide an essentially consistent picture of diminishing land-value gradients in a variety of types of cities. Hoyt times the beginning of 'the decentralization of land values' in Chicago as being after the First World War[26] and Yeates reveals a steady decline in the relation between land values and distance from the CBD in that city between 1910 and 1960.[27] Similar tendencies have been revealed in Christchurch, New Zealand[28] and Munich[29] over much the same period. It might be expected in non-Western cities, where the adoption of transport innovations has generally been retarded, that these tendencies would be more recent.

They are apparent in the 1970s, however, in several Korean cities[30] and in the Colombian cities of Bogotá and Cali (figure 4.5).[31] In Bangkok between 1958 and 1971, although the absolute increase in land values was greatest in or near the city centre, the percentage increase was greater near the limits of the urban area.[32]

These generalized relationships conceal a great deal of complexity and, although they are consistent with improved transport, they do not enable a causal relationship to be confirmed. Many other factors are at work. Nevertheless, if our argument concerning the relationship between land value and intensity of use is valid, then the tendency for land-value gradients to lessen in recent times should have a parallel in the gradient of intensity of use. In practice within an existing urban area intensity of use is much less amenable to rapid change than is land value. Furthermore, if cyclical movements in land values are excluded, absolute reductions are not common in either land values or intensities of use, with the possible exception of zones of older housing close to major Western city centres. A more readily observable manifestation of transport improvements and associated flattening of land-value gradients is to be found in low-density 'sprawl' at the urban fringe. Few attempts have been made to quantify this, but the development of the urban fringe of north-west Glasgow considered previously (figure 3.12) strongly suggests the abrupt appearance of this phenomenon during the housebuilding boom that marked the introduction of the electric tramcar at the turn of the century. However, it is doubtful if there was any sign as early as this of CBDs undergoing lower absolute rises in land values than peripheral urban areas. In Chicago, during the sharp rise in land values in the course of the building boom of the late 1880s and early 1890s, when the rapid spread of the cable car and electric street railway brought the urban fringe within quick reach of the CBD,[33] city-centre land values rose, in both percentage and absolute terms, more than anywhere else in the urban area. The flattening of the land-value gradient took place beyond the CBD as suburban areas underwent greater improvements in accessibility than older-established residential areas.[34]

While transport innovations transformed the urban area and its environs in terms of accessibility, thereby influencing the intensity at which sites were developed, innovations in constructional technology and architectural style influenced the urban landscape directly in terms of the physical characteristics of the structures erected. Changes in constructional technology, like those in transport, have implications for the model of urban development considered in chapter 3. Most importantly they affect the feasibility of developing sites at a high intensity. The rise in the value of city-centre sites before the First World War was paralleled by the adoption of major innovations in methods of construction. The ability of Chicago's city-centre organizations to exploit the increases in nodality brought about by the cable car and the electric street railway in the late 1880s and early 1890s was related in part to the more or less simultaneous adoption of a constructional innovation – the use of load-bearing frameworks of iron and steel – and the lift, or elevator.[35] These innovations permitted the development of sites at much higher densities than was previously practicable. During the corresponding building boom in New York City the largest buildings were about 50 per cent taller than those built in the boom of the 1870s.[36] In the next national building boom, during the decade preceding the First World War, reinforced concrete began to be widely adopted in America and even higher buildings were erected.[37]

PLANNING

These connections between innovations, land use and land value exemplify a web of relationships that is essentially unplanned. Simultaneously, but not independently, and perhaps varying as much over both space and time, there is a more or less continuous stream of innovations that represent conscious attempts by some form of national or local authority to control urban development. Such 'planning' is generally associated with governmental action, though it may, especially in individual cities, involve other forms of corporate action and attempts by individuals, especially large landowners, to exercise control over the landscape.

The way in which local building regulations may exercise an influence on housebuilding cycles has already been referred to. As well as influencing the timing of developments such regulations exercise an influence on building design.[38] Central government legislation has also had an effect on the timing and character of building activity, as Barras has shown for the City of London in the post-war period.[39] However, there are two interrelated types of spatial planning that are particularly relevant to the argument that has been developed so far about land use and land value. These are controls on the intensity or density of development and the designation of green belts – zones in which all or most types of urban building are precluded.

Density controls – expressed for example in terms of plot ratio (floor-space concentration), plot size or dwellings per unit area – have a long history of private and governmental use in many countries. Their implementation usually causes changes in the land-value surface. Sites whose development is limited to a density below that which would otherwise have occurred fall in value. The lower density will mean that more land is required to accommodate the same number of people and activities. Therefore other sites, not limited to a density below that which would occur without density restrictions, rise in value. The degree to which value is transferred between sites depends on the extent of the density controls and the availability of substitute sites.[40]

Green belts are an extreme form of density control applied specifically to the edge of the urban area. Probably their earliest manifestation is the 'glacis' – an open zone outside town walls, on which building other than of a defensive kind was prohibited. Such defences were a feature of pre-industrial cities in widely divergent culture areas. The cordons that they placed on city growth have been important in several different ways. In one respect they acted as density controls. As cities grew the constraining influence of the fortifications increased the pressure on land within the walls and building densities increased. In many major cities the pressure was ultimately released by the construction of a zone of fortifications further out, sometimes followed, in cases of additional city expansion, by a third zone even further out. The imprint of these zones on the urban landscape has remained strong in modern cities even after the fortifications themselves have been dismantled, especially in Europe and China,[41] for not only densities but much of the street system was related to them.

Viewed historically, planned physical limitations on urban growth manifest a series of innovations, first primarily military, but most recently relating to the control of urban sprawl. As weaponry developed so did the elaboration and width of the fortification zone, until by the eighteenth century a glacis extending several hundred metres beyond the main defence line was not uncommon.[42] Long before fortifications had ceased to have military significance they formed a social and economic barrier, in much of Europe at least, between the city and the suburbs, town gates serving as control posts for the movement of people and goods.[43] As they became obsolete the zone they occupied took on a new significance. Following their demolition in Paris, a boulevard-ring was completed on their line in the early eighteenth century.[44] By the end of that century the Renaissance fortification zone of Vienna, already leapfrogged by the growing built-up area, was converted into a recreation zone for the people living in the Old Town. The idea of utilizing the glacis as a zone for amenities and especially as a boulevard-ring was adopted widely on the continent of Europe in the nineteenth century. This was the formative phase in the development of the ring roads lined by public buildings, promenades, parks, public utilities and transport termini that were to become a striking feature of many major European cities. Meanwhile the idea of a surrounding amenity zone, or parkland belt, was being taken up in certain nineteenth-century new towns, most notably in South Australia and New Zealand, though seemingly with both intellectual origins and at least one antecedent in Britain.[45]

The modern green belt may be seen as the latest in this long chain of related innovations, though itself having different forms. In Vienna at the beginning of this century the green-belt concept was primarily about the provision of recreational space for people living in the densely built-up city.[46] At the same time proposals for a green girdle around London were probably influenced by the broad boulevards around Chicago, Boston and other American cities.[47] But it was not until 1938 that London's green belt achieved legal status.[48] In post-war Britain green belts have been viewed primarily as a means of controlling urban growth. Their implications for the theory of urban development discussed in chapter 3 are similar to those of the other encircling zones that have characterized the history of cities and are related to those of density controls. The concentricity of all these zones is of peculiar interest to our building-cycle/bid-rent theory because that theory too gives rise to essentially zonal patterns in the landscape. An important difference is that whereas our theory envisages a periodic shifting outward of density zones with each housebuilding boom, the planned belts of low density or quasi-rural character that we are now considering are for the most part fixed, though in some cases they may have been succeeded outward by belts of similar character as the urban area has expanded.

The effects of the imposition of green belts on land values have been the subject of several studies.[49] In a growing city without other density controls the effect is to raise land values and intensity of use on both sides of the green belt. Thus, in figure 4.6, instead of the land-value curve rising from *AA* to *BB* as the population of the city increases, it rises further to *CC*. Because of the high rents within the existing built-up area potential users of land are willing to pay the extra transport costs

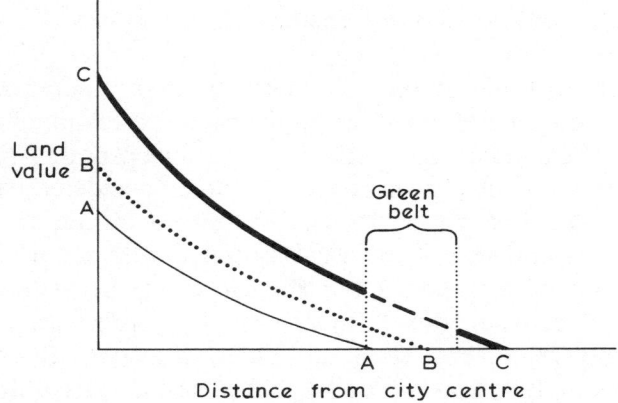

Figure 4.6 Influence of a green belt on land values
Source: Adapted from Evans, 1973, p. 254.

incurred at locations beyond the green belt.[50] The value of green-belt land will in most instances fall because the value that would have attached to it in the event of uncontrolled urban growth will be transferred to other areas. Nevertheless, the inclusion of a site in a green belt may add amenity value to land in its existing use, even though its exchange value, which reflects the potentialities for more intensive use, falls.

Clearly green belts, whether in a twentieth-century sense or in the sense of a glacis surrounding a town wall, have an impact that extends well beyond their physical boundaries. They merit attention in any realistic theory of urban development not only because they are obstacles to the physical expansion of urban areas and constitute distinctive land-use zones but because they influence the nature and intensity of land use elsewhere within the urban and peri-urban area.

Attempts to control densities and to place constraining girdles around cities are just two of the more important aspects of planning that affect the form taken by the urban landscape. The effects on land values of various other forms of legislation, such as rent control and compulsory purchase powers, also deserve note.[51] In the light of these influences and the effects of other innovations discussed previously it is necessary to address the problem of assessing the significance of innovations for the essentially economic explanations of urban development discussed in chapter 3.

INNOVATION ADOPTION AND ECONOMIC EXPLANATIONS

Although at least some of the effects of statutory limitations on the growth of the built-up area are clear, in the case of many innovations it is difficult to disentangle their effects from one another and from underlying economic mechanisms such as those considered earlier. For example, the spread of the garden-city movement during the first four decades of the twentieth century was associated with reduced dwelling densities in new developments, but the causes of such trends are not readily separated from the influence of the spread of motor-car ownership and motor-bus services. These transport improvements increased the supply of accessible sites and caused a relative shift in land value from the outer urban area to a wide penumbra of surrounding countryside. They are thus likely to have been important factors underlying reduced densities. Over a much longer period of time there are the higher average dwelling densities (and associated differences in building types) in Scottish as compared with English cities. It is problematic how far these differences may be explained by purely economic considerations. Although Birmingham and Glasgow were of similar size and had major housebuilding booms in the 1870s,[52] the resulting new developments differed markedly both in intensity and structural type. The dwelling densities in Glasgow were, at a conservative estimate, on average probably twice as high[53] and the structures were largely tenements,[54] while in Birmingham the terrace predominated.[55] According to our earlier argument concerning the economics of development, the densities should have been comparatively little higher in Glasgow. It is true that a considerable part of the density difference may be accounted for by differences in per capita incomes and by a higher demand for land in Glasgow, reflected in a higher rate of dwelling construction, but examination of the building types involved suggests that regional barriers in the diffusion of working-class house types have been influential, as perhaps have differences in types of site tenure.[56]

These examples illustrate the complex intertwining of innovation adoption and economic factors. Innovations and their adoption are interrelated with cyclical aspects of urban form that are strongly economic in basis. Furthermore, it is often difficult in practice to separate the effects in the landscape of innovation adoption from those of an economic mechanism such as the building-cycle/bid-rent theory developed in the previous chapter. It is necessary therefore to explore alternative types of explanation of urban landscape development. Urban-rent theory and innovation diffusion theory can take us only so far in our search for explanation. The next chapter will therefore examine a notion – the fringe-belt concept – that obviates some of the problems identified here. Its application yields findings both consistent with and, at first sight at least, at variance with those described so far, and prompts a reappraisal and extension of that part of our argument concerned with the economics of development.

5
Fringe belts

The ideas about the development of the urban landscape considered so far have drawn heavily on the work of economists and economic historians. The urban landscape has been viewed in large part as an outcome of economic cycles and innovation adoptions, in which forms have been distributed according to a Thünen-like conception of urban-rent theory. Such an approach is somewhat mechanistic. It is true that, in so far as it incorporates the findings of economic historians, it takes some account of the uniqueness of historical periods. But the landscape remains diagrammatic in representation and essentially passive in its role, reflecting rather than shaping developments. Such a view of the landscape is at variance with the urban morphogenetic tradition in geography described in chapter 1. This tradition offers a counterpoise to the economically infused theory that has dominated our discussion so far and provides an alternative perspective on some of the matters considered in preceding chapters.

The fringe-belt concept is arguably the most important single contribution to urban morphology to arise out of the German morphogenetic tradition. It has its origins in the recognition of the long-term significance of the physical limitations on urban growth discussed at the end of chapter 4. Unlike much of our argument so far, which has been concerned primarily with drawing inferences from temporal sequences, the fringe-belt concept is rooted in the reconstruction of landscape development. In 1936, Louis recognized, within the urban structure of Berlin, a number of land-use zones representing former peripheral urban uses encompassed by later accretions to the built-up area and separating older from younger residential areas.[1] He described these zones as urban fringe belts (*Stadtrandzonen*). Their land use varied, especially according to position within the urban area: institutions, country houses and their parks, public utilities, recreational areas and allotment gardens were

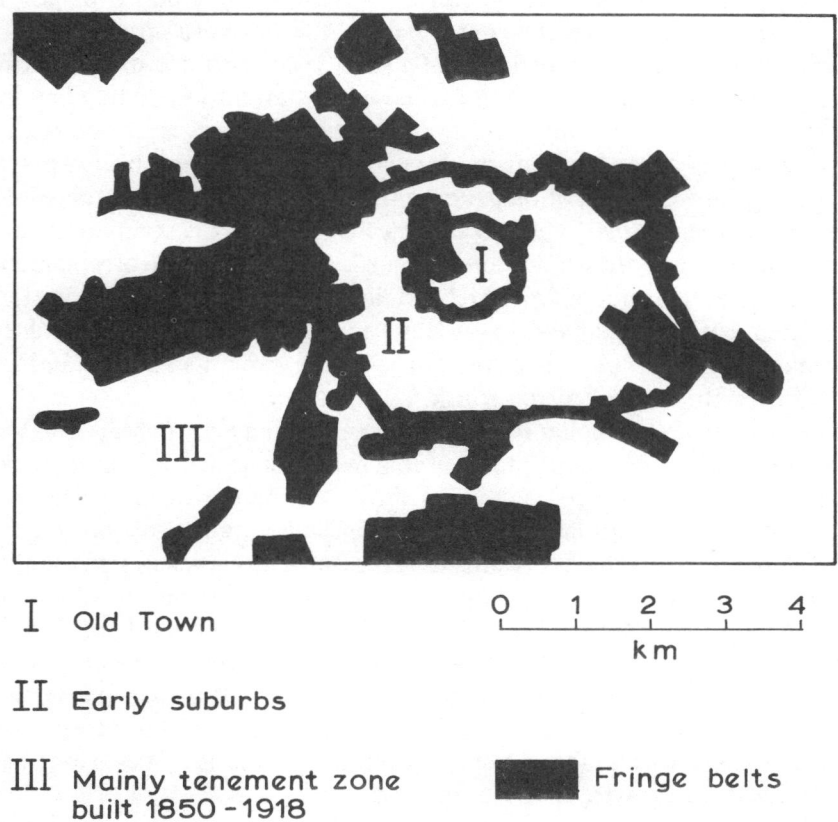

I Old Town

II Early suburbs

III Mainly tenement zone built 1850-1918

■ Fringe belts

Figure 5.1 The fringe belts of inner Berlin, c.1936
Source: Louis, 1936.

among existing or former uses. Two continuous fringe belts were associated with former fortification zones (figure 5.1). Further out, similar belts of extensive land use were discontinuous, including a broad zone of intermixed urban, quasi-urban and agricultural land at the rural–urban fringe.

In the hands of Conzen, Louis's idea of urban fringe belts became a means of putting order into the complexity of urban development.[2] By reconstructing the past development of urban areas he recognized that changes taking place in the landscape contained a cyclical element. The urban fringe did not extend outward steadily but underwent periods of acceleration, deceleration and even standstill, according to such factors as a city's economic well-being and constraints placed upon the use of land at the urban fringe. During a halt in the outward advance of the built-up area a varied assortment of urban land uses normally seeking large, cheap, peripheral sites tended to occupy land immediately beyond the stationary urban fringe. Once established, the existence of such a fringe belt was an obstacle to the renewed advance of the built-up area and during a resurgence of urban growth was leapfrogged by subsequent residential accretions. The repetition of phases of stagnation and resurgence of outward growth created a roughly concentric arrangement of distinctive integuments in which predominantly residential accretions alternated with fringe belts of mixed, initially peripheral, land uses. Conzen draws an analogy between this cyclical growth structure and the annual growth rings of a tree trunk.[3]

The sequence in which a fringe belt develops may be divided into two principal phases. The first phase is that when land at the fringe of the built-up area is taken up for the first time by urban or quasi-urban land uses. It continues until land under these uses no longer abuts on to rural land. Broadly equivalent to Conzen's fixation and expansion phases,[4] it may be termed the phases of fringe-belt formation. Further development of the fringe belt by the addition of new plots at the actual fringe of the built-up area is thereafter precluded, and the second phase, that of fringe-belt modification, commences. In fact modifications may occur before the fringe belt is sealed off, but most modifications are associated with changes of location that result from the enveloping of the fringe belt by the outward growth of the built-up area.

FRINGE-BELT FORMATION

Certain periods have been characterized by fringe-belt formation, and so have certain areal conditions: the two are clearly interrelated. A further factor influencing this phase is the mutual attraction and repulsion of various land uses.

Areal conditions conducive of fringe-belt formation include obstacles to the normal outward growth of the residential area. Continuous inner fringe belts have been particularly associated with fortification zones, which acted as powerful fixation lines during the pre-industrial era.[5] Less common, but often having comparable effects, have been parkland belts in the nineteenth century and green belts in the twentieth century. Williams has shown the pronounced effects of the nineteenth-century parkland belt in Adelaide, South Australia, surviving around the core of the present city as a girdle of public open spaces, transport installations, recreation areas and cultural and educational institutions.[6] The much wider post-war green belts around British cities have been less sharply identifiable on the ground, owing to several decades of rampant urban sprawl that preceded them. Over the last two centuries corporate decision making has probably been less important in delineating new fringe belts than it was in the era of town fortifications. In nineteenth-century Aberystwyth the fixation line for the town's middle fringe belt reflected a combination of landownership, land tenure, a specific fringe land use (ropewalks) and sharp breaks of slope.[7] During the same period on the eastern fringes of Newcastle upon Tyne the gorge and valley of Jesmond Dene was the fixation line of what is now the city's middle fringe belt (figure 5.2).

While in individual cities it is clear that particular periods have been characterized by fringe-belt formation, the extent to which local as opposed to national, or even international, factors are responsible has not been systematically analysed. It is apparent that in the second decade of the twentieth century and the years immediately preceding and following it, pronounced fringe belts came into existence in the Tyneside conurbation.[8] Many of the factors responsible were at work in Great Britain as a whole and some more widely. This was the culmination of a period of major expansion in the use of land by a wide variety of public and private institutions – for instance, educational establishments, hospitals, sports clubs, public parks, cemeteries and public utilities – virtually all of which were taking up spacious sites within a zone extending some 2–3 km beyond the edge of the built-up area. At the same time new housing, for a large proportion of the population at least, was still taking the form of high-density terraces and, in Scotland, tenements. Furthermore, the long hiatus in housebuilding over the period just before, during and just after the First World War meant that the outward spread of residential areas was minimal. Under these conditions it would be surprising if strongly developed 'Edwardian' fringe belts, such as have been identified in Tyneside,[9] were not also a feature elsewhere in Britain.

From the inception of a fringe belt the mutual attraction or repulsion of certain land uses plays an important part in its internal differentiation. Again taking examples from Tyneside, country houses and residences acquired adjacent sites in the vicinity of Jesmond Dene, while industries and warehouses concentrated in a quite separate area near the confluence

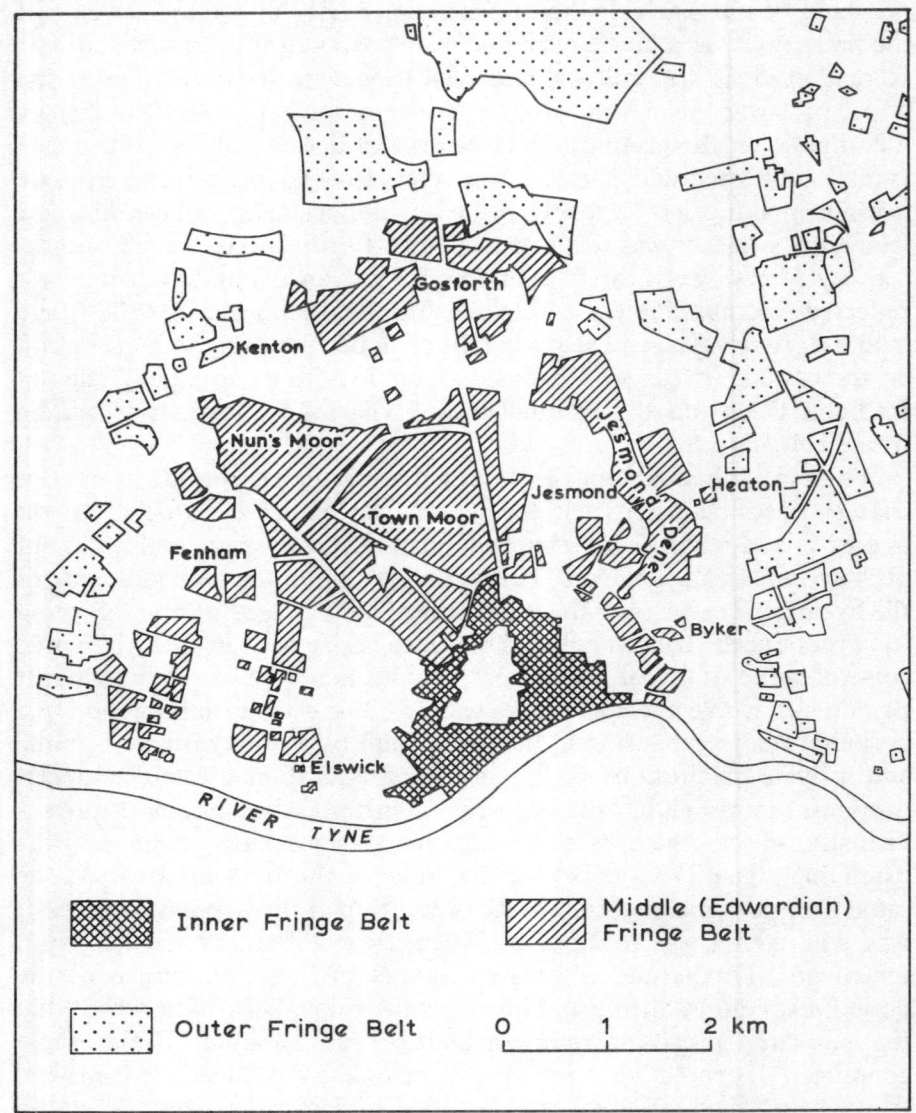

Figure 5.2 The fringe belts of Newcastle upon Tyne in 1965

of that valley with the Tyne valley. Some types of fringe-belt land uses, for example brickworks and certain industries, have been incompatible with the development of middle-class residential areas and are thus likely at times to have delayed the envelopment of fringe belts by the outward spread of housing. Such delays would allow more time for the character of fringe belts to become established.

At the end of their formation phase fringe belts provide landscapes that generally stand in marked contrast to those of residential accretions. Their admixture of land uses results in a more varied physiognomy. They exhibit considerably lower building densities and a coarse-grained pattern of plots. This results from the common requirement of large sites for such uses as parks, cemeteries, colleges, golf courses and public utilities. Such functions require few if any new streets and the existing rural framework of roads and boundaries requires little change except for the occasional amalgamation of adjacent fields. Thus a free fringe belt, namely one still abutting on to countryside as distinct from an occluded fringe belt inside the built-up area, may for many years preserve some of the seclusion of its rural origins.[10] Large villas or even country houses generally fit without difficulty into such a landscape.

While these factors affecting fringe-belt formation are applicable to a wide variety of situations, the outcome in the landscape reflects the economic and social history of the particular city. Whereas a series of relatively distinctive fringe belts is commonplace in the cities of north-west Europe, in southern Europe major differences of social and economic history, in particular a marked time lag in the onset of the Industrial Revolution, tend to be associated with a different spatial pattern. Clermont-Ferrand, in south-central France, underwent none of the large-scale nineteenth-century residential accretion so characteristic of cities in north-west Europe. In 1920 the population was still almost entirely concentrated within the town's medieval confines. Population growth just before a late and largely post-1918 Industrial Revolution was mostly accommodated by the multi-occupation of dwellings in the old town.[11] Instead of the extensive medieval fringe belt being encompassed by nineteenth-century residential accretion, as was the norm in cities of comparable size in north-west Europe, it remained open for augmentation by the institutions and related open spaces that developed in the later nineteenth century in response to growing economic needs and especially the growing social consciousness of the time. This extensive fringe belt, comprising plots of widely differing ages (figure 5.3), was not closed off until the inter-war period, when a rash of low-density housing, encroaching on to large areas of surrounding countryside, released the population pressure within the old town. Here was a different outcome from that created by a series of growth pulsations during the same period in cities that have been investigated in north-west Europe. The basic

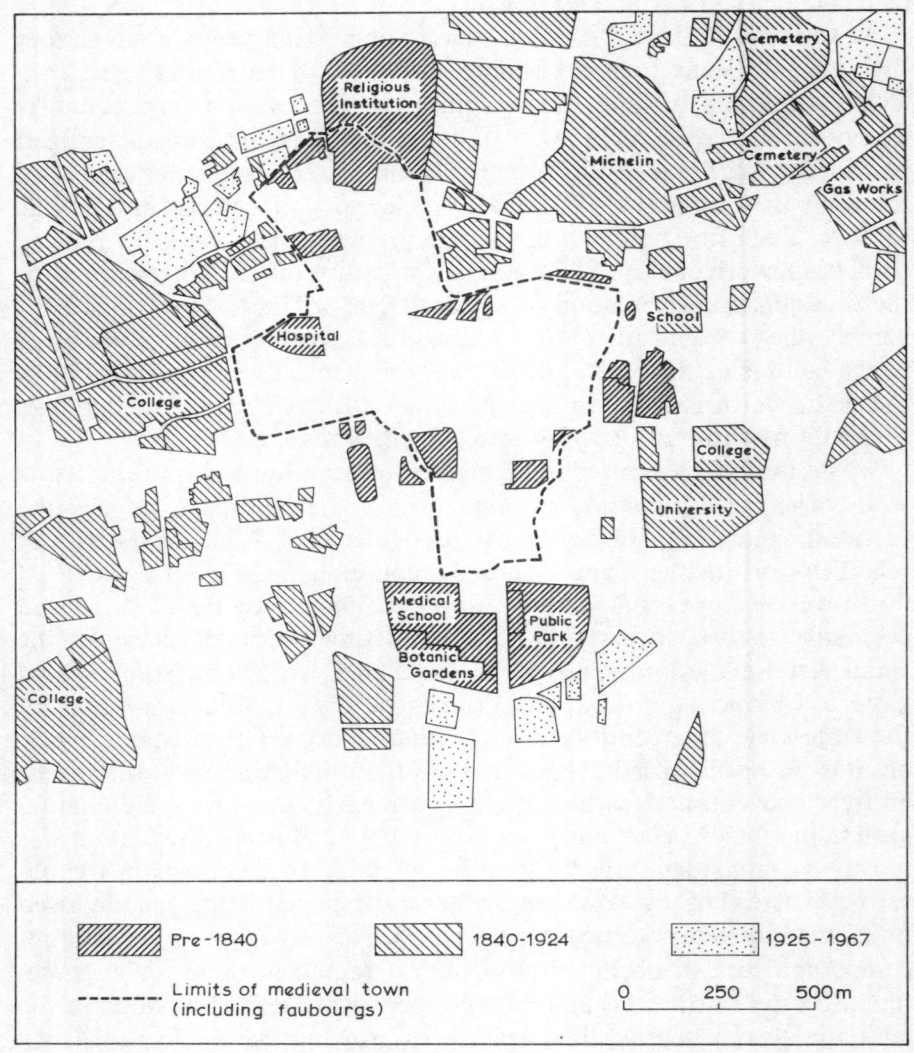

Figure 5.3 The inner fringe belt of Clermont-Ferrand in 1967. Beyond the medieval limits most of the blank areas are post-1924 residential accretions

Source: Unpublished plans and maps supplied by M. Robert Léon, Ingénieur de la Ville, Clermont-Ferrand; land-use survey by the Department of Geography, University of Glasgow, 1967; Bird's Eye View of Clermont-Ferrand in 1574 by F. Fuzier, in BelleForest, *La Cosmographie Universelle, Tout le Monde* (Paris, 1575), reproduced in Arbos, 1930, p. 39.

mechanism would appear to be consistent, however, with that suggested elsewhere.

How is such a conception of urban development to be reconciled with the theory of building cycles and bid rents explored in chapter 3? In many respects it is a morphogenetic, inductive approach to what in our earlier discussion was a matter of deductive, spatial analytics. Conzen's residential accretions have their parallel in the Thünian housing growth-rings generated by each housebuilding boom. Similarly fringe belts resemble the institutional zones that tend to consolidate at the urban fringe during housebuilding slumps. But, as Sutcliffe has pointed out,[12] cycles of residential accretion and fringe-belt development are considerably longer than housebuilding cycles. Between the occlusion of an inner fringe belt in the mid-Victorian period and the present, most British cities have experienced four housebuilding cycles but, assuming studies undertaken so far to be representative, they are unlikely to have acquired more than two further fringe belts.[13] It has already been shown that in nineteenth-century Glasgow each building cycle phase did not necessarily synchronize neatly with a particular land-use zone. The relative proportions of institutional development and residential development over time are not translated into clearly defined rings on the ground. The scale of housebuilding booms and slumps, the characteristics of the pre-existing rural landscape, and the tendency for land uses to attract or repel one another influence the outcome.[14] For much the same reasons, it is unlikely that each fringe belt could be related neatly to a particular housebuilding slump. A hiatus in housebuilding is an important condition in the formation of fringe belts, at least during the industrial era, but it is not a sufficient condition. It tends to be over a longer time-span than a housebuilding cycle that a pronounced slump in housebuilding combines with other conditions, notably in the past the existence of a fixation line, to give rise to the formation of a fringe belt.

FRINGE-BELT MODIFICATION

Fringe belts retain their distinctiveness long after they cease to be at the actual fringe of the built-up area. Although their character inevitably changes, and though they often expand or contract, except in unusual circumstances, they remain distinctive from adjacent areas. According to Conzen, 'it is as if such a belt, once established, created its own environment and imposed its own conditions of further development on its area in terms of shape and size of plots, types of land use, and degree of opening-up by streets'.[15]

The changes that take place depend to a considerable extent on the existing character of the fringe belt. One of the first changes is fringe-belt consolidation. Areas of agricultural land frequently remain within a fringe belt after it ceases to be at the actual edge of the built-up area, but are often eventually occupied by a use akin to that of adjoining fringe-belt plots. A knowledge of landownership often helps to illuminate this process. Such residual farmland has frequently been purchased with an urban use in mind while still at the urban fringe. In north-east Newcastle the Ministry of Public Building and Works acquired approximately 60 ha of land at the time of the Second World War, nearly half of which was still awaiting urban development as a hospital and a school some 20 years later.[16]

Existing fringe-belt plots, like other parts of an urban area, are subject to a cycle of adaptation and redevelopment that frequently involves a change of land use. Such a cycle may have already run its course several times in an old-established inner fringe belt, but in the Edwardian fringe belts of Tyneside relatively few sites had experienced redevelopment by the mid-1960s. Many were still in their original use or in a first stage of adaptation – for example, the country houses converted to institutions in Jesmond Dene. Such changes, by causing exchange values to rise relative to existing-use values, often precipitate similar changes in adjoining plots. Among the factors influencing such changes are the fact that as an urban area grows existing plots change their position in relation to the rest of the built-up area. The older the fringe belt the greater the relative change. In a city that has grown rapidly during the industrial era, an inner fringe belt is much more likely in the twentieth century to be located on the fringe of the modern CBD than on the fringe of the built-up area. When this occurs, land uses seeking locations on the edge of the CBD tend to acquire the conveniently placed and often relatively spacious plots of the inner fringe belt, which thus becomes part of the CBD frame.

A further fringe-belt modification involves changes near the boundaries between fringe belts and adjoining areas. The conversion of plots not associated with fringe belts to uses compatible with them is an instance of the more general and continuous process of change that is particularly characteristic of boundaries between land-use regions. A common example is for a growing institution, such as a hospital or college, to expand into nearby residential areas, often first converting existing houses and then redeveloping the sites with purpose-built institutional structures. The reverse process – the acquisition of fringe-belt sites for unrelated uses – is often associated with the increasing commercial land requirements of expanding city centres. It is also associated with the redevelopment for housing of fringe-belt sites occupied by uses entailing relatively small capital investment in site improvements, such as allotment gardens and parks attached to country houses.[17]

Evidence from America of the influence of fringe belts on land-use patterns long after they cease to be at the fringe of the built-up area is provided by M. P. Conzen.[18] In his study of Madison, Wisconsin he particularly examined the view that fringe belts are augmented by attracting 'sympathetic' land uses despite their loss of fringe location. He found that although most additions were to the outer fringe belt, located at the current edge of the built-up area, there was a strong tendency for the inner fringe belt of Madison to expand by the addition of new plots and kindred land uses (figure 5.4).

At first sight the tendency for fringe belts to be perpetuated and augmented long after they cease to be at the edge of the built-up area seems inconsistent with our earlier argument about the relative abilities of institutions and housebuilders to bid for sites. Although the implications of this argument were only considered in relation to the conversion of rural land to urban use, the reasoning can be extended to apply to existing urban land. Given a growing city and fixed bid-rent gradients, existing institutional sites would soon become attractive to housebuilders. Having acquired a fringe site during one housebuilding cycle, perhaps during its slump phase, an institution would receive increased bids for its site as housebuilding recovered. Our theory would lead us to suppose that the institution would therefore relinquish its site for one sub-marginal to the housebuilder. On this basis zones of institutional land use would be ephemeral. However, studies of the long-term development of fringe belts suggest that this is far from being the case in reality. Modification of the building-cycle/bid-rent mechanism previously outlined is therefore necessary. A further study of part of north-west Glasgow helps to clarify the timing of actual developments in the landscape that any such modification must account for.[19]

In a sample area of approximately 15 km^2, divided into northern and southern parts according to the period when the conversion of land from rural to urban use was at its height, the history of 100 fringe-belt plots between 1840 and 1968 was reconstructed. This revealed the extent to which fringe-belt uses either lost land to housing or gained land from it.

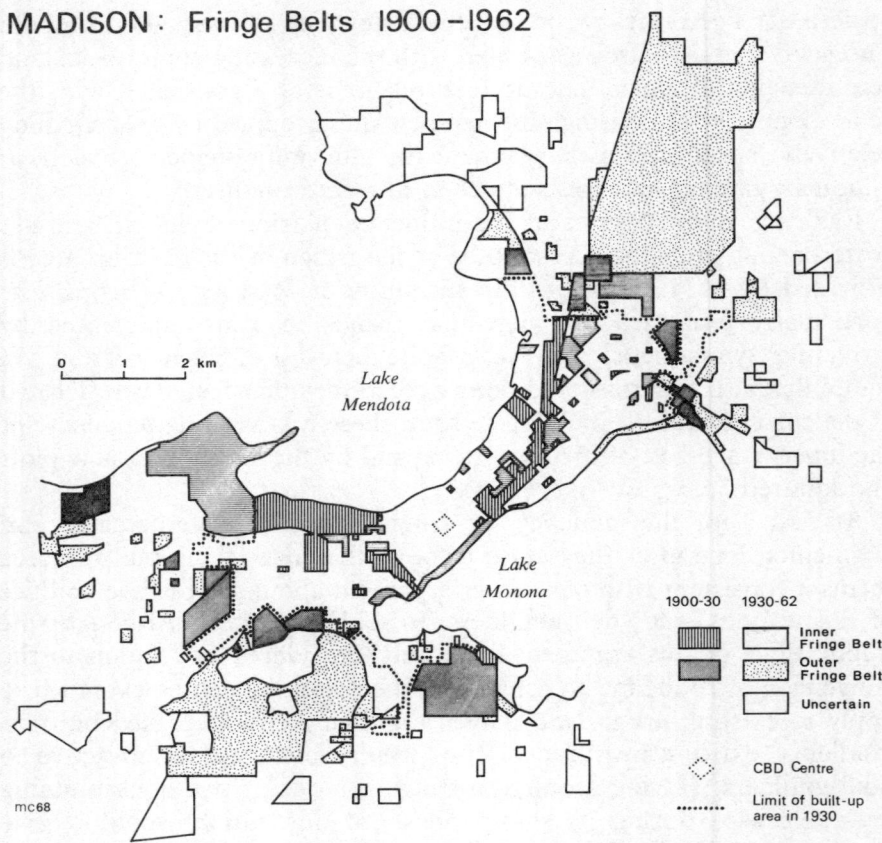

Figure 5.4 The fringe belts of Madison, Wisconsin in 1962
Source: Reproduced from Conzen, 1968.

The redevelopment of fringe-belt plots for housing was related to housebuilding cycles and the passage through the area of the main wave of housebuilding activity (figure 5.5). As the conversion of rural land to housing reached its peak, so did the redevelopment of fringe-belt plots for housing. Thereafter resurgences of decreasing magnitude were associated with succeeding booms until such redevelopments reached a negligible level.

In the case of fringe-belt expansion (figure 5.6) any influence of housebuilding cycles appears to have been subordinate to longer-term trends relating to the peak period of rural-to-urban land conversion.

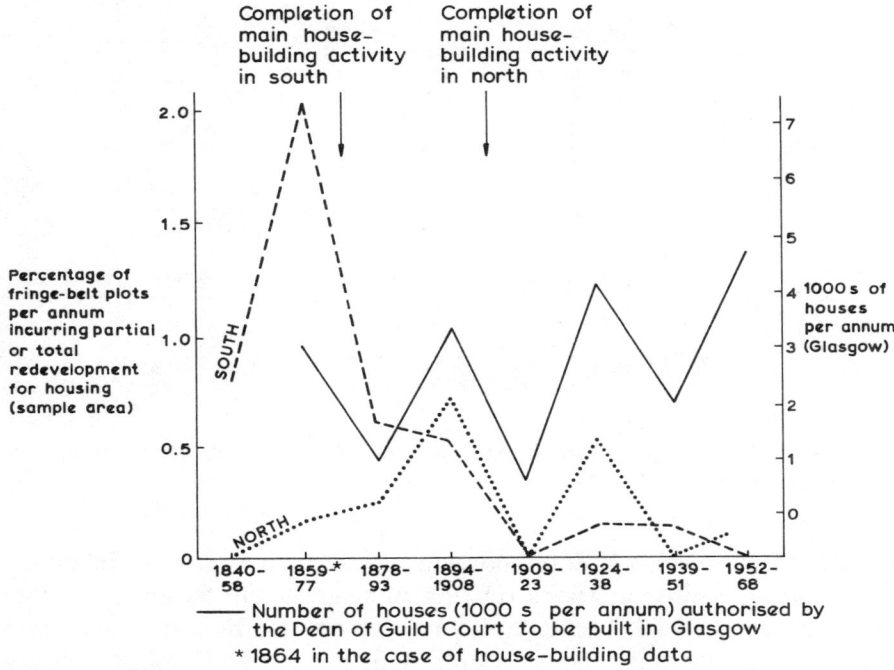

Figure 5.5 The redevelopment of fringe-belt plots for housing in a sample area in north-west Glasgow related to the building cycle, 1840–1968

During and immediately following this there was little expansion, but expansion was renewed within a few decades. Taking losses and gains together, it would appear that some fringe-belt uses, notably country houses and their parks, were vulnerable to redevelopment during the peak period of land conversion. Subsequently there may have been a period of equilibrium during which few fringe-belt sites were acquired by housebuilders and there was relatively little expansion of fringe-belt uses into adjoining areas. After this, and sometimes without such a period intervening, there was an increasing likelihood of fringe-belt uses actually expanding their site areas at the expense of adjacent housing areas by converting or redeveloping these.

Various explanations may be offered for these changes. An important consideration is the different requirements of owners and occupiers of housing on the one hand and institutions and most other fringe-belt occupiers on the other, and how these relate over time to the characteristics of the sites they occupy. The basic requirements of

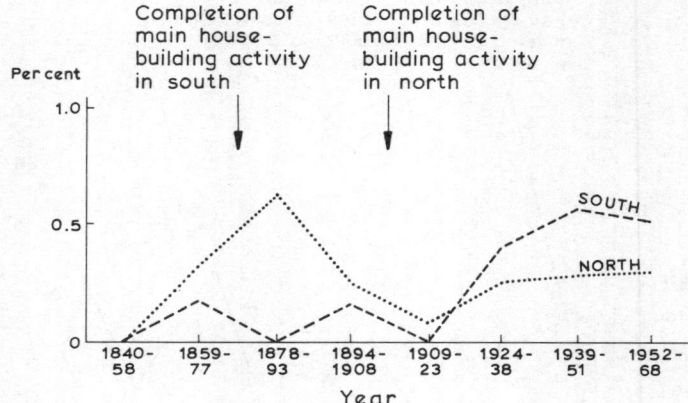

Figure 5.6 Percentage of fringe-belt plots per annum incurring expansion in a sample area in north-west Glasgow, 1840–1968

households for living accommodation are in many respects relatively invariable. Despite variations relating to stage in the family life cycle, family size and social class, housing accommodation has, at a basic level at least, a considerable degree of both homogeneity and exchangeability between one occupier and another. Institutional property is diverse and specialized by comparison and institutions themselves are subject to considerable growth and change in their physical requirements. These requirements are more likely to have been met initially by bespoke structures and when they change it is not as feasible for an institution as it is for a household to fulfil them by moving to another site.

Most of the institutions that took up sites on the fringe of north-west Glasgow during the first half of the study period had increased their activities by the end of it, and there had been associated increases in capital investment in their sites. Each investment tended to strengthen the bond between specific institution and site, often reducing the facility with which the site might be occupied by another user, other than perhaps a similarly specialized institution. The effect in bid-rent terms would be to create a local peak in the bid-rent curve of an individual institution associated with its existing site and perhaps neighbouring sites on to which expansion might take place. Similar deformations in the bid-rent curves of individual householders for their own sites would be comparatively slight owing to the much greater availability of substitute sites.

In addition to the greater inertia of institutions engendered by investment in relatively specialized and non-transferable structures, account must be taken of changes in the organization of institutions over time, especially their increasing size. Bound up with this there is the transformation of individual institutions from a peripheral point on the edge of the urban communication network to a minor, or even major, node within it. This would be reflected in a general steepening of the bid-rent gradients of individual institutions as they became more deeply embedded within the urban area. It is in this light that we should view the ability of institutions within old-established fringe belts to outbid competitors for nearby sites.

This long-term perspective on the bidding strengths of institutions and housing should also be viewed in relation to the different potentialities of housing sites and institutional sites for more intensive use. These relate to differences in capital investment per unit of land involved in their original development. Even low-density housing sites tend to have less space for adding new accommodation than the average institution, which will have initially devoted only a small fraction of its site to buildings. In fact, if investment in additional buildings on housing and institutional sites is plotted over time, generalized curves resembling those in figure 5.7A might be expected to obtain. Direct empirical confirmation of this is not available, but figure 5.7B shows the cumulative number of major investments in additional buildings for seven institutions established in north-west Glasgow in the period 1840–77 and surviving on the same sites in the post-war period.[20] The adding of new buildings took place throughout the period of approximately 100 years,[21] although on a slightly reduced scale during housebuilding slumps. Investment in additional buildings on housing sites in the same area was small by comparison, although population density increased in association with the subdivision of large dwellings.

This suggests that the average age of buildings will tend to increase more slowly on an institutional site than on a house site (figure 5.8). This will be associated with a quite different phasing of building obsolescence in which it is unlikely that the whole building stock will become obsolete at one time. Once a normal pattern of periodic additional building has been established, it is probable that the capital value of an institution's building stock as a whole is rarely at a sufficiently low level to make it economic for the institution to sell its site to a housebuilder and develop a cheaper site at the urban fringe. For similar reasons the redevelopment by an institution of its entire site at one time tends to be uneconomic.

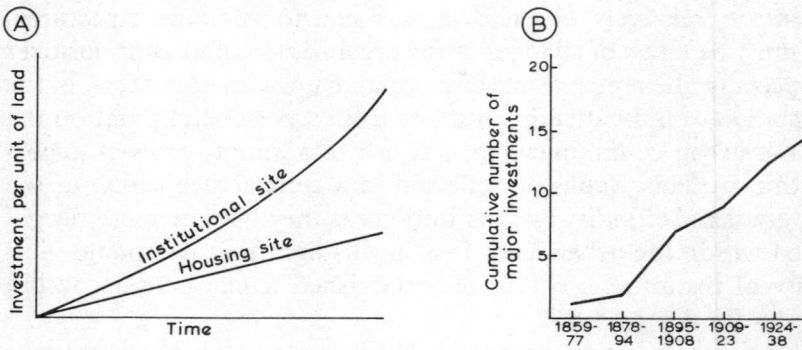

Figure 5.7 Investment in additional buildings over time: (A) hypothetical trends for institutional and housing sites; (B) cumulative number of major investments in additional buildings on seven institutional sites in north-west Glasgow, 1859–1968

If changes over time in the relative bidding strengths of users offer a plausible interpretation of the longevity of fringe belts and of secular changes in their intensity of use, how does this relate to our argument about building cycles? If an institution on an internal site eventually develops at a higher intensity than neighbouring housing areas, then part of the explanation offered for differences between housing and institutions in the timing of investment at the urban fringe is not applicable to internal sites. Indeed, the excess of an institution's bid rent over that of housing might be thought of as actually diminishing during housebuilding slumps. Although there is no empirical evidence to support it, this supposition is made in figure 5.9, in which the bid rent of an institution for its own site is compared over time with that of housebuilders. In fact any advantage in bidding strength during a housebuilding boom that an institution might acquire as it became a more intensive user of land would have to be balanced against financial and other advantages it might have over housebuilders during a housebuilding slump.

The growing space requirements of an institution are not necessarily satisfied by expanding on to adjacent sites. It is in the nature of at least part of the function that many institutions perform that substantial areas of land are required for low-intensity use, such as for playing fields. As an institution expands it becomes increasingly uneconomic to use parts of its site, or expensive adjacent sites that have been acquired subsequently, for low-intensity use. It seems plausible that it will

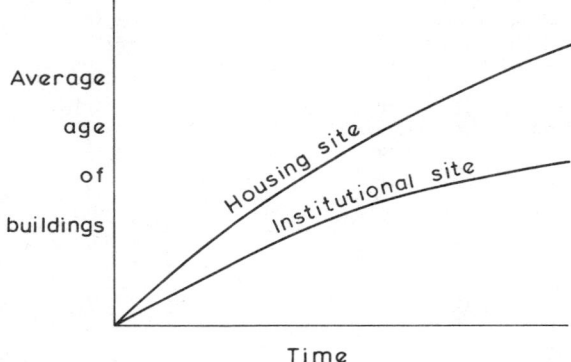

Figure 5.8 Hypothetical trends in the average age of building stock over time

increasingly differentiate between on the one hand those parts of its function requiring higher accessibility and amenable to higher-intensity development and on the other those land-extensive facilities for which accessibility is a lower priority. In a housebuilding slump, when credit is short but land is cheap, a growing institution will tend to concentrate on acquiring new sites at the current urban fringe for activities requiring less accessibility, even allowing some of this land to remain temporarily in agriculture or undeveloped. During a housebuilding boom, when land values are high, capital will tend to be invested in the more concentrated development of sites already acquired. In this respect the locational decisions of a large institution may resemble those of local government in that sites for activities with varying priorities in terms of space and accessibility are being financed from a single budget.

This theoretical discussion must be viewed in relation to the variations that exist in the adaptability to growth of both sites and activities. If from the beginning a site is small relative to the size of the organization occupying it, this is likely to limit the scope for adding buildings and to increase the probability of a stage being reached when the whole building stock is obsolete. There is a greater chance that the bid rent of an institution for such a site will be exceeded by that of a housebuilder. In the case of some types of organization, space for the intensifying of activities may be strictly limited by the nature of the activity. Where land, rather than buildings, remains by far the main asset, as is the case with many sports grounds, the potential return on redevelopment for housing is likely to exceed rapidly the value of land and buildings to the

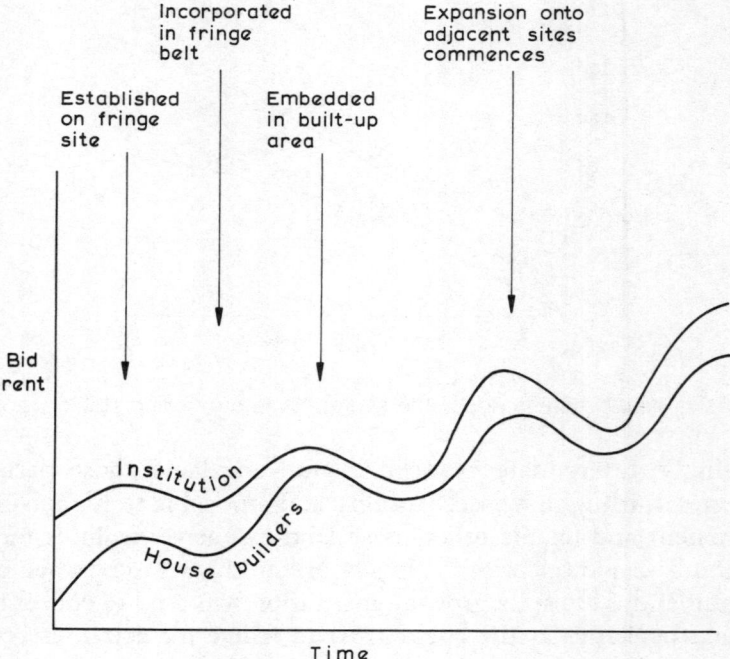

Figure 5.9 Hypothetical bid rent of an institution for its own site over time compared with that of housebuilders. Major events in the locational history of the institutional site are indicated by arrows

existing user. Such sites are especially likely to be redeveloped for housing.

Although the competition for sites between fringe-belt users and housebuilders is a major consideration in fringe-belt modification, it is not unusual for fringe-belt sites to be acquired by a second or even a third institution. One reason for this is that some of the site assets that accrue to a particular land use over time can be passed on to a related use. For example, the buildings will often be more readily adaptable by a related use and the immediate environment is more likely to be compatible with it than with a different type of use. Such factors will tend to increase the prices that related uses are prepared to pay for the site and may reduce those that other uses are prepared to pay. In addition planning authorities often seek to maintain less densely built-up spaces within the urban area and this may lead to radical departures from an 'economic' landscape, such as were discussed in our consideration of the effects of green belts. The net result of these and other factors is that, in addition to the large majority of institutions that occupy fringe sites during the outward growth process, a small but significant number of institutions move to internal sites. When this happens the subsequent institutional use tends to be more intensive than its predecessor.

The tendency for there to be sequences of related types of uses on the same site, and for sites near the city centre to become outgrown and increasingly vulnerable to competition from commercial uses, is associated with the gradual displacement of some institutions to sites progressively further from the city centre. An incomplete record of institutional movements in Glasgow since 1800 reveals several institutions (including a university and botanic gardens) that have occupied three successive fringe belts, each progressively further from the city centre. More than twenty have made one outward shift. Thus, in addition to the changes undergone by institutions that remain on the same site, the relocation of specific institutions from one fringe belt to another is a significant aspect of fringe-belt modification.

OTHER DEVELOPMENTS OF THE FRINGE-BELT CONCEPT

This discussion has concentrated on the traditional conception of fringe belts, relating this to interpretations of urban-fringe development and intra-urban change in which bid-rent theory and building cycles play a major part. This has involved a consideration of the developmental characteristics of housing, viewed essentially as undifferentiated 'residential accretion'. It is appropriate to conclude this chapter by referring to two developments of the fringe-belt concept that offer springboards from which to examine more closely in the next chapter the character of residential areas.

In one of these Slater has related the timing of the creation, modification and redevelopment of a single category of fringe-belt land use – the nineteenth-century ornamental villa – to significant stages in the life cycle of the occupants.[22] He concluded that the stage reached in the family life cycle was a significant factor in determining the timing of the adjustment of the landscape to changes of intra-urban location and more general economic climate such as we have already discussed. Marriage was in this respect the most significant event and in large towns generations of villas occupying fringe belts successively further from the town centre could be envisaged as resulting from the consequent new household formation, though in a small country town a sequence of additions to a single nineteenth-century fringe belt was more likely. The other significant event to 'trigger' change was the death of a villa owner, which in particular provided opportunity for changes to an existing villa – notably, change of tenure, renovation of the buildings, extension of the grounds, change of use and, the greatest change of all, redevelopment. The urban landscape is thus viewed primarily as the outcome of an interaction of land economics and family life cycles, and some of the unexplained residuals in a purely economic conception of fringe-belt development are thereby explained.

The other development of the fringe-belt concept is concerned directly with the differentiation of residential areas through its concern with the relationship between fringe belts and social areas. Carter and Wheatley conceive of much of the physical structure of their study town of Aberystwyth in terms of fixation lines and fringe belts, but they then link this to the evolution of the distribution pattern of social classes.[23] Whereas hitherto in fringe-belt studies there has been a tendency to view residential accretion as undifferentiated, their work suggests that it may be possible to integrate the fringe belt as a concept for structuring the development of the form of cities with aspects of the differentiation of residential areas. However, much groundwork remains to be done, including a closer examination of a range of aspects of residential areas. It is to this that we turn in chapter 6.

6
Residential growth and change

At least as important as fringe belts in the structure of cities is the differentiation within residential areas. Like the differentiation between fringe belts and residential accretion, this may be interpreted as a cyclical phenomenon, in which the character of each addition to the residential area is related to long swings in the economy and cycles of innovation adoption. Similarly, internal change within residential areas may be viewed as paralleling the modification of fringe belts. It is appropriate, however, at this stage in our argument not only to examine our previous perspectives in relation to residential areas but to consider other perspectives, notably on the one hand those that give particular attention to property ownership and on the other those that emphasize cultural and regional variations. The aim of this chapter will therefore be threefold. First, to apply to residential areas arguments developed in previous chapters; secondly, to view residential development in relation to individual property ownership; and thirdly, to consider inter-urban and international variations between residential areas, especially within the Western world.

CYCLES AND RESIDENTIAL DEVELOPMENT

Our consideration earlier of land values and the economic basis of different types and intensities of land use revealed considerable cyclical variations. Comparable variations in the types of dwellings constructed would also seem likely to exist. A number of writers have broached this subject. One of the distinctions most frequently made is between working-class and middle-class housing. Gauldie, for example, has noted the immediate effect on working-class housing of an industrial recession and the paying off of employees on the ability of tenants to pay rents.[11]

In general, middle-class housing might be expected to be less severely affected in a depression and this would compound any tendency for average plot sizes to increase during a period of reduced land values. Within middle-class housing the tendency for the proportion built speculatively to fall during housebuilding slumps would have a similar effect on plot sizes, since speculatively built houses are on average smaller than those that are bespoken, a fact noted by Cannadine, for example, in his study of a major estate in Birmingham in the nineteenth century.[2]

Quantitative data on the incidence of different types of residential construction are limited. At the national scale, Long's attempt to compile long-term series for the United States is still one of the few.[3] His separate series for detached dwellings and multi-family dwellings cover the period 1868–1935 but, as with his series for other types of building, the number of cities upon which the nineteenth-century parts of the series are based is too small to justify placing much reliance on them.[4] Nevertheless, the greater fluctuations in the construction of multi-family dwellings compared with detached dwellings that his findings reveal[5] tend to accord with more recent data for the first three decades of the twentieth century.[6] These reveal a clear tendency for the mixture of dwelling types to alter between housebuilding booms and slumps. During the housebuilding slump at the end of the First World war there was a marked rise in the proportion of single-family dwellings constructed, whereas during the housebuilding boom of the late 1920s the proportion of tenement dwellings constructed rose sharply (figure 6.1). Rodger too, in his examination of the Scottish building industry between 1860 and 1914, draws a sharp contrast between the volatility of working-class housebuilding and the relative stability of middle-class housebuilding.[7] If the fragments of evidence are pieced together it does appear that there have been considerable variations over time in the relative proportions of middle-class and working-class houses constructed, the latter comprising a large proportion of dwellings built during booms but a smaller proportion of those built during slumps. In the long term the pattern seems to have been one of marked fluctuations in the building of working-class dwellings underlain by a more stable pattern of middle-class housebuilding.

On balance evidence on variations between sub-categories of residential construction in individual cities adds support to this view. However, long-period data have been compiled for few cities and the conclusions drawn must be qualified in each case. Beresford's series for Leeds for the

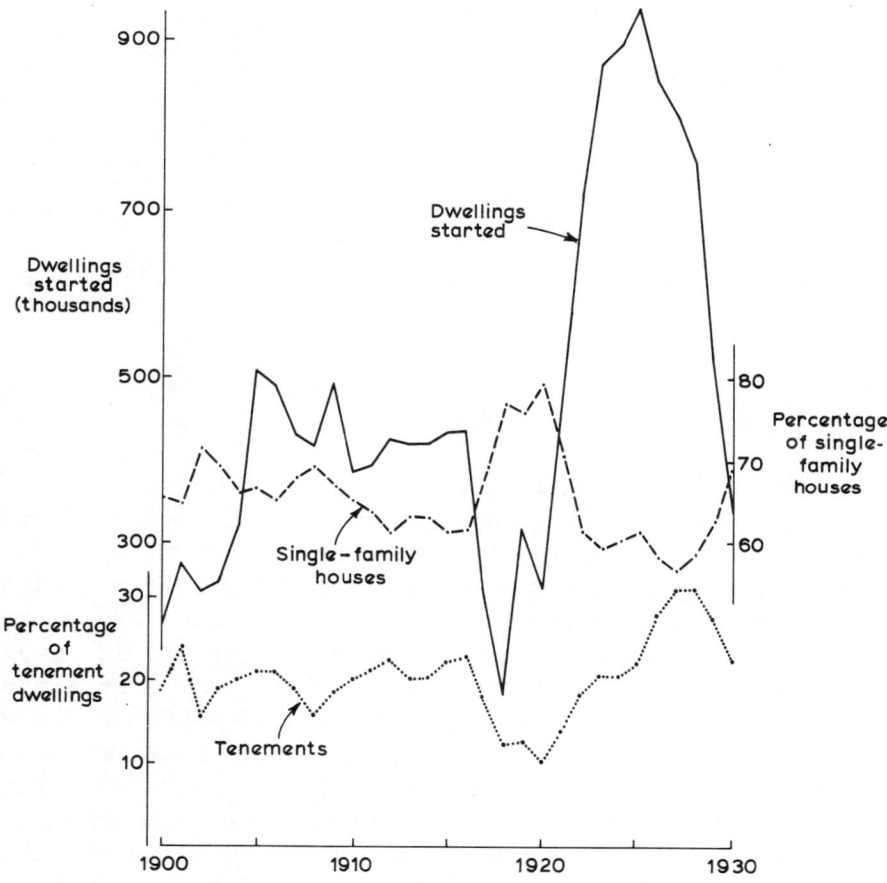

Figure 6.1 Changes in the percentages of tenements and single-family houses constructed in the United States 1900–1930, related to housebuilding fluctuations
Source: Barrows, 1983, figs 1 and 2.

period from 1886 to 1914 reveal on the whole a fairly constant number of plans approved for new villas (detached houses) compared with the large variability in the number of semi-detached houses, the large majority of which were concentrated in the housebuilding boom at the turn of the century (figure 6.2). However, the dominating relationship was the secular upward trend in the proportion of these two house types compared with the main working-class types (the back-to-back houses and through houses).[8] Similarly, White's series for Liverpool for the

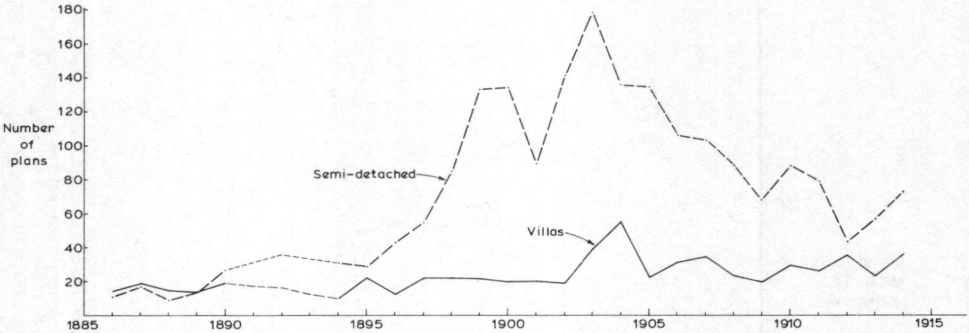

Figure 6.2 Number of building plans approved for villas and semi-detached houses in Leeds, 1886–1914. *Source:* Beresford, 1971, p. 117.

period 1814–70 show a relatively high proportion of dwellings of under £12 annual rental during the housebuilding boom of the early 1840s but the series are of insufficient length to attempt to separate a possible cyclical element from a strong secular downward trend in the proportion of dwellings in this rental category.[9] Data for Glasgow also require qualification. Although Cairncross's series for Glasgow for the period 1833–1914 reveal that the average number of rooms per new house was higher during the troughs in housebuilding in the early 1880s and early 1910s[10] and this would seem to indicate that increased proportions of middle-class houses were constructed at these times,[11] other data indicate that the number of houses constructed with more than four rooms fell to negligible levels in several years during the slump of the 1880s.[12] Indeed, it has been suggested that in particular local instances there was little difference between high-class and low-class houses in the extent to which their construction was affected by a housebuilding slump. Jahn suggests that this was the case in part of west London during the housebuilding slump of the late 1880s and early 1890s.[13] Thus, although in general the market shares of different classes of housebuilding varied considerably according to the total amount of housebuilding, in specific local circumstances this may not have been so.

The cyclical variations in the relative amounts of speculative and bespoke housebuilding and the greater sensitivity to the economic climate of private building for working-class occupation need to be viewed in conjunction with our discussion of the relationship between land values and land use in chapter 2. Clearly the strong speculative element in much housebuilding and the effects of economic depression on the ability of low-income households to pay for housing are by no means unrelated to fluctuations in land values. Indeed, although our building-cycle/bid-rent theory was couched primarily in terms of land value, these other factors are implicit. It may be argued, however, that speculation and economic climate have a direct effect on the incidence of different types of development that is independent of the indirect effect they have through their influence on land values. Thus changes in average intensities of development over time may well be related both to changes in the relative numbers of dwellings built for middle-class and for working-class occupation and to changes in land values. The separating of these two elements in reality would not be easy.

LANDOWNERSHIP AND RESIDENTIAL DEVELOPMENT

While the major influence of economic considerations in residential development is undeniable, there is a reluctance among many historians of the development process to assign them a primary role, at least of the type that has dominated our discussion hitherto. We have already seen how the family life cycle sometimes played a significant role in fringe-belt development in the nineteenth century. Some consider that the circumstances surrounding individual landownership, especially in the case of major landowners, take on a significance that either overrides market forces or leads to their modification in ways that render untenable the notion of land being developed in accord with the swings of the building cycle and the prescriptions of bid rent.

That the landscape upon which the process of urban development takes place is highly differentiated in terms of landownership, topography and a host of other characteristics is almost a platitude. As long ago as 1962 Ward showed the effect of the size and shape of landholdings on the outward growth of Leeds.[14] More recently interest has reawakened in the roles of individual landowners, especially in the nineteenth century.[15] One view of major landowners is that they imposed their will on the landscape largely independently of the interplay of economic forces. This view of the conversion of rural land to urban use has often been seen as being in opposition to interpretations of urban development in terms of the operation of the land market, especially the building-cycle/bid-rent mechanism.[16] Cannadine has examined aspects of this polarization of views in the light of evidence from a variety of studies, especially of aristocratic landowners in Britain.[17] He concluded that high-class residential areas developed under various ownership conditions: under fragmented landownership, such as in suburban Boston, Massachusetts and west Sheffield, and concentrated landownership, such as in London's West End, and parts of Manchester, Birmingham, Nottingham, Liverpool and Oxford. Similarly, mainly low-class residential areas developed both in areas in which large landowners predominated, such as on the Duke of Norfolk's estate in east Sheffield and in much of Cardiff, and in areas of highly fragmented ownership more commonly associated with this type of development. The inference drawn was that the market process was more important than landownership.[18]

This is a welcome attempt to stand back from those particularities of individual estates that have absorbed many historians of urban development. However, the artificiality of setting up market forces and landownership as alternative explanations remains insufficiently acknowledged. It is undeniable that at many times and in many places landowners have had a large degree of control over the development of their own land. A more pertinent issue in understanding the developments that take place is the extent to which decision makers, among whom landowners are of major importance, are influenced by economic factors. More specifically, since various economic arguments exist, how far do landowners conform to the type of mechanisms that make up the theory set out in previous chapters?

In considering this question it should be noted that our approach so far has been for the most part to see whether developments in the landscape are consistent with our theory. This is by no means full proof, since other theories may be equally compatible with the facts of landscape development that we uncover. The plan developed by the Calthorpes for their Edgbaston Estate in Birmingham illustrates this point (figure 6.3). The distinctive residential zones that it identifies in c.1910, with an inner working-class zone, intermediate middle-class zones and an outer 'aristocratic' zone intermixed with large institutional sites is presented by Cannadine primarily in terms of the aspirations of the aristocratic Calthorpe family to convert its large landholding on the fringe of Birmingham into an exclusive suburb.[19] The reality emerging in the early twentieth century differed considerably from the original conception of the early nineteenth century, as Cannadine points out. The zonal pattern, however, is viewed by him primarily in terms of 'the élitist preference of nineteenth-century urban landlords, more anxious to

Residential growth and change 101

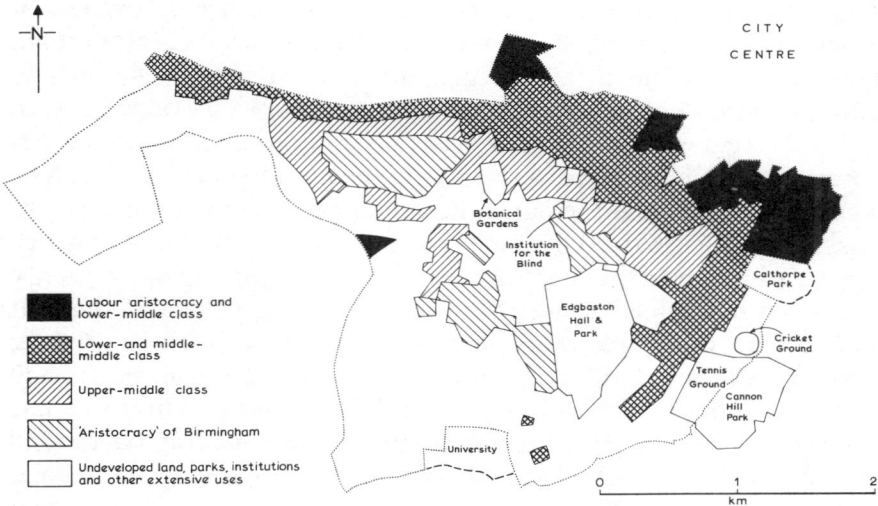

Figure 6.3 The zoning pattern of Edgbaston Estate, Birmingham, c.1910
Source: Cannadine, 1980, p. 114.

maximize prestige than profit, and thereby acting as major agents of social segregation'.[20] Thus the lower-middle-class and upper-middle-class zones are viewed as 'buffers' between the working-class inner city and the mansions of the aristocracy amid the agricultural land and parklands of the rural–urban fringe.[21] A problem for the analyst of the urban landscape is that the outcome is much as might have been anticipated from our argument about bid rent. Inaccessible sites away from main roads and distant from the edge of the built-up area of the time were on the whole developed at low intensity (notably for houses in large grounds and institutions) or remained in agricultural use. Accessible sites close to the built-up area and along main roads were on average developed more intensively, with a larger proportion of small and medium-sized dwellings. In the light of our discussion in chapter 3, the social objectives of the Calthorpes would seem to conform reasonably well to a strategy based on an assessment of the type of development likely to yield the greatest profit in different locations.

In the polarization between land-market explanations of residential development and landownership explanations, the former have generally been associated with a nomothetic approach and the latter with an idiographic approach. Studies of the development activities of an individual landowner have tended to eschew comparisons and the search for large-scale regularities. But the existence of recurrent features at various scales, from national, or even international, down to intra-urban, makes it hard to justify restricting attention to individual units of landownership. Comparisons of these units can provide a bridge between the highly aggregated data that have been utilized in much of our analysis and considerations of the pecularities of each local area. Thus, for example, if we return to our earlier findings on plot sizes in northern Kensington, discussed in chapter 3, we can consider the extent to which the regularities apparent at an aggregate level are made up of distinctive patterns on individual estates. We find, in fact, that each of the four estates in the study area possessing enough plots to justify a separate analysis (Ladbroke, Phillimore, Norland and Holland) had secular and cyclical variations in plot sizes consistent with our theory. On each estate the mean size of new plots decreased during housebuilding booms and increased during housebuilding slumps, and in each case the secular trend was for the size of new plots to decrease. An analysis of a number of smaller estates in the area, grouped together in order to provide sufficient data, produced the same result. Thus, although each estate had its individual characteristics, there are strong grounds for believing that forces of a more general order were at work. As Rodger has pointed out in his analysis of housebuilding and public building in Scotland, if regularities are apparent over a number of distinctive areas it is hard to believe that they are the product of processes peculiar to each area.[22]

The fact remains that, whatever the influences at work, most decisions on developments in the landscape are taken locally and will reflect circumstances peculiar to individual landowners. It is appropriate, therefore, to consider briefly these more particular circumstances that have not been taken into account in our argument so far, looking first at the decision to undertake development and secondly at factors influencing the nature of development.

In our theory of land development at the urban fringe accessibility is of overriding importance in the timing of development. If this were the only factor and accessibility were purely a function of distance, then clearly all development would be contiguous and take place sequentially according to distance from existing development. In reality, even where accessibility is largely determined by distance, as in the era before suburban railways became important, development frequently leapfrogs over intervening agricultural land. The factors responsible for this are multifarious, including legal restrictions on the development of land, ignorance of the land market, and the deliberate withholding of land from the market, perhaps as an investment. Where land is in the hands of only a few large landowners, they have a special ability to influence the market and thereby influence the intensity of development and the degree to which pockets of undeveloped land remain within the urban area.[23]

After the decision to convert land to urban use a number of other decisions affecting the development process are taken over a period ranging from months to decades. In the case of a large estate the time span between the initial and final phases of urban development may be spread over several building cycles. A lapse of over a year between the preparation of plans for specific houses and their completion is quite common. Under these circumstances time lags between changes in economic conditions and adjustments in dwelling types and plot sizes are to be expected. This raises the more general question of the responsiveness of the development process to the mechanisms embodied in our argument.

Detailed studies of particular developments suggest that in fact plans were frequently modified to suit the exigencies of changing circumstances. Activities (both on the drawing board and on the ground) concerned with the development of parts of northern Kensington have been reconstructed in detail for a period covering several decades during the nineteenth century.[24] It was not uncommon for streets to be staked out and then realigned or completely replanned. Subdivision and amalgamation of plots, changes in plot boundaries, and alterations in the proposed numbers and types of dwellings and in the intensities of use were commonplace. Sometimes changes took place on the drawing board before developments were initiated on the ground; on other occasions a plot pattern already staked out on the ground was modified. In his study of Boston, Massachusetts, Warner emphasizes the flexibility of the 'frontage lot and grid system' that was used over the whole suburban area between 1870 and 1900.[25] It readily enabled lot sizes to be adjusted to changing circumstances by longitudinal subdivisions or amalgamations. Thus scope seems to have existed for development to adjust to changes in the property market. How general this flexibility was remains to be investigated. Widespread dislocation in the development industry in the early years of a slump might well exacerbate time lags in the adjustment of new development to changed economic conditions.

INTERNAL CHANGE

As in the case of fringe belts, the initial form of residential development has a major effect on subsequent changes. This has long been recognized by geographers adopting a morphogenetic approach, and is increasingly being acknowledged by scholars primarily concerned with the economics of urban areas.[26] One of the most striking changes in a growing urban area is the repletion of existing plots. The form this takes is strongly influenced by the shape of the original plot and the position of buildings within it.

The plot type that has been subjected to the most detailed analysis is the English burgage – the elongated strip plot occupied by an enfranchised member of a medieval borough and still familiar today in various residual forms in the oldest parts of the majority of English towns and cities. It was by examining the development of burgages in a variety of medieval towns and cities, most notably the Northumberland market town of Alnwick, that Conzen recognized the burgage cycle.[27] The first, or institutive, phase of this normally commenced in the pre-industrial era and consisted essentially of a single dwelling at the head of its garden plot, facing on to the street. The second, repletive, phase included the construction behind the dwelling of additional buildings, such as back-to-back houses, workshops and outbuildings, to which access was gained by an alleyway running along the length of the plot, at right angles to the street. It was succeeded by a climax phase in which the plot became densely built-up, often as far back as its rear boundary. Finally, there was a more or less abrupt recessive phase, when the existing fabric became obsolete and was cleared and the plot became temporarily unused or 'fallow', prior to a redevelopment cycle.

As more studies of the development of plots have been undertaken it has become clear that Conzen's burgage cycle is a particular regional and historical variant of a widespread phenomenon in growing towns and cities. As plots become embedded within the built-up area and circumstances change, so a re-evaluation is made of their potentialities for more intensive use. In Istanbul, Stewig has shown how the process of piecemeal subdivision and repletion of much wider, and therefore less constraining, original plots has given rise to the creation of complex and highly irregular culs-de-sac linking internal derivative plots to the original street.[28] In Melbourne, Australia, where the rectangular grid was the main method of plot division for many decades, a system of

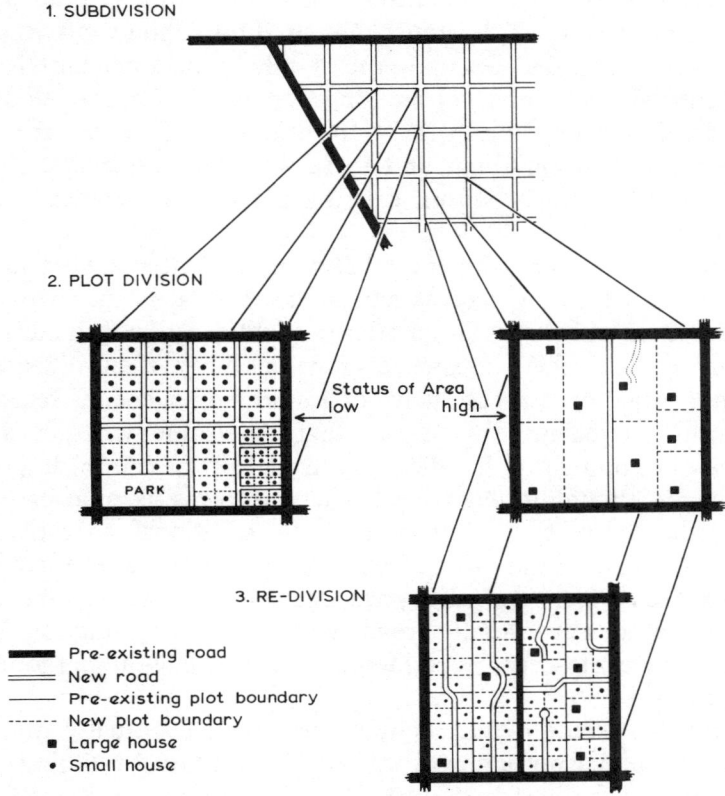

Figure 6.4 Stages of street- and plot-pattern development in Melbourne, Australia
Source: Johnston, 1968, p. 454.

subdivision into smaller rectangular plots was the normal means of achieving a more intensive use (figure 6.4). The large plots of the high-status areas provided scope for more varied forms of adaptation than the small plots of the low-status areas.[29]

It is more difficult in the United States than in Europe to recognize a clear separation between an initial phase of residential accretion, in which house plots are laid out for the first time, and a subsequent phase of modification for more intensive use. M. P. Conzen attributes this to the existence, in the nineteenth century at least, of an extremely fragmented land market and the small-scale structure of construction enterprise, both of which emphasized disaggregated decision making about the location and timing of individual residential development.[30]

Nevertheless, a progressive intensification of plot use over time is just as evident. For example, Boston's North End underwent thorough repletion in the four decades up to the middle of the nineteenth century. In 1852 substantial numbers of buildings remained from the colonial and early federal periods, but by 1874 the interiors of plots were almost entirely covered by buildings and there was rapid replacement of old buildings, either largely within existing plots or associated with plot amalgamation.[31]

Notwithstanding the differences between residential areas and fringe belts, it is clear that the processes of intensification in the two types of areas have many parallels. The similarity of different households in their requirements and their greater average mobility than organizations occupying fringe belts is conducive of a more homogeneous response to changes in the balance of factors that determine whether a more intensive development is justified. Nevertheless, of central importance in both cases, though it may take a variety of forms, is an assessment of whether the value of the property with additional or replacement buildings will exceed the value of existing structures and the cost of new buildings.[32] The factors affecting this decision can change substantially over a few decades in a rapidly growing city and it is common for the use of large, nineteenth-century residential plots to have undergone some intensification.

Despite this, some old residential areas have eventually undergone periods of minimal investment, not only in additional buildings but in maintenance of the existing fabric. This is generally associated with a particular type of intensified use, involving social downgrading and the letting of subdivided dwellings for rent. There is a limit to the extra rent that can be derived from compressing more households into existing floor-space and, given the low rent-paying ability of households likely to be attracted to the area, redevelopment at higher floor-space concentrations is liable to be uneconomic. A point may be reached when capital invested by landlords in the maintenance of these areas yields a lower return than capital invested in areas farther out or in some other sector of the economy. The interaction of factors that are at work in these circumstances, including the reluctance of financial institutions to make loans and the detrimental effects on neighbouring areas has been portrayed by Smith.[33] Instead of land values continuing to rise, they actually fall, at least relative to the city centre and residential areas further out, creating a land-value trough around large parts of the city centre. This feature was noted by Hoyt as appearing in Chicago by the late 1920s[34] and it eventually characterized many large Western cities, especially in the United States.

Deterioration of this type was already beginning by the time of the First World War in the inner parts of the Calthorpe Estate in Birmingham.[35] In some large urban areas in the United States the decay of older residential areas has, since the Second World War, extended several kilometres out from the city centre. As in the case of the development of fringe belts, the ageing of buildings is not in itself the crucial factor in this process. Many older residential areas have been occupied without interruption by high-status residents. What is of key importance is the return on investment in such areas, by comparison with alternative investments.[36] In an assessment of this the condition of neighbouring areas and the fashionability of building types and living styles are likely to be considerations.

Just as the decline of older residential areas is not inevitable, so the continuation of that decline is by no means inexorable. It may be interrupted by local government action as was commonly the case in major cities in the United Kingdom during the 1950s, when comprehensive redevelopment became fashionable. If this does not occur the time is likely to come when the rents to be derived from slum property become low enough for existing use value to fall sufficiently far below potential value to make attractive capital investment in redevelopment or refurbishment. Since the mid-1960s, or even earlier, there has been a relationship between this change in investment preferences and the diffusion of the fashion for conservation. Thus although the current wave of refurbishment in older residential areas by private organizations and individuals may be viewed as a sound financial investment, it would be wrong to regard this as independent of innovation diffusion. As at the urban fringe, economic factors and fashion are thoroughly intertwined.

INTER-URBAN AND INTERNATIONAL VARIATIONS

While broad generalizations have been made about intra-urban residential variations, inter-urban differences remain to be considered. Here the relation between innovation adoption and economic factors is no less important. Both these factors are fundamental to Lichtenberger's view of major inter-city and international differences in residential building types in Europe. Indeed the interpretation she offers is similar in tenor,

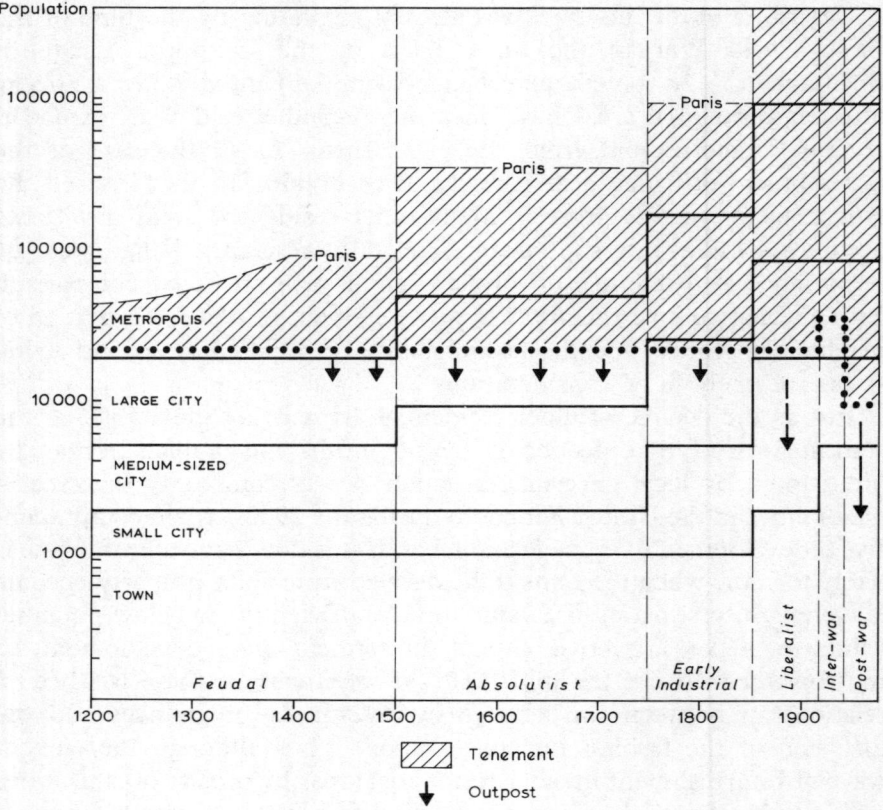

Figure 6.5 The spread of the tenement within the urban hierarchy of continental Europe
Source: Lichtenberger, 1970, fig. 3.

if not in the precise terms in which it is presented, to the argument offered thus far in an intra-urban context.

In her interpretation the key issue in the historical geography of residential building forms in Europe is the relation over time and space between the tenement and the single-family house.[37] Over space there are striking differences between the main regions and countries: for example, England has a low proportion of tenement dwellings and Italy has a high proportion. In terms of the urban hierarchy, major cities are much more likely to have tenements than small cities (figure 6.5). Since land values tend to increase with city size, this is consistent with our argument about the relationship between land values and intensity of use. But neither spatial nor hierarchical thresholds have remained constant. The tenement has tended to spread northward and, associated with a secular increase in land values, it has been adopted at lower levels in the urban hierarchy. These changes have taken place at uneven rates, however, reflecting a complex pattern of diffusion of both different types of tenement dwelling and numerous other innovations.

Probably the earliest tenements to be constructed north of the Alps were multi-storey apartment houses with arcaded patios, designed for the rich. This style spread in the sixteenth century from Italy to Vienna, and to Crakow, Warsaw and Lublin in Poland. Another line of diffusion can be traced from Italy and Spain to the south of France and Paris. Naples provided the prototype of the standardized large-scale tenement blocks that were constructed for the upper-middle class from the late eighteenth century onward. It was at this time too that the first tenements were being constructed in medium-sized cities. By the second half of the nineteenth century the tenement had completed its diffusion down the social hierarchy, almost completed its diffusion down the urban hierarchy, and its geographical spread within continental Europe was close to its maximum extent. Capital cities, such as Paris, Berlin and Vienna, had distinct regional types of tenements that were adopted by smaller provincial cities in their vicinity.[38]

There are two exceptions to this predominance of the tenement. These are England and eastern Europe. In the former the single-family house dominates, the tenement still being a rarity outside the East End of London. In the latter the tenement is largely restricted to the capitals and major industrial cities. Despite their remoteness from the presumed source region of the tenement, these exceptions would not seem to conform neatly to any crude explanation purely in terms of the effects of distance on diffusion, particularly as the tenement has a long history in Scottish cities, even more remote than many cities that lack tenements. Clearly many other factors are relevant. Among these are the tendency for pressures on land to have been greater in continental Europe, associated with restrictions on the extension of cities beyond their fortification zones, in some cases well into the industrial era. In the case of the contrast between Scotland and England it may be that differences in land values are again important. Rodger gives particular emphasis to this, attributing the higher cost of land in Scotland in the nineteenth century largely to the peculiar feudal tenure system.[39] This is not to exclude the influence of cultural factors either here or elsewhere. For although the Scottish tenement enables higher densities to be achieved than any of the forms of terrace housing in England, there are considerable regional differences in types of terrace housing within England that are not necessarily associated with differences in dwelling densities and land values.[40]

During the inter-war years of the twentieth century the English garden-city idea had more impact on the continent of Europe than the 'continental' tenement has ever had in England. The limited constraints on urban sprawl and in particular the increasing use of motor transport made possible the use of the single-family house on the continent to an extent unequalled before or since. But in the post-war period rising land values have been associated with a reversion to the construction of very high proportions of flats in continental cities.[41]

Average dwelling densities have been consistently lower in North America than in Europe. In the United States the tenement is a relatively minor dwelling type.[42] This almost certainly reflects both the greater influence of English traditions, by comparison with those of continental European countries,[43] and the relative cheapness of land. The prevalence of the single-family dwelling in North America is associated with a greater physical separation of social classes than in continental Europe, where several social classes may be contained within the same tenement block, differentiated by position in the building and dwelling size. The low density of the American city in comparison with its European counterpart is relevant to the internal changes already discussed. The scope for intensification of use by building upon garden land, and by dividing for working-class occupation dwellings designed for the middle class, is much greater in North America than in continental Europe.

These continental and international differences are an important addition to our general argument. They have received insufficient attention from geographers, particularly during the period when attempts to construct theories of city structure encouraged the fiction that the Western city and the North American city were synonymous. It is clear that to ignore some of the differences of housing type identified here would be to risk overlooking important processes. While building cycles and bid rents have a prominent place in understanding the various aspects of residential development that have been considered, they should be viewed in a wider context. Economic factors act in conjunction with social and cultural factors, from which they may seldom be separable in practice. To try to encapsulate social and cultural factors entirely within the notion of innovation diffusion is, of course, to simplify greatly. Nevertheless, the complementarity of our essentially economic mechanism of development with innovation diffusion appears to be important. This is so not only in relation to the enlarging outer integuments of urban areas and the process whereby these zones are adapted, augmented, and redeveloped or recycled as they become embedded within the urban area, but also in relation to inter-urban and international variations. It remains to be seen whether our argument can be extended to apply to the commercial cores of cities.

7
Commercial cores

By comparison with residential areas, commercial areas are of limited extent. However, they have an importance out of proportion to their size. In addition to frequently comprising part or all of a city's historical nucleus, the city centre or commercial core reflects the character of the much wider, mainly residential, areas it serves and is part of the life of virtually every resident in a city. It would be surprising therefore if it were not affected by many of the processes that have been identified in earlier chapters. But whereas most of the types of area to which attention has hitherto been given, including most residential areas, began their urban lives by performing functions similar to those they perform today, it is commonplace for large parts of commercial cores to occupy areas originally developed for different purposes. This reflects in large part their outward expansion into surrounding areas in the course of city growth. In addition their centres of gravity may shift, occasionally resulting in the original centre being left outside the modern commercial core. Thus the main part of the development of the commercial core of most cities has consisted of the transformation or replacement of existing urban structures. These structures generally comprise an even more complex surface, especially in physical form and ownership, than the rural landscapes that provide the starting point for most other types of urban development. This does not negate the use of the economic arguments already discussed, but it does require that they be viewed with circumspection.

As an entity, the city centre may be viewed in terms of the kinds and quantities of goods and services that the population of its hinterland is able and willing to purchase. Clearly, changes in the size and purchasing power of that population and in the ability and willingness of organizations to provide various goods and services in city-centre locations are of fundamental importance. However, although in broad terms a relationship between city-centre developments and economic and demographic trends, both nationally and in the city and its region, would seem plausible, for various reasons this relationship is unlikely to be simple in character. For instance, additions to the population of a city may have a less than proportional effect on floor-space requirements in the city centre. This relates to the fact that as the population of a city grows its average distance from the city centre tends to increase, as does city-centre congestion, thereby tending to increase the relative attractiveness of suburban centres. Furthermore, there are different effects on floor-space requirements for different functions. Thus an increase in a city's population may engender an increase in demand for more-specialized goods in the city centre but a reduction in demand for less-specialized goods, which may now be more economically provided in suburban centres. Clearly, the effects will vary according to city size and transport systems, although the differing post-war histories of the CBD in America and its counterpart in Europe suggest that other factors must be taken into account.

It is evident that there must be a close connection between the form of city-centre developments and the diffusion of the many and varied innovations that relate either directly (for example, through building technology) or indirectly (for example, through the development of new functions) to the nature of the visible creations in the townscape. These innovations may themselves be manifested in the city-centre townscape, often with different streets and sub-areas being affected at different times. Alternatively they may occur elsewhere, for example in out-of-town shopping centres, and have an indirect effect on the city centre through changes in trading patterns. Clearly there is a relationship between the adoption of innovations and economic trends, albeit that the direction of cause and effect at the national level is still an open question,[1] but there has been little research on the relationship between local economic trends and the spread of innovations.

REDEVELOPMENT

The replacement and modification of city-centre structures may be seen in the context of the relationships just considered. Particular attention will be paid initially to redevelopment, including both the replacement of individual buildings on existing plots and the usually more extensive form of renewal in which a new plot pattern is created. This is usually the most substantial type of change to the physical fabric, although it cannot be separated entirely from a variety of other changes to which it is closely related.

The profit obtainable from a change to the physical fabric varies considerably from site to site. The probability of structural modification and renewal tends to increase as physical structures diverge from the 'optimum' (or most profitable) for the sites they occupy. Physical structures may diverge from the optimum in terms of the *amount* of floor-space and/or in terms of the *suitability* of that space for a particular function. These two aspects are related but may be considered separately for clarification.

Changes in the optimum amount of floor-space for a particular site are intimately bound up with changes in demand for that site. These are related to changes in the population of the hinterland of the city centre and changes in the spending power of that population. The secular trend since the Industrial Revolution has been a rapid rise in both population and income in the hinterlands of most Western city centres. This has enhanced the profitability and value of city-centre sites and has been paralleled by long-term increases in floor-space concentrations.[2] A major way in which increases in floor-space have been obtained is by redevelopment. Sites that have undergone major increases in value since the buildings on them were last altered tend to be susceptible to this type of change. However, although in a growing city the greatest increases in land values tend to occur in the most accessible central sites,[3] account must be taken of the development of subsidiary nodes, as cities become large enough to have suburban centres, and of the effects of transport innovations, which may occasion disproportionately high increases in peripheral areas.[4] Nevertheless, inferences may be drawn concerning the declining susceptibility of sites to redevelopment with increasing distance from the core of the CBD.[5]

In considering the tendency for physical structures to decline over time in their suitability, it is necessary to observe the changes in the uses that buildings are required to perform. First, uses change their structural needs; for instance, the building requirements of retailing have changed considerably during the twentieth century. Secondly, certain functions decline and new ones emerge. Although the adaptation of existing buildings for new uses is commonplace, this may not be practicable where there are specialized building requirements, as for example is frequently the case with cinemas, which emerged as an important new use and rapidly declined again within three-quarters of a century.

The susceptibility of sites to changes in building requirements because of use changes may only be appreciated from a detailed knowledge of the uses occupying different parts of the city centre at different times. While the relatively rapid changes in the building requirements of retailing areas[6] and entertainment areas make these parts of the city centre susceptible to change, a variety of other types of site, not necessarily as agglomerated in distribution as the areas just mentioned, are occupied by declining functions with specialized building requirements – for example, churches. There would seem to be some basis here for inferring sites that are susceptible to redevelopment within a particular period of time, although the bids of other users for sites occupied by declining uses would need to be taken into account.

Many other relevant factors may not be susceptible to generalization to the same degree. These include the role of central and local government, which ranges from controls exercised through building regulations to planned development of extensive areas,[7] and the role of property owners,[8] although neither of these participants in the development process may be regarded as independent of the market forces previously outlined. Damage by bombing[9] and fire may or may not be significant factors, scarcely related, it would appear, to the aspects mentioned earlier, and the significance of topographical factors would also seem difficult to incorporate into generalizations. The complexities relating to inheritances from earlier socio-economic conditions, certainly pre-industrial (in Europe frequently medieval),[10] add further to the problems of generalization.

It is apparent that the forces just mentioned could distort and, in exceptional cases, dominate the sort of development of city-centre form envisaged in our discussion of theoretical issues. It is desirable, therefore, in selecting an actual city centre in which to examine our notions about economic forces and innovation that the effects of the 'distorting' factors just described be minimized.

A CASE STUDY

Glasgow, the second city by population in Britain during most of the industrial period, has a central area which, for a number of reasons, is particularly suited to this type of study (figure 7.1). The great majority of the Victorian and modern city centre was in an area that had

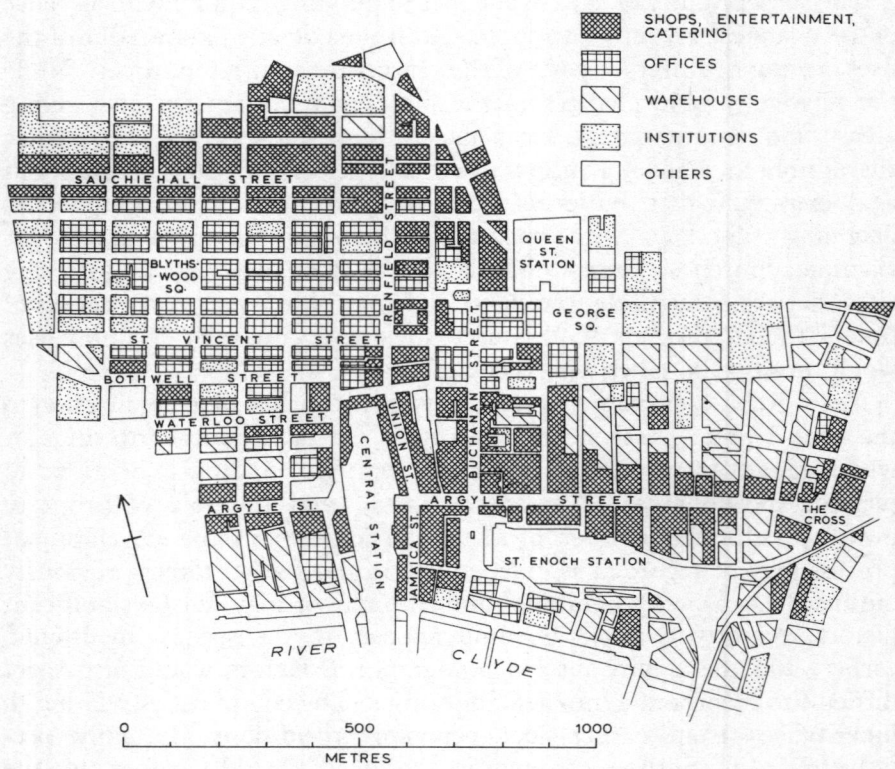

Figure 7.1 Generalized ground-level land use in central Glasgow in 1969. Warehouses include storage and wholesale. Institutions include all public services (except transport) and churches

undergone rapid initial urban development during a period of approximately 60 years prior to 1840. This development had taken place on a regular, essentially gridiron, plan, to the north-west of the medieval core. With its almost entirely late Georgian (1770–1839) buildings and rectangular plots, much of the city centre had the unity of a 'new town'. By the standards of European cities it was unusually homogeneous, being relatively free from the intricate medieval antecedents that greatly complicate developmental studies. Damage to buildings by bombing and direct state involvement in redevelopment were rare. No comprehensive central-area plan existed until 1975.[11] Although a substantial redevelopment of the decaying medieval core was undertaken by the local authority during the late nineteenth and early twentieth centuries,[12] in general piecemeal building replacements were overwhelmingly predominant, particularly before the 1970s. These involved a multitude of individual concerns and affected a few plots at a time.

The economic history of Glasgow during the nineteenth and twentieth centuries makes it feasible to consider a number of the relationships that would seem to bear upon the process of redevelopment. Population and economic growth were rapid during most of the nineteenth century, the marked hiatus in economic development in the 1880s being succeeded by a major resurgence of activity in the Edwardian period.[13] In contrast, a combination of minimal population change and economic stagnation in the inter-war years provided a condition as close to a stable economic state as is likely to be attained in the real world.[14] This provides the opportunity to assess the effects on the city centre of innovations, such as the variety store and the cinema, which were diffusing on a national scale. Post-war economic revival was slow but ultimately pronounced, albeit less so than in Britain as a whole. Although the size of the population changed little, its average distance from the city centre increased. As in many Western cities, this was associated with slum clearance in inner areas and considerable housebuilding at the urban fringe.[15]

Data on redevelopment in central Glasgow are available for the period 1840–1969,[16] and may be compared with more limited information available for other cities. The average building life span was about 130 years. This was almost twice as long as the norm suggested by the tables of building depreciation of the United States Department of the Treasury,[17] and longer than for other major cities with which it is possible to make comparisons. Holden and Holford recorded that about four-fifths of the buildings existing in 1855 in the City of London (which comprised much of the commercial core of the metropolis in the nineteenth century) had been rebuilt by 1905.[18] Hoyt suggested that there were few sites in the CBD of Chicago that had not been occupied by at least three different buildings between 1830 and 1933, and one exceptional site had undergone at least five redevelopments during that time: this was a remarkable rate of renewal, even allowing for the widespread effects of the fire of 1871.[19] Van Hulten reported that if the speed of rebuilding in the canal zone of the inner city of Amsterdam between 1957 and 1962 were continued a total renewal would have taken place in 50 years.[20] Even in a much smaller city, Hobart (Tasmania), Solomon revealed that relatively few of the buildings existing in the 1840s survived in the CBD in 1963,[21] suggesting a replacement rate not

118 *J. W. R. Whitehand*

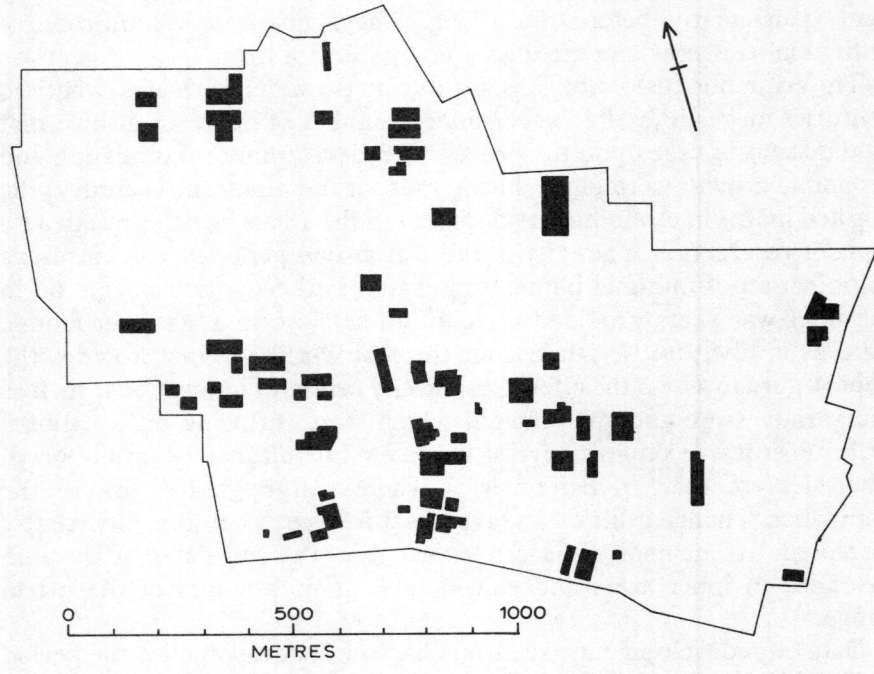

Figure 7.2   Sites redeveloped twice or more in central Glasgow, 1840–1969

dissimilar from that in Glasgow. Leeds City Planning Department estimated that normally one-fifth of the central-area buildings could be expected to be renewed in a 20-year period,[22] certainly a faster rate than that actually experienced in Glasgow.

Glasgow's relatively slow replacement rate in the long term needs to be seen in the light of variations over space and time. The spatial pattern was characterized by a high incidence of redevelopment within or close to the two main east–west shopping streets of Sauchiehall Street and Argyle Street (figure 7.2). In the intervening, predominantly office area between Blythswood Square and George Square there was a low incidence. But there was considerable short-distance variation within streets. Within the main shopping streets replacement was greatest on central sites (figure 7.3). Within the street containing the main financial offices, St Vincent Street, there was again a central peak, although, in contrast to Chicago during the period 1830–1933,[23] both this and average levels were slightly lower than in the two main shopping streets (figure 7.3).

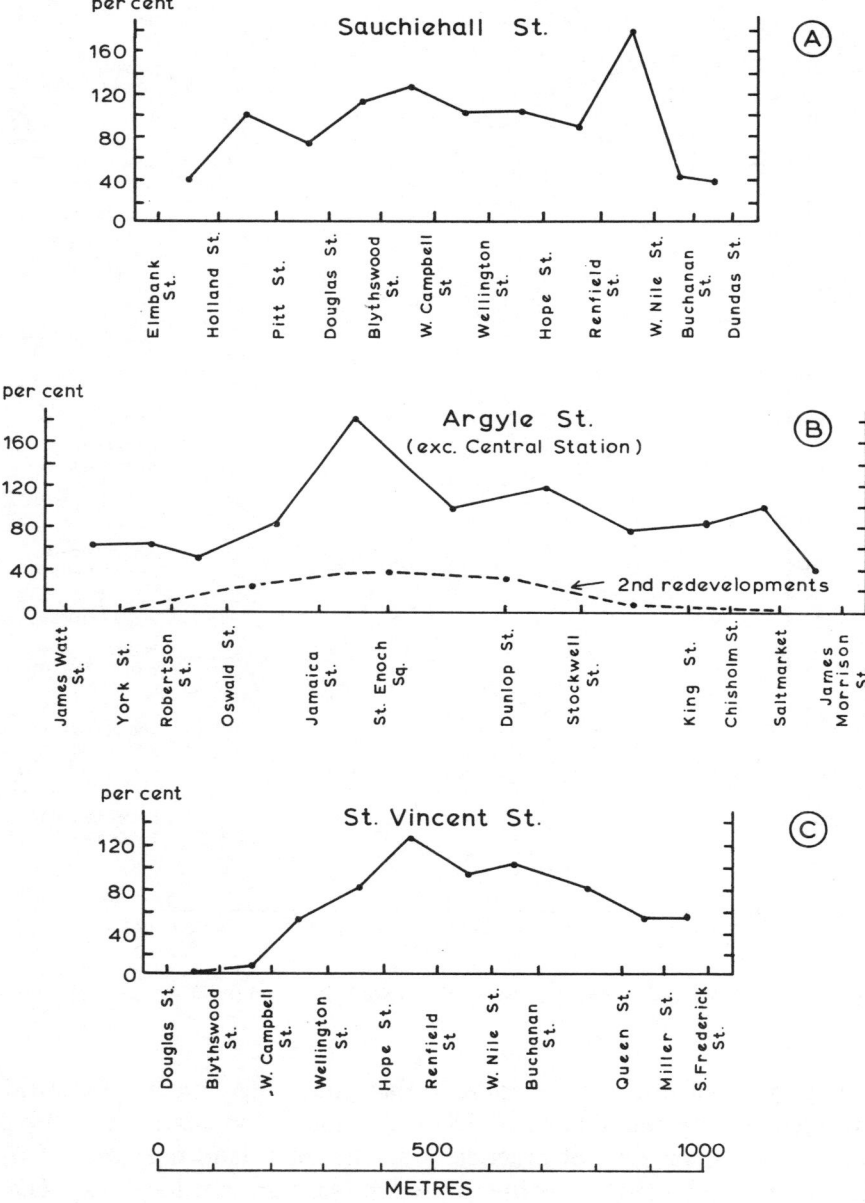

Figure 7.3 Percentage of frontage redeveloped 1840–1969 in selected streets in central Glasgow

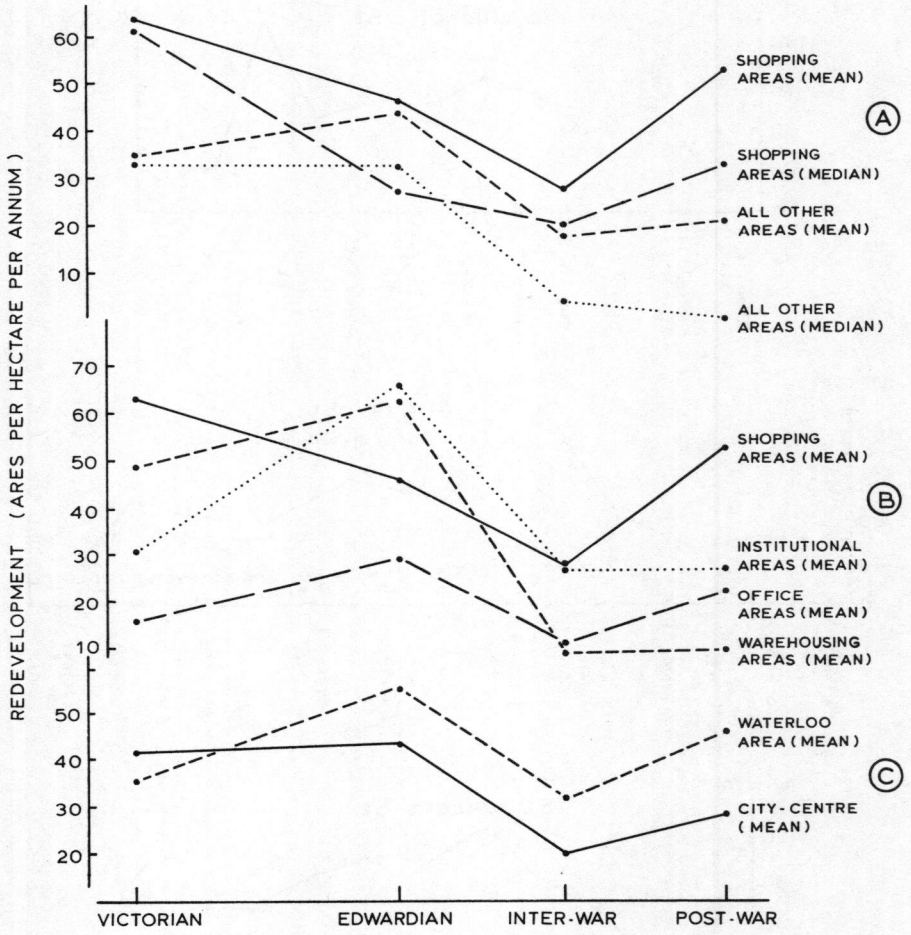

Figure 7.4 Changes over time in rates of redevelopment in different parts of central Glasgow

The bulk of the redevelopment that made up this configuration occurred during the Victorian (1840–94) and Edwardian (1895–1918) periods. This was true of practically all the main land-use areas of the city centre (delimited according to predominant ground-level use). Over the 130-year period the shopping areas collectively had significantly higher rates of redevelopment than other land-use areas combined, except in the Edwardian period (figure 7.4A).[24] In explaining these patterns, the interplay of innovation and changes in demand for space is best considered in relation to each historical period in turn.

Victorian redevelopment was dominated by the shop and the warehouse. The form of the latter was a major innovation,[25] being in almost all respects a pronounced departure from previous dwelling-like designs. Except for bank buildings, redevelopment for offices was comparatively rare and most offices occupied adapted premises. The purpose-built shops erected during the large-scale renewal of the main shopping streets contrasted with the converted dwellings and dwelling-like structures they replaced. There was a large increase in floor-space and pronounced changes in shop architecture associated with a changed conception of the scale and, in some respects, the nature of retailing.[26] This was most apparent in those streets that in 1840 had been occupied by commercial functions for a relatively short time. For example, 75 per cent of the street frontage in Union Street/Jamaica Street was renewed during the Victorian period, 66 per cent of that in Buchanan Street, south of West George Street, and 61 per cent of that in Sauchiehall Street between Blythswood Street and West Nile Street. In contrast, in the older-established commercial thoroughfare of Argyle Street (between the present Central Station and the Cross) only 40 per cent of the frontage was renewed, perhaps related to the fact that this street had undergone large-scale renewal in the preceding half-century.[27] The evidence for the Victorian transformation is unusually complete in the case of Buchanan Street, owing to the survival of engravings of the façades of virtually every building in the predominantly retail part of the street as they existed in about 1840.[28] A street of mainly two- and three-storey buildings, comprised of both Georgian town houses with shop-fronts inserted and elegant small-scale Regency shop-front buildings, often with private gardens at the rear and some with their upper floors still in residential use, was transformed by 1894 into a street of mainly four-storey Victorian buildings. These had continuous shop-fronts, almost entirely commercial use of their upper floors, approximately treble the floor-space concentrations of the buildings they replaced (since the whole of plots were built over) and even greater increases in cubic capacities, since ceilings were higher.

During the Edwardian period the rate of redevelopment in the shopping areas fell, both absolutely and relative to that in the warehouse, office and institutional areas, all of which reached their highest rates of redevelopment at this time (figure 7.4B). The boom in office redevelopment was associated with a combination of rapid commercial growth, which led to pressure on central office sites, many of which were still two-storey buildings designed for residential purposes, and the innovation of multi-storey office blocks. The new office blocks were of up to nine storeys in height and had architectural styles quite distinctive from those characterizing the bank buildings that had comprised a major share of the less rapid Victorian office redevelopment.[29] No conclusive evidence is available to explain the falling rate of rebuilding in the main shopping streets at a time when redevelopment in almost all other parts of the city centre was rising, even in the warehousing areas which had undergone rapid renewal in the Victorian period. It is possible that it was part of a cyclical trend so familiar in the building industry as a whole, reflecting in this instance overprovision of accommodation earlier in the century, combined with the fact that the buildings constructed at that time would still have been relatively new, making their demolition unlikely in the short term and thus temporarily reducing overall rates of redevelopment. However, this argument has considerably less force in this particular case. Most of the Victorian redevelopments took place during the first two-thirds of that period (much of the last one-third, broadly from 1878 to 1894, comprising an economic slump) and the scale of the Edwardian boom[30] was such that, if any vacant space still existed in 1895, it is likely that it would soon have been occupied.

The inter-war period (1919–45) in Glasgow is of especial interest since it provides an opportunity to consider the effects of innovation separately from those of economic growth. During this period Scotland 'came near to realizing in practice the imaginary stationary state that has so occupied theoretical economists'.[31] Yet it was also a period when a large range of innovations relating to townscape development achieved their greatest impact in Britain as a whole, a situation related, in part at least, to the considerable economic growth experienced in southern and midland England.[32] Important among these innovations of national significance were department and variety stores[33] and cinemas,[34] since they tended to have major structural requirements often most economically met in large cities by redevelopment. Furthermore, a greater absolute increase than in any previous period in the number of branches of multiple stores[35] had structural implications because of the large areas of floor-space that many of them required. The multiple stores also had an important effect in introducing both capital and decision-making from other cities.

In central Glasgow, the retailing innovations widely adopted in the inter-war period were almost exclusively restricted in their direct effects on the townscape to existing shopping areas and were associated with the replacement of buildings on sites with long histories of retail use. In the case of the cinemas, the same areas or their immediate environs were affected, with buildings used for a variety of commercial purposes being replaced. Several innovations in communications also experienced peak periods of adoption at this time. Redevelopments for bus stations, commercial garages, car showrooms and telephone exchanges generally took place on the periphery of the city centre and in all cases involved the demolition of buildings designed for substantially different purposes. Elsewhere in the city centre the virtual cessation of redevelopment may be related to the absence at this time of innovations with comparable structural effects in either the office or warehouse areas. Thus, after at least a century in which the demand for increased space was generally so great that in many respects it had a controlling influence on the spatial pattern of redevelopment, even in an era of many structurally significant innovations, in the inter-war period there was a major change in the relative significance for the townscape of increased space requirements and innovation. The hiatus in the demand for more space was reflected in the fact that a much smaller proportion of redevelopments involved substantial increases in floor-space than in the Victorian and Edwardian periods. Changes in ways of using space, involving both new uses and new types of facilities for certain existing uses, assumed greater significance and the suitability of structures and locations for these changed functional requirements became of major importance in determining those areas in which redevelopment took place.

Redevelopment in the post-war period (1946–69) was predominantly for shops and offices, the latter being underrepresented in figure 7.4B owing to the fact that by no means all new office building was confined to the area predominantly in office use. The office redevelopments generally involved substantial increases in floor-space. The comparatively small increases in retail floor-space reflect large-scale rehousing of the population of the inner zone of the city in areas much less accessible to the city centre, thereby reducing the population catchment for certain of its retailing services, although there was a tendency in the urban area as a whole for per capita retail sales to rise.[36] However, more noteworthy in the shopping areas, as in the inter-war period, were the effects on physical structures of changes in the nature of activities. In these changes the role of the variety chain stores (notably Woolworth, Littlewoods, British Home Stores, Marks & Spencer, and Boots, if it may be grouped in this category) was even greater than during the previous period: large areas of uninterrupted ground floor were created, often by redevelopment of the sites of several small shops of the type that had dominated the nineteenth-century city centre.

The economics of redevelopment for offices was much more closely linked to the profitability of creating *additional* office accommodation, relating to the increase in employment in this field.[37] However, as with redevelopment for other uses, a significant consideration was the comparative cost of refurbishing and extending existing buildings according to contemporary fashions and standards, including some embodied in legislation, such as the Offices, Shops and Railway Premises Act, 1963. In the case of offices, innovations relating to the nature of the function did not have structural implications on the scale of those affecting the shopping areas. In the case of redevelopment for other purposes, the relatively low rate was probably strongly influenced by an apparently almost stationary demand for warehouse space in the city centre,[38] coupled with relatively few innovations in this function of the type that would have had the effect of accelerating obsolescence in the existing stock of buildings.

In considering the differences between various parts of the city centre in relation to changing rates of redevelopment over time, attention has been focused on regions characterized by the predominance of a single use throughout the study period. However, a good deal of redevelopment in any city centre is associated with a change of use.[39] Some areas have changed sides on a land-use boundary, while others have a long history of mixed land use. The extent of the association between redevelopment and change of use depends in part on the extent to which one use may occupy accommodation designed for another. Certain uses, for example, churches, cinemas and bus stations, tend to have specialized buildings that are readily adaptable for few other purposes. If in addition the use itself is one with a short life span, then the likelihood of redevelopment is clearly increased. The area with relatively high rates of development lying approximately between Bothwell Street and Argyle Street in the south-west part of the city centre (the 'Waterloo Area' in figure 7.4C) exemplifies this. Containing the Corn Exchange and a host of both closely related and apparently unrelated uses, this area was marginal to the city centre throughout the study period and in 1840 included sites used for low-intensity purposes such as the storage of stone, slate and timber. Some of these uses were unlikely to survive long within 300 m of the most valuable commercial sites in the city, but the replacement uses, numbering among them a theatre, a bus station and a post office, tended themselves not to belong to the main categories of land use with already established foci within the commercial core. Furthermore, there was a high incidence of ephemeral uses and of relatively specialized buildings, such as churches, ill-adapted for possible subsequent users seeking similar sites. A history of rates of redevelopment broadly following the general trend but, except for the Victorian period, at a higher level, continued into recent times (figure 7.4C). It may be that the very heterogeneity of the area discouraged the establishment of the sorts of uses that tended to occur in major concentrations elsewhere in the city centre. Although this area was exceptional within central Glasgow, its history suggests that a combination of ephemeral uses and specialized buildings can result in a relatively high rate of redevelopment over a long period on sites outside the areas of highest land value.

The tendency for redevelopment to take place more rapidly within certain parts of the city centre has implications for the rates of replacement of buildings of different ages. Clearly a random occurrence of replacement throughout the whole building-age range would be inconsistent with our findings so far. Also inconsistent would be a model in which the rate of replacement increased with building age. It is true that the replacement of new buildings is rare; but it is also true that younger buildings in certain locations are more susceptible to replacement than older buildings elsewhere. This should result, for the city centre as a whole, in a rise and then a fall in the death rates of buildings of particular ages. The death rates of old buildings would eventually fall below those of younger buildings since the younger buildings would be on average on sites more susceptible to redevelopment.

Although the relative slowness of building replacement in central Glasgow means that our study period is rather short for examining this process, such data as are available (table 7.1) are broadly consistent with such a view in that during the post-war period Victorian buildings were apparently about to succeed Georgian buildings as the most vulnerable to replacement. However, certain deviations from the suggested model are apparent. For instance, it would appear that buildings constructed during different periods differed in their susceptibility to replacement, with Edwardian buildings showing no sign of a rise in their rate of replacement at the end of the study period in spite of the lapse of half a century since these buildings were constructued. Indeed, in the post-war period they were actually less vulnerable than inter-war buildings, perhaps owing to the fact that Edwardian buildings were proportionately

Table 7.1 Average annual replacement rates* in central Glasgow

| | | Age of building | | |
Period	Georgian	Victorian	Edwardian	Inter-war
1840–1894	0.84			
1895–1918	1.46	0.21		
1919–1945	0.61	0.19	0.04	
1946–1969	0.67	0.58	0.00	0.25

*$R = 100b/By$ where R = average annual replacement rate, b = buildings (site area) replaced, B = buildings (site area) existing at the beginning of the period, y = length of period (years).

fewer than inter-war buildings in the most vulnerable retailing areas. Many of them were high office blocks, on the whole less susceptible to changes of fashion and in any case more difficult, with their high floor-space concentrations, to redevelop economically within the 3.5:1 guide-line for plot ratios adopted by the Corporation in 1955.[40]

The suggestion that the change over time in the replacement rates of different age categories for the city centre as a whole may relate to the existence of different life spans in different locations is consistent with table 7.2 in which changes over time in the ratio of Georgian to post-Georgian buildings replaced are shown separately for the shopping areas and all other areas. Large-scale replacement of post-Georgian buildings began earlier in the shopping areas and such buildings constituted a substantial majority of those replaced in these areas between 1946 and 1969. In the remainder of the city centre, Georgian buildings still comprised the majority of those replaced even in the post-war period. However, the fact that the ratios for the two areas did not diverge markedly until the post-war period suggests that the interplay of forces is more complex than our previous generalizations might suggest.

Figure 7.5 represents schematically one aspect of the rate of replacement of buildings of different ages over time that seems plausible in the light of the Glasgow findings. Rather than conforming to a normal probability distribution that might conceivably obtain if inter-regional differences in rates of redevelopment did not exist, the curves are positively skewed, relating to the fact that away from the shopping areas the onset of replacement of any age category tends to be retarded and its incidence over time more spread out. This simple perspective may be taken a stage further by incorporating changes over time in the extent of spatial variations in rates of redevelopment and by taking account of other variations between periods. The latter, in particular, may have major long-term implications

Table 7.2 Ratio of Georgian to post-Georgian buildings replaced in central Glasgow

	Shopping areas		Other areas	
Period	Georgian	Post-Georgian	Georgian	Post-Georgian
1895–1918	83	17	88	12
1919–1945	76	24	77	23
1946–1969	37	63	57	43

and in some circumstances, such as in the case of Edwardian and inter-war buildings in central Glasgow, contribute to a younger building age group undergoing a substantial rate of replacement before an older one.

AMOUNT AND CHARACTER OF SECULAR CHANGE

The Glasgow data provide a rare entrée into central redevelopment in a specific city over an extended period. But redevelopment is only one aspect of change and for recent decades it is possible for British cities and to a lesser extent other Western cities to piece together a picture of the wide variety of changes that commercial cores have undergone.

The main land-use change in the post-war period has been the growth in floor-space devoted to offices, especially professional and scientific services, insurance, banking and finance, and public administration,[41] reflecting an increase in both office employment and the amount of space per office worker. In contrast, declines have been evident in the amount of floor-space in industry and wholesaling.[42] In the latter case they reflect a decreasing dependence of retail establishments on separate centrally located wholesaling facilities,[43] and in both cases they reflect increased demand for central office space.[44] Retailing has occupied an intermediate position, with many city centres undergoing moderate increases in floor-space but some experiencing declines. There have been considerable variations over short distances, for example within parts of the English Midlands.[45] Within Great Britain as a whole, the great variation between city centres in the extent of their changes in retail turnover[46] suggests that a pattern of considerable variation in changes in their amounts of retail floor-space is likely to continue.

These changes in the admixture of city-centre land use have been accommodated by a variety of forms of building adaptation and

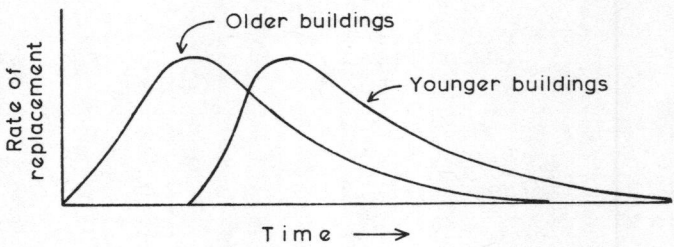

Figure 7.5 Rates of replacement of buildings over time – schematic

redevelopment. In the case of offices, the main increases of floor-space have resulted from the construction of large, generally free-standing office blocks, particularly on sites formerly occupied by lower-density offices or by warehouses, industrial establishments and transport installations. In the City of London this has further accentuated the domination of offices, which by 1978 comprised three-quarters of the City's floor-space, and has restored floor-space concentrations to their pre-war levels.[47] Indeed in the City of London and in Manchester the limited scope for further major office redevelopments in the core office area has forced new schemes further out into the zone around the core which is largely occupied by warehouses and small factories.[48] This has happened even during periods of reduced demand for office space by users, and largely reflects the growing demand by financial institutions for office property in city centres as an investment, the limited number of sites in such areas ensuring the growth of rents and the increased value of existing investments.[49] Thus the investment policies of the financial institutions have had a major effect on the scale and location of new office building. One of the effects on users, particularly in the City of London, has been to reduce the number of small units of accommodation that are available, thereby further increasing the rents of small businesses and displacing them from central sites.[50]

In the case of retailing, the major variety chain stores have continued to undertake their own redevelopments of key sites. But the main additions to floor-space since the mid-1960s have resulted from shopping schemes intended for more than one, usually many, tenants. Although retailing has been the most common single former use of the sites that have been developed in this way, considerable amounts of land formerly in other uses have been incorporated.[51] Furthermore, on average less than 8 per cent of all tenants of town-centre shopping schemes formerly traded on the site[52] and the character of the new retail uses differs considerably from that of those displaced. Many specialized retailers, such as antiquarian bookshops, stamp dealers, antique shops, art dealers and musical instrument shops, that are able to afford the rents in old property have been unable to meet the high rents that generally obtain after redevelopment.[53] The same is true of craft and specialist services,[54] and it has been estimated that about half of the industrial firms whose sites are taken over for such schemes close down.[55] The tenants replacing them tend to comprise a much higher proportion of shops selling high-turnover goods of a type available in large suburban centres.[56] Thus the variety of goods and services available is being reduced,[57] small traders are being displaced and the socio-cultural role of the city centre is diminishing.[58] A further problem is the integration of shopping schemes into the townscape, since they have a tendency to be inward looking, sometimes presenting a blank face to the established streets on to which they have a frontage. They have also tended to attract retailers away from existing streets, some of which are suffering as shopping streets from an excessive influx of 'service trades', such as employment agencies, travel agents, betting offices, estate agents and building societies, which may have the effect of isolating parts of streets from the main pedestrian flows.[59] The new shopping schemes have also highlighted the existing problems of traditional shopping streets, notably their frequently great length – in contrast to the compactness of most shopping schemes – exposure to weather and traffic, and difficulties of service access.[60]

The new shopping schemes, even more than the new office blocks, have brought major land-use change and physical renewal. But going on simultaneously has been a great deal of other change that has been more widely spread over the city centre. Some of this has involved the small-scale replacement of individual buildings or small groups of buildings, but a great deal has consisted of the much more numerous other types of changes that the building fabric undergoes, notably change of use, façade changes, and the extension of existing buildings.

The role of individually minor, but in aggregate important, changes to the fabric of buildings has been even less studied than complete building replacement. Buissink and de Widt in their study of central Utrecht over the period 1910–61 found that buildings in shopping streets were consistently and markedly more prone to frontal alterations than buildings in other streets.[61] A similar result later emerged from Sim's study of façade changes in central Glasgow between 1950 and 1969.[62]

Within the shopping streets Buissink and de Widt also found that buildings in the most central streets were consistently more prone to frontal alterations than buildings in more peripheral streets, a finding with which both Sim in Glasgow and Alexander[63] in Perth, Australia subsequently concurred. Buissink and de Widt also found that buildings in shopping streets had consistently more internal alterations than those in other streets, although in this case the difference was comparatively small. Differences between streets in the rate of frontal alterations seem bound to persist in the foreseeable future, related as they are to the more intimate connection in retailing than in any other city-centre function between the attraction of trade and the external appearances of buildings.

FLUCTUATIONS

The temporal trends and spatial patterns that have been referred to, some of them with a history extending over the post-war period and some much longer, must not obscure the fact that many types of changes in city centres are, like changes elsewhere in the urban area, very uneven over time. This is inevitable given the long life of physical structures. Some fluctuations are very long term. For example, it was commonplace for British city centres to undergo major redevelopments associated with major road building, and occasionally railway construction, in the nineteenth century – Birmingham and Newcastle upon Tyne are examples – but not to undergo further major redevelopments on this scale until well into the post-war period. It would not be surprising if cities such as Birmingham that have been subject to major redevelopment schemes in their commercial cores in recent years underwent no further changes of this type until well into the twenty-first century. Even where the replacement of physical structures throughout Victorian and modern times has been overwhelmingly piecemeal, as in the commercial core of Glasgow, there have still been major long-term fluctuations in its incidence.

Superimposed on these long swings have been marked short-term fluctuations which, despite inter-city and regional variations, are evident in national aggregate figures for commercial building. Thus the value (at constant prices) of new orders obtained for commercial construction in Britain reached a peak in 1964, fell to less than two-thirds this figure by 1967, rose to another peak in 1971, fell to little more than half this value by 1975, and then rose again in the late 1970s and early 1980s.[64] These data do not distinguish between new building and the great variety of alterations that take place. Data for central Huddersfield suggest that alterations may be less erratic than the construction of new buildings in their incidence over time, at least at the scale of the individual town centre,[65] a finding that would seem to hold for building generally.[66] Time series of building completions naturally show a time lag relative to plans submitted and orders obtained by contractors, and the peak year for the opening of shopping centres was actually 1975,[67] the lowest year of the decade for new orders for commercial buildings.[68] The redevelopment of sites on speculation, as in the case of many office blocks, combined with a lag of 3 or 4 years between the drawing up of plans and building completion, are major factors underlying the short-term cyclical element in city-centre redevelopment.[69] The marked fluctuations in speculative office building are underlain by a more stable pattern of bespoke office building (including that for owner occupation) which, as in bespoke building generally, comprises a higher proportion of developments initiated in slumps than of those initiated in booms.

Arguably, in the case of the cycles in office redevelopment in Britain, there has been a tendency for public policy to reinforce the peaks and troughs.[70] Thus in the City of London the development charge and building licence regulations of the 1947 Town Planning Act held back the post-war redevelopment boom until the early 1950s, and the introduction of Office Development Permits to some extent delayed the beginning of the second boom in the late 1960s, the end of which was followed in 1973/74 by the new Labour government ordering a review of this policy and its strict enforcement in the interim. The abolition of Office Development Permits by the Conservative government in 1979 encouraged a new speculative boom and added fuel to a further resurgence of activity.

The extent of future booms and slumps and inter-city variations in their incidence will depend on a variety of factors, including the extent to which oversupplies of office space have been whittled down and the extent of investment in real estate abroad. The continued flow of international capital into the City of London is likely to maintain the growth in demand for prime space from the financial sector in that city, and the further concentration of the headquarters of firms in south-east England is likely to maintain the demand for office space in that region as a whole. But reductions in expenditure by the public sector in Britain, a major user of speculative redevelopments in most provincial cities during the boom of the early 1970s,[71] has curtailed the demand for office space in other regions. However, the demand for property by users has a far-from-perfect correlation with the demand for property as an investment[72] and there is not a simple relation between cycles of redevelopment and the general state of the economy. The strength of the speculative element in commercial property development almost guarantees the continuation of cyclical tendencies.

Cycles are sometimes more pronounced on the ground than appears from data aggregated for whole city centres, since there is a tendency for an area once selected to receive the concentrated efforts of developers until its potentialities are exhausted, whereupon activity shifts to another location.[73] A 'neighbourhood effect' of this kind has been evident in the post-war period in shop redevelopments (almost entirely individual shops) in central Glasgow, although not in office redevelopments,[74] and the tendency for such an effect to exist in alterations to the façades of buildings has been observed in small town centres.[75]

INNOVATIONS

As in other parts of the urban area, the unevenness that characterizes the development of the city centre is by no means simply historical repetition. Although the continuance of fluctuations seems inevitable, each future cycle will differ in some way, much as cycles have done in the past. One reason for this is the adoption of innovations. Apart from their effects on the whole process of change, these tend to endow particular booms and slumps with their own characteristics.

Included among these innovations are the controls and laws that govern change. The changing legislation relating to building in Britain is one instance. For example, present daylighting codes and controls over building heights and plot ratios combine to make it difficult to develop a small site.[76] Often fundamental but, since legislation is not necessarily involved, sometimes indeterminate, are changes in planning fashions. Among the most important of these has been the swing from a widespread espousal of comprehensive redevelopment in the first 25 years after the war[77] to an approach that is more concerned with adapting and supplementing the existing urban fabric.

Even more significant in some respects are technical innovations, particularly in the construction industry, communications and retailing. It has been estimated, for example, that the introduction of business machines has been responsible for an increase of about 3 per cent per year in the amount of space needed per office worker.[78] Furthermore, there is the growth of agents of change that are largely new, at least within property development. Looking back over several decades one may note, for example, the rise to prominence of the shopfitters in the 1920s, the consulting engineers in the 1950s, and the insurance companies and pension funds in the 1960s. It would be surprising if another agent of change did not rise to importance before the end of the century.

Perhaps most obviously, there is the advent of new types of land use in the city centre, sometimes entailing the erection of purpose-built structures. For example, the cinema came and largely went within well under a century,[79] and the multi-storey car-park appeared on a large scale in the 1960s and is likely to be with us in large numbers until well into the twenty-first century. These and many more innovations add qualitative variety to the trends and fluctuations that characterize the city centre and require taking into account in any balanced appraisal of change and how it can be managed.

INTER-URBAN VARIATIONS

There remains the need to assess the significance of these changes for inter-urban variations. There are grounds for supposing that the adoption of many of the innovations affecting physical change will occur first in major cities and only later, if at all, in small towns. Not only are awareness of innovations and adoption-proneness likely to be greater in large cities,[80] but a substantial population catchment is frequently a major economic factor in the viability of an innovation. Thus, in addition to the effect of population change on the form of a commercial core, there is likely to be a hierarchical effect, town centres serving large populations having a higher proportion of their buildings altered or replaced, and having higher floor-space concentrations, than town centres serving small populations. Such a hierarchical effect is likely to be compounded by increases in personal mobility, especially associated with rapidly increasing car ownership in the post-war period, which in general might be expected to be associated with an expansion in the trade of larger, at the expense of smaller, centres.

Although in the long term the form of town centres is likely to be associated with both the urban hierarchy and population change, the strength of the correlations is likely to vary over time and space. This is a reflection in particular of the considerable variations in the extent of the differences between towns in respect of population change and innovation adoption, both of which are affected by a wide variety of factors. In the case of innovations, not only must their specific nature be taken into account but also the timing of their introduction in a particular region and at different levels in the urban hierarchy. For example, in Britain there was a strong tendency for the earlier department stores, mainly founded during the few decades preceding the First World War, to be located in the major city centres, whereas the main phase of their proliferation, during the inter-war period, was characterized by widespread diffusion into medium-sized towns.[81] The major banks, in contrast, were rapidly opening branches in the smallest towns by the inter-war period,[82] although the impact of this on building replacement was probably smaller than had been associated with the opening of branches in large and medium-sized towns in earlier periods. Regional differences in the timing of the introduction of an innovation may be largely short-term, reflecting the presence of a neighbourhood effect,[83] but long-term spatial contrasts must also be considered. For example, not only did Scotland have an appreciably greater percentage increase in cinema provision than other parts of Britain during the inter-war period but it retained a higher per capita provision into the post-war period when cinema construction had virtually ceased.[84] And in retailing, although Scotland was one of the first areas to experience the growth and spread of co-operative societies during the later nineteenth century, it remained one of the main areas of their further development in the inter-war period.[85] Such regional variations, together with the various temporal and hierarchical variations already referred to, must be borne in mind when assessing the results of research on particular areas.

Examination of two groups of small town centres, 25 centres in southern Scotland and 34 centres in East Anglia, helps to clarify the effects of population change and the urban hierarchy on building fabric change.[86] Both areas have undergone lengthy periods of contrasting economic conditions within the twentieth century. In aggregate the populations of both groups of towns were essentially stable during the inter-war years but increased appreciably in the post-war period associated with considerable economic growth. The adoption of functional innovations with important structural implications for town centres, such as variety chain stores, department stores, cinemas and commercial garages, was particularly characteristic of the inter-war

Table 7.3 Spearman's rank correlation coefficients between building fabric change and population characteristics among town centres in southern Scotland and East Anglia in the inter-war period. Partial correlation coefficients are shown in italics*

	Population, 1931		% population change 1921–51		% population change 1921–31	
	Southern Scotland	East Anglia	Southern Scotland	East Anglia	Southern Scotland	East Anglia
% building replacement	+0.60 *+0.60*	+0.09 *−0.12*	+0.11 *+0.02*	+0.07 *−0.01*	+0.19 *+0.02*	−0.29 *−0.25*
% façade conversion	+0.35 *+0.33*	−0.03 *−0.04*	+0.29 *+0.26*	+0.10 *+0.10*	+0.41 *+0.34*	−0.12 *−0.12*

*Percentage population change 1921–51 is controlled in relationships with population in 1931, and population in 1931 is controlled in relationships with percentage population change in 1921–51 and 1921–31.
Source: Luffrum, 1980, p. 172, table III.

period, though some, for example Woolworth's stores, were adopted more widely among the towns in southern Scotland, reflecting at least in part the inclusion of some larger towns in that area.

In the inter-war period in southern Scotland there was a fairly strong relationship between the urban hierarchy and the percentage of buildings replaced and a weaker one between the urban hierarchy and the percentage of façade conversions (table 7.3). No such relationships existed, however, in East Anglia. In neither group of towns was there a correlation between percentage population change and percentage of buildings replaced. The hierarchical effect in southern Scotland was partly a manifestation of the geographical spread of new functions that required population catchments larger than those of the smaller towns. The accommodation requirements of these functions (for example, cinemas, Woolworth's stores and co-operative stores) were often not readily met by the adaptation of existing structures and the firms and organizations concerned frequently initiated developments specifically for their own occupation, particularly in the 1930s. Among the East Anglian towns this response was on average slightly delayed, occurring less in the inter-war period and more in the post-war period.

In the post-war period in both groups of towns there were positive correlations, mostly sizeable, between both the urban hierarchy and percentage population change on the one hand and percentage of

Table 7.4 Spearman's rank correlation coefficients between aspects of the building fabric and centrality, population size and population change among town centres in southern Scotland and East Anglia in the post-war period.[a] Partial correlation coefficients are shown in italics.[b]

	Centrality index[c]		Population 1971		% population change 1951–71	
	Southern Scotland	East Anglia	Southern Scotland	East Anglia	Southern Scotland	East Anglia
% building replacement	+0.64 *+0.46*	+0.54 *+0.51*	+0.79 *+0.64*	+0.70 *+0.65*	+0.67 *+0.36*	+0.34 *−0.04*
% façade conversion	+0.66 *+0.58*	+0.41 *+0.39*	+0.58 *+0.44*	+0.32 *+0.29*	+0.42 *+0.08*	+0.14 *−0.03*
Floor-space concentration[c]	+0.54	+0.50	+0.48	+0.19		

[a] 1946–76 in southern Scotland and 1946–75 in East Anglia.
[b] Percentage population change 1951–71 is controlled in relationships with population in 1971 and centrality index, and population in 1971 is controlled in relationships with percentage population change.
[c] Measured in 1976 in southern Scotland and in 1975 in East Anglia.
Source: Luffrum, 1980, p. 171, table II.

buildings replaced and percentage of façade conversions on the other (table 7.4). However, whereas in East Anglia this reflected the inter-correlation of population change and the urban hierarchy, in southern Scotland population change had an influence on building replacement independent of any hierarchical effect. In the 1960s and 1970s in both groups of towns large speculative developers assumed major importance and tended to select both faster-growing and larger centres for their activities. In both areas, both percentage population change and the urban hierarchy were correlated more strongly with percentage of façade conversions than in the inter-war period, but on average these correlations were still lower than those with percentage of buildings replaced. The relative cheapness of façade conversions may have made them less subject to economic factors than complete building replacement.[87]

These observations should be seen in the light of the slowness with which the building fabric has been changed in both areas. Of the town-centre buildings existing in the mid-1970s, in both groups of towns some 80 per cent were constructed before 1918. This accounts at least in part for the relatively low correlations between floor-space concentration and the urban hierarchy (table 7.4). Indeed recent floor-space concentrations actually correlate more closely with measures of the urban hierarchy before the First World War than with recent measures.

This last finding underlines the slowness with which physical change takes place even in the most focal parts of urban areas. It flaws any attempt to explain the townscape solely in terms of current processes. A much longer term view, covering decades and often centuries, is required. This is also relevant to the consideration of future townscapes. Although we cannot forecast the discoveries that will underlie future innovation, the main physical structures upon which future processes will work are already strongly rooted in the landscape.

8
Conclusion

We have begun to weave the fabric of a theory of urban form by threading together a number of social and economic variables. Considerable attention has been given to land values and how these relate to long waves in the economy and the adoption of innovations. The conjunction of these elements provides a structure that helps to disentangle the complexities of urban form. The empirical basis consists of the examination of a number of fairly explicit propositions in individual cities and groups of towns, and less detailed reference to a wide range of relevant case studies. In this final chapter we shall make a critical assessment of the perspective that has been adopted, review and amplify the main findings, and consider some implications of those findings for the management of townscape change.

THE PERSPECTIVE

The importance of land value and similar concepts is acknowledged in a variety of perspectives on urban development, albeit that there are differences in the way that these concepts are developed.[1] The evidence presented here confirms that importance. Land value is a convenient method of expressing the more general phenomenon of pressure on space that is by no means confined to urban environments or for that matter to human affairs.[2] It is not suggested, however, that in combination with economic fluctuations and innovation adoption it provides a complete explanation of urban form. Although much of urban form may be construed in terms of the economics of land use, some fairly substantial differences between and within urban areas remain unexplained. Quite apart from architectural styles, the rich spatial variety of which has received relatively little mention, variations such as occur in the heights and types of buildings have only been explained to a limited degree. It is not hard to pose questions, for example about the distribution of the skyscraper or the tenement (as distinct from the single-family house), that are more complex than would appear to be explicable by the conjunction of relationships that have been postulated here. In some cases it is necessary to elicit cultural factors for which a crude explanation in terms of innovation diffusion is inadequate. Although the adoption of innovations may reflect the presence of economic thresholds, of major importance are the value judgements that are placed on different, especially qualitatively different, forms. While the incidence of city-centre skyscrapers within North America and Europe reflects city size, the differences between the heights of buildings in city centres of similar size in the two continents are marked. They reflect different attitudes and antecedents, some of them embodied in legislation concerning building heights. In part related to this, buildings have a symbolic value,[3] seldom separable from their economic value. Contrasting attitudes to the status of living near the city centre, for example between Europe north of the Alps and Mediterranean Europe, should also be seen in part in this light.

In addition to having limitations as an explanation of cultural differences, innovation diffusion is an imperfect explanation of change, particularly over long time spans. Although the recognition of the relationship between clusters of innovations and their diffusion can provide a plausible retrospective view of the changing form of cities, forecasting innovations and their adoption is a far greater problem. At the core of the problem are the changes that take place in the relationships between variables, especially in the long term but even within decades. Compounding the difficulty, changes take place in the characteristics of the categories that we use. For example, although it may be revealing to trace the fluctuations that have taken place in industrial building over long spans of time, it is necessary to bear in mind that 'industry' as a category has changed substantially, both as an activity and in location, even within the post-war period. Furthermore, the same land-use categories have varied considerably in the ways in which they have been brought into being and in the motives for which they have been created. In Britain, for example, the production of housing by private enterprise has changed from being largely for an investment market before the First World War, with rental income accruing to landlords, to being largely for a user market (that is, for owner occupation) in the 1980s. There have also been major changes in the relative amounts of housing produced by the state and by private enterprise. Most of these changes are inseparable from the roles of the agents responsible for change in the urban landscape which are the subject of a complementary volume that is in preparation.

MAIN FINDINGS

Despite these caveats, it is possible to make a variety of generalizations, many of which are supportable over long periods of time at least within Western countries if not more widely. Some of these provide valuable bases upon which to view the future. It is also possible to identify certain enduring attributes of the urban landscape that may well provide a basis for making the major intellectual leap from monitoring developments and identifying those that are likely to continue into the future to formulating principles for managing change and suggesting possible procedures for their implementation.

For quite fundamental reasons that are unlikely to change in the foreseeable future the different elements that make up the urban landscape change at different speeds. This is partly related to the time lag between changes in function and changes in form that is a general characteristic of the cultural landscape. The occupation of buildings by land uses for which they were not designed is one example. More generally, however, a spectrum of susceptibility to change can be recognized, with structures entailing a large capital investment, such as street systems, changing rarely and those involving a relatively small capital investment, such as shop-fronts, undergoing quite frequent changes. These changes are seldom the result of physical decay. Their root cause is the endless succession of changes in society generally and in local circumstances in particular.

If we take a long-term view it is possible to recognize certain recurrent features in the speed of change of different types of forms that have remained in evidence in spite of major changes in the functioning of society. The most common change to street systems is the addition of subsidiary streets, often culs-de-sac, associated with intensified use – for example, the construction of additional dwellings within the gardens of houses originally developed at low density. Even where an exceptionally radical reshaping of an area has taken place, as in central Newcastle upon Tyne in the mid nineteenth century, or in central Birmingham in the 1950s and 1960s, or indeed in cities whose centres were almost razed to the ground by bombing, the lines of the majority of the main streets have remained unaltered. The building fabric is on average less resistant to replacement, although in Europe, where building life spans well in excess of 100 years are quite normal even in city centres, buildings would seem to survive longer than in the United States. Alterations to the existing fabric, as distinct from complete replacements, are comparatively frequent. Extensions to buildings and façade changes are both more numerous than complete building replacements and, if all alterations to buildings are combined, building replacements are numerically insignificant by comparison, although individually their cost and impact on the townscape is usually substantially greater.

Changes of building user and, in parts of the city centre, changes of use occur more frequently than building replacements. Most buildings are occupied by several users during the course of their lives, and the arrival of a new occupier increases the likelihood of physical change to the premises. Most building replacements are associated with a change of site user.

The most important single finding to emerge from our analysis is the widespread unevenness of development. Not only do individual morphological elements not change at the same speed, but both the amount and character of the forms created and the modifications that they subsequently undergo are subject to cycles. Many of the examples we have examined occurred between the mid nineteenth century and the mid twentieth century. Since this was a period in Western countries in which both centralized planning and local planning were, with few exceptions, on a minor scale, it might be argued that what has been studied is essentially the consequence of the operation of a free market. Indeed in our examination of British commercial cores we deliberately sought to minimize the effects of post-war 'planning' in our selection of a case study. However, there is no reason to suggest that planning is in some way outside the cyclical patterns that have been discussed. On the contrary, it would seem that planning itself is subject to cycles, related to, and often hard to distinguish from, those in the uncontrolled economy. Sutcliffe identifies two upswings in planning activity since the development of modern planning at the end of the nineteenth century.[4] These have been in 1890–1914 and 1945–70. The downswings have been in 1918–39 and from 1970 to the present day. There is an evident synchronism with morphological periods. The present concern with conservation, renovation and Post-Modern architecture, which has provided such a powerful reaction to the Modern Movement, may be seen as a reawakening of the conservationist and historicist concerns of the 1880s.[5] In so far as 'planning cycles' may be distinguished from those apparent in the adoption of innovations more generally, they have on balance had the effect of reinforcing the annular structure of urban development created by the alternation of fringe belts and residential accretion and by the cyclical rhythm of innovation adoption. They have tended to emphasize the unity of morphological periods and thereby of the morphological regions that are their correlates on the ground.

Both in planning and in other aspects of urban development it is useful to make the distinction between new growth and changes to what already exists. The cessation of population growth in many Western cities and the considerable age attained by their inner areas has been associated with some shift in attention from new growth to internal change. Fitting the creations of new societies within the framework created by previous societies is a problem of increasing importance. The morphogenetic record provides an indispensable basis for addressing this problem.

Perhaps the most obvious influence of the past is the actual survival of forms created when an urban area was initially developed. However, features may leave a legacy long after they have ceased to have a physical existence. It is quite common for major post-war redevelopments in British city centres to have boundaries that conform at least in part to the lineaments of plot series laid out in medieval times. Sometimes it is plot size rather than plot shape that is important: the tendency for users of large sites on the edges of commercial cores, such as government departments and transport installations, to occupy inner fringe-belt plots is one instance. Both legacies relate to the difficulty of assembling large sites from numerous small plots in different ownership. In other cases it is the intensity of initial development that is crucial. For instance, the scope for more intensive development without redevelopment tends to be much greater on fringe-belt sites and in areas of large detached houses than in areas of working-class housing.

These are in a sense 'environmental' explanations of the form taken by the urban landscape. But the influence of existing forms also needs to be seen in the light of the interests of the users and, more particularly, the owners of property. If an owner's interest is in investment, decisions about whether to invest in the urban fabric will be influenced by the return obtainable from alternative investments. This is subject to change. A notable feature is the degree to which owners invest or disinvest in concert within a given part of the city. This partly reflects the nature of the original development. If, as is often the case, forms over a sizeable area have been brought into existence by similar decision makers, those forms and decision makers may well have similar subsequent histories. The interdependence of decisions is also relevant. Change on one site is liable to affect the environment of nearby sites. Recent patterns of decline and renewal in the older areas of cities show this to a marked degree.

However, if homogeneous areas are one of the products of the growth process so are the boundaries between them. The boundary between a fringe belt and a particular type of residential accretion is an example. Such an area of contact is frequently a place of conflicting interests. Institutions in fringe belts have frequently colonized adjacent residential accretions, their existing capital investment in an area being a major factor in their ability to outbid potential residential users. But like other processes this needs to be seen not only in the context of the historical development of areas but in relation to the life histories of institutions and owners. House owners tend to have greater mobility and shorter life cycles than institutions. Especially when expanding, institutions are predominantly interested in the existing-use value of their property unless a change of site is contemplated. Households tend to be mainly interested in the existing-use value of their property until they reach old age. At that point the realization of the development value of a large garden may initiate a cycle of more intensive development. As far as the owners of sites nearby are concerned, this may well be contrary to their interests as occupiers but may enhance the development value of their land.

The implications for urban renewal of the cyclical nature of the way in which urban areas are created are more a reflection of the nature of the forms created during a particular boom or slump than of the fact that structures close to one another tend to be of similar age. Age alone is a poor indicator of the need for renewal. It has tended to be a more important factor where tenure is leasehold. In this case, where a number of neighbouring plots have been developed at about the same time and conveyed by a single ground landlord on leases of the same term, the more or less simultaneous reversion of the plots increases the feasibility of completely re-planning an area. Thus in Birmingham, on the Calthorpe Estate, several groups of house plots conveyed on 99-year leases during housebuilding booms in the early 1850s, early 1860s and mid 1870s were 'comprehensively' redeveloped some 100 years later. However, the strengthening of the rights of leaseholders, especially as a result of the Leasehold Reform Act of 1967, has made it more difficult for landlords and developers to assemble sufficient contiguous plots for large-scale redevelopments to be undertaken.[6] On the majority of land, freehold and leasehold, the most common form of renewal, unless powers of compulsory purchase have been acquired, is piecemeal, involving building replacement or refurbishment or additional building. In such small-scale renewal, the physical characteristics of the initial development, especially the types of buildings and their relation to plot boundaries, have a particularly important influence.

MANAGING CHANGE

Although it is more realistic to view 'planning' in Western cities as an integral part of this historical process than as an independent force, that is not at all to say that planning has been without effect. Its effect has sometimes resembled that intended, as in the case of London's green belt. Sometimes the effect has been unintentional – arguably 'planning' has exacerbated booms and slumps in office building in post-war London. The main point, however, is that planning has been heavily influenced by powerful forces within the uncontrolled economy, especially in democratic countries.

Planning begins with a predisposition towards the *status quo*. As far as the internal structure of urban areas is concerned most planning 'policy' takes as its starting point the existing land-use map. The 'Town Maps' that have provided the basis for the majority of post-war planning in existing towns in Britain, at least until recent years, were essentially maps of existing land use. Interests represented in the existing townscape therefore tended to be reinforced. 'Precedent' is an even more crucial concept in the many cases in which a more recent formal Local Plan is lacking.[7] As far as the creation of individual forms in the townscape is concerned, most British planning consists of 'development control' by local authorities. As the term suggests, this is essentially regulatory. It is, perhaps above all else, a procedure for resisting departures from precedent.

Positive planning, in the sense of seeking actively to initiate change, is comparatively rare, although there have been notable cases in Britain of the creation of 'new towns' on predominantly greenfield sites. Positive planning is mainly associated with the insertion of new lines of communication, notably ring roads around commercial cores in the post-war period, and slum clearance. Here again, however, the hand of

Conclusion 145

history plays a major part in the choice of location. Slum clearance in Britain has consisted mainly of an eating outward through the earliest acccretions of industrial housing. The sharp boundary with housing surviving from the late nineteenth century and the twentieth century reflects primarily the point where the early post-war fashion of comprehensive redevelopment had run its course and was replaced by the fashion of conservation and refurbishment in the 1970s and 1980s.

A major lesson from these developments is that attempts to remove the existing townscape and start anew have generally been made with difficulty and at considerable economic and social cost. The more successful they have been in erasing the past, the less satisfactory the new landscape has generally proved to be as an environment to live in. Where comprehensive redevelopments adjoined city centres, they frequently exposed to full view a motley collection of rear elevations that would have been better left in the concealment for which they were intended. Practically no consideration was given to the fact that communities are interrelated with their physical surroundings historically as well as functionally.

In this context it is instructive to look back over the span of history covered in this volume and consider the relationship between morphogenesis and the way in which societies develop self-awareness. The development of urban landscapes that we have followed is one in which change takes place in cycles, but these are themselves subject to other cycles in the way in which their effects in the landscape are viewed. Sometimes history is respected; sometimes it is quite consciously rejected. No society can detach itself completely from its past and the landscape is never a blank sheet on which a society can draw unfettered. To seek to achieve such a condition is a profligate waste of past human endeavour. Each society leaves its mark on the landscape, reflecting the aspirations and problems of its day. These marks are part of the inheritance of future societies, which they in their turn alter, add to, preserve and erase. In this way the landscape, whether that of a large area, like a conurbation, or a small locality, like a single street, acquires its own *genius loci*. This is the product not only of the present occupants but also of their predecessors. Far from being just a reflection of the requirements of the society currently occupying it, the urban landscape is a cumulative, albeit incomplete, record of the succession of booms, slumps and innovation adoptions within a particular locale. Urban landscapes are thus a means by which both individuals and societies can set their own needs and aspirations within a historical and geographical context.

This perspective brings us back to the justification for urban morphology with which this volume began and to Conzen's development of the morphogenetic tradition. For Conzen, the historical unfolding of the townscape is not only fundamentally important in itself but it becomes the starting point in the search for a theoretical basis for the future management of townscapes.[8] The past provides the key to the future. The idea of the townscape as the 'objectivation of the spirit of a society' is fundamental. This concept can be traced back to studies on the philosophy of culture by German philosophers in the 1930s but first appeared in geography in the work of Schwind.[9] The spirit of a society is objectivated in the historico-geographical character of the townscape and becomes the *genius loci*. In Conzen's view this is an important environmental experience for the individual even when it is received unconsciously. It enables individuals and groups to take root in an area. They acquire a sense of the historical dimension of human existence. This stimulates comparison and encourages a less time-bound and more integrated approach to contemporary problems. Landscapes with a high degree of expressiveness of past societies exert a particularly strong educative and regenerative influence.[10] The Conzenian townscape is a stage on which successive societies work out their lives, each society learning from, and working to some extent within, the framework provided by the experiments of its predecessors. Viewed in this way townscapes represent accumulated experience, historical townscapes especially so. A responsible society therefore acts as the custodian of the urban landscape for future generations.

Although the translation of this standpoint into a fully-fledged theory has scarcely begun and the practical problems of its application in planning are likely to be great, Conzen has indicated the main elements to which consideration needs to be given.[11] It is on the historical expressiveness or historicity of the townscape that he places most emphasis. It is accordingly the nature and intensity of the historicity of the townscape that provides his main basis for devising proposals for future townscape management. This is articulated in practical terms by utilizing his division of the townscape into three basic form complexes – town plan, building forms and land use. These are regarded as to some extent a hierarchy in which the building forms are contained within the plots or land-use units, which are in turn set in the framework of the town plan. These three form complexes, together with the site, combine at the most local level to produce the smallest, morphologically homogeneous areas that might be termed 'townscape cells'. These cells are grouped into townscape units, which in turn combine at different levels of integration to form a hierarchy of intra-urban regions. Since the three form complexes change at different speeds, their patterns frequently differ. Particularly in old towns, the delimitations of cells, units and regions are complex, although the commercial core, fringe belts and different types of residential accretion are recurrent features. The hierarchy of areal units is the geographical manifestation of the historical development of the townscape and encapsulates its historicity. It is the reference point for all proposals for townscape change. The approach, therefore, is essentially conservative. The accent is on the transformation, augmentation and conservation of what already exists.

Preoccupied as most societies are with current practical problems rather than long-term values, it is easy for such an approach to be overlooked. The problem becomes especially acute in societies ever more technically capable of producing substantial change, especially in phases of economic buoyancy. Thus in the economic boom of the 1950s and 1960s Britain turned its back on its *genius loci*. Mesmerized by the capabilities of technical innovations and the driving force of rapid economic growth, Britain, like most other Western countries, allowed long-term social and cultural needs to take second place to short-term material goals.

Now, in the economic depression of the 1980s, we are experiencing a wave of interest in historicism and conservation reminiscent of that in the economic depression of the 1880s. This would seem to provide more fertile ground for the management of change in a way that is sympathetic to the *genius loci*. It would be unrealistic, however, to expect Conzen's ideas on townscape management to be widely appreciated, let alone adopted in planning practice. The most that can be hoped for is that wider promulgation of his ideas and the development of an improved understanding of long-term aspects of urban development will promote greater appreciation of the historico-geographical context of townscape development.

Notes

CHAPTER 1 BACKGROUND TO URBAN MORPHOLOGY

1. J. Fritz, 'Deutsche Stadtanlagen', *Beilage zum Programm 520 des Lyzeums Strassburg* (Strasbourg, 1894); O. Schlüter, 'Bemerkungen zur Siedlungsgeographie', *Geographische Zeitschrift*, 5 (1899), pp. 65–84.
2. J. W. R. Whitehand, 'Taking stock of urban geography', *Area*, 18 (1986), pp. 147–51.
3. J. E. Vance, *This Scene of Man: the role and structure of the city in the geography of western civilization* (New York, 1977).
4. J. W. R. Whitehand, 'Urban geography: the city as a place', *Progress in Human Geography*, 9 (1985), pp. 85–98; P. Jackson, 'Social geography: the rediscovery of place', *Progress in Human Geography*, 10 (1986), pp. 118–24; P. J. Larkham, 'Review of *The Past is a Foreign Country*', *IBG Urban Geography Study Group Newsletter*, May (1986), pp. 9–12.
5. See, for example, R. U. Ratcliff, *Urban Land Economics* (New York, 1949), pp. 149–53; H. W. Richardson and D. H. Aldcroft, *Building in the British Economy between the Wars* (London, 1968), pp. 275, 298–9.
6. L. Needleman, *The Economics of Housing* (London, 1965), p. 13.
7. M. R. G. Conzen, 'Geography and townscape conservation', in H. Uhlig and C. Lienau (eds) *Anglo-German Symposium in Applied Geography, Giessen-Würzburg-München, 1973* (Giessen, 1975), pp. 95–102.
8. For a rare attempt to draw together the distinctive traditions of urban morphology within geography and urban morphology within urban design, see I. Samuels, 'Urban morphology in developed countries', unpublished paper, Joint Centre for Urban Design, Oxford Polytechnic, 1985.
9. R. Blanchard, *Grenoble: étude de géographie urbaine* (Paris, 1912).
10. P. Pinchemel, 'Geographers and the city: a contribution to the history of urban geography in France', in J. Patten (ed.) *The Expanding City: essays in honour of Jean Gottmann* (London, 1983), pp. 295–318.
11. Schlüter, p. 67.

12 H. Hassinger, *Kunsthistorischer Atlas von Wien*, Österreichische Kunsttopographie 15 (Vienna, 1916).
13 G. Schaefer, *Kunstgeographische Siedlungslandschaften und Städtebilder: Studien im Gebiet zwischen Strassburg-Bern-Dijon-Freiburg i. Br.* (Basle, 1928).
14 W. Geisler, *Danzig: ein siedlungsgeographischer Versuch* (Danzig, 1918).
15 W. Geisler, *Die deutsche Stadt: ein Beitrag zur Morphologie der Kulturlandschaft*, Forschungen zur deutschen Landes- und Volkskunde, 22 (Stuttgart, 1924).
16 R. Martiny, *Die Grundrissgestaltung der deutschen Siedlungen*, Petermanns Mitteilungen, Supplement, 197 (Gotha, 1928).
17 J. W. R. Whitehand, 'Background to the urban morphogenetic tradition', in J. W. R. Whitehand (ed.) *The Urban Landscape: historical development and management*, Institute of British Geographers Special Publication No. 13 (London, 1981), pp. 5–7.
18 H. Bobek, 'Grundfragen der Stadtgeographie', *Geographischer Anzeiger*, 28 (1927), pp. 213–24.
19 W. Christaller, *Die zentralen Orte in Süddeutschland* (Jena, 1933).
20 K. Scharlau, *Siedlung und Landschaft im Knüllgebiet* (Leipzig, 1941).
21 H. Bobek and E. Lichtenberger, *Wien: Bauliche Gestalt und Entwicklung seit der Mitte des 19. Jahrhunderts* (Graz, 1966); E. Lichtenberger, *Die Wiener Altstadt: von der mittelalterlichen Bürgerstadt zur City* (Vienna, 1977).
22 W. Krings, *Innenstädte in Belgien: Gestalt, Veränderung, Erhaltung*, Bonner Geographische Abhandlungen, 68 (Bonn, 1984); E. Sabelberg, *Regionale Stadttypen in Italien*, Erdkundlichen Wissens, Geographische Zeitschrift, Beihefte, 66 (Wiesbaden, 1984).
23 M. R. G. Conzen, 'Towards a systematic approach in planning science: geoproscopy', *Town Planning Review*, 18 (1938), pp. 1–26.
24 M. R. G. Conzen, 'Modern settlement', in P. C. G. Isaac and R. E. A. Allan (eds) *Scientific Survey of North-eastern England* (Newcastle upon Tyne, 1949), pp. 75–83.
25 M. R. G. Conzen, 'The growth and character of Whiteby', in G. H. J. Daysh (ed.) *A Survey of Whitby and the Surrounding Area* (Eton, 1958), pp. 49–89.
26 M. R. G. Conzen, *Alnwick, Northumberland: a study in town-plan analysis*, Institute of British Geographers Publication No. 27 (London, 1960).
27 Ibid., p. 7.
28 For example, T. R. Slater, 'Medieval new town and port: a plan-analysis of Hedon, east Yorkshire', *Yorkshire Archaeological Journal*, 57 (1985), pp. 23–41.
29 W. Hartke, 'Die soziale Differenzierung der Agrarlandschaft im Rhein-Main-Gebiet', *Erdkunde*, 7 (1953), pp. 13–22; W. Hartke, 'Die Sozialbrache als Phänomen der geographischen Differenzierung der Landschaft', *Erdkunde*, 10 (1956), pp. 257–69.

30 See, for example, I. Möller, *Die Entwicklung eines Hamburger Gebietes von der Agrar- zur Groszstadtlandschaft: mit einem Beitrag zur Methode der Städtischen Aufrissanalyse*, Hamburger Geographische Studien, 10 (Hamburg, 1959).
31 I. Möller, 'Review of *Alnwick, Northumberland: a study in town-plan analysis*', *Petermanns Geographische Mitteilungen*, 108 (1964), pp. 112–13.
32 C. T. Onions (ed.) *The Shorter Oxford English Dictionary* (Oxford, 1950), p. 445.
33 J. W. R. Whitehand, 'Conzenian ideas: extension and development', in J. W. R. Whitehand (ed.) *The Urban Landscape: historical development and management*, Institute of British Geographers Special Publication No. 13 (London, 1981), pp. 127–52.
34 H. J. Fleure, 'Some types of cities in temperate Europe', *Geographical Review*, 10 (1920), pp. 357–74.
35 A. E. Smailes, 'Some reflections on the geographical description and analysis of townscapes', *Transactions of the Institute of British Geographers*, 21 (1955), pp. 99–115.
36 W. K. D. Davies, 'The morphology of central places: a case study', *Annals of the Association of American Geographers*, 58 (1968), pp. 91–110; R. J. Johnston, 'Towards an analytical study of the townscape: the residential building fabric', *Geografiska Annaler*, 51B (1969), pp. 20–32.
37 H. Carter, *The Towns of Wales* (Cardiff, 1965).
38 J. B. Leighly, 'The towns of Mälardalen in Sweden: a study in urban morphology', *University of California Publications in Geography*, 3 (1928), pp. 1–134; J. E. Spencer, 'Changing Chungking: the rebuilding of an old Chinese city', *Geographical Review*, 29 (1939), pp. 46–60.
39 C. C. Colby, 'Centrifugal and centripetal forces in urban geography', *Annals of the Association of American Geographers*, 23 (1933), pp. 1–20; R. E. Murphy, 'Johnstown and York: a comparative study of two industrial cities', *Annals of the Association of American Geographers*, 25 (1935), pp. 175–96.
40 E. W. Burgess, 'The growth of the city', in R. E. Park, E. W. Burgess and R. D. McKenzie, *The City* (Chicago, 1925), pp. 47–62.
41 H. Hoyt, 'The pattern of movement of residential rental neighborhoods', in *The Structure and Growth of Residential Neighborhoods in American Cities* (Washington, DC, 1939), pp. 112–22, reprinted in H. M. Mayer and C. F. Kohn (eds) *Readings in Urban Geography* (Chicago, 1959), pp. 499–510.
42 C. D. Harris and E. L. Ullman, 'The nature of cities', *Annals of the American Academy of Political and Social Science*, 242 (1945), pp. 7–17.
43 For example, J. W. R. Whitehand, 'Urban-rent theory, time series and morphogenesis: an example of eclecticism in geographical research', *Area*, 4 (1972), pp. 215–22.
44 Leighly, pp. 1–134.

45 Spencer, pp. 46–60; J. E. Spencer, 'The houses of the Chinese', *Geographical Review*, 37 (1947), pp. 254–73.
46 J. E. Rickert, 'House facades of the northeastern United States; a tool of geographic analysis', *Annals of the Association of American Geographers*, 57 (1967), pp. 211–38; R. W. Bastian, 'The Prairie style house: spatial diffusion of a minor design', *Journal of Cultural Geography*, 1 (1980), pp. 50–65; J. A. Jakle, 'Twentieth century revival architecture and the gentry', *Journal of Cultural Geography*, 4 (1983), pp. 28–43.
47 H. J. Dyos, *Victorian Suburb: a study of the growth of Camberwell* (Leicester, 1961).
48 For example, F. H. W. Sheppard (ed.) *Survey of London*, 40, The Grosvenor Estate and Mayfair, part 2 (London, 1980).
49 R. Barras, *The Returns from Office Development and Investment*, Centre for Environmental Studies Research Series, 35 (London, 1979), p. 1.

CHAPTER 2   FLUCTUATIONS IN URBAN DEVELOPMENT

1 For example, W. H. Newman, *The Building Industry and Business Cycles* (Chicago, 1935); L. Grebler, 'House-building, the business cycle and state intervention: I', *International Labour Review*, 33 (1936), pp. 337–55.
2 M. Gottlieb, *Long Swings in Urban Development* (New York, 1976), pp. 12, 192, 322. See also D. Parkes and N. Thrift, *Times, Spaces, and Places: a chronogeographic perspective* (Chichester, Sussex, 1980), pp. 424–5.
3 B. Thomas, *Migration and Economic Growth: a study of Great Britain and the Atlantic economy* (Cambridge, 1973), p. 244.
4 M. Abramovitz, 'The nature and significance of Kuznets cycles', *Economic Development and Cultural Change*, 9 (1961), p. 230.
5 H. J. Habakkuk, 'Fluctuations in house-building in Britain and the United States in the nineteenth century', *Journal of Economic History*, 22 (1962), pp. 198–230.
6 S. B. Saul, 'House biulding in England 1890–1914', *Economic History Review*, 2nd Series, 15 (1962), p. 136.
7 J. P. Lewis, *Building Cycles and Britain's Growth* (London, 1965), p. 203.
8 T. Ellison, *The Cotton Trade of Great Britain* (London, 1886), pp. 34–5.
9 Lewis, p. 315.
10 Ibid., pp. 129–36; Habakkuk, pp. 228–30.
11 Thomas, p. 347.
12 Lewis, pp. 212–33.
13 Habakkuk, pp. 208–9.
14 Lewis, p. 222.
15 J. H. Niedercorn and E. F. R. Hearle, *Recent Land-use Trends in Forty-eight*

Large American Cities, RAND Corporation Memorandum RM-3664-FF (Santa Monica, Calif., 1963).

16 This compilation of data was first discussed in J. W. R. Whitehand, 'Fluctuations in the land-use composition of urban development during the industrial era', *Erdkunde*, 35 (1981), pp. 129–40.

17 C. D. Long, *Building Cycles and the Theory of Investment* (Princeton, NJ, 1940), appendix B, section 2; R. E. Lipsey and D. Preston, *Source Book of Statistics Relating to Construction* (New York, 1966), pp. 20–1; C. H. Feinstein, *National Income, Expenditure and Output of the United Kingdom 1855–1965* (Cambridge, 1972), table 48; H. W. Richardson and D. H. Aldcroft, *Building in the British Economy between the Wars* (London, 1968), p. 56, table 1 and p. 62, table 3; N. G. Butlin, 'Some structural features of Australian capital formation 1861 to 1938/39', *The Economic Record*, 35 (1959), pp. 397–8, table II and pp. 403–4, table IV. See also Long, pp. 168–75; R. U. Ratcliff, *Urban Land Economics* (New York, 1949), pp. 154–5.

18 Based upon Lipsey and Preston, appendix B, section 2.

19 Based upon Lipsey and Preston, appendix B, section 2 and Butlin, pp. 397–8, table II and pp. 403–4, table IV.

20 R. G. Rodger, 'The building cycle and the urban fringe in Victorian cities: another comment', *Journal of Historical Geography*, 5 (1979), pp. 72–8.

21 Gottlieb, p. 77.

22 S. T. Delaney, personal communication. The time series of golf *course* creation and golf *club* foundation are broadly similar. Data are not available on the creation of rugby union *grounds*, as distinct from clubs.

23 Gottlieb, p. 77.

24 G. F. Warren and F. A. Pearson, *World Prices and the Building Industry* (New York, 1937), p. 121, fig. 2.8.

25 A. K. Cairncross, *Home and Foreign Investment 1870–1913* (Cambridge, 1953), p. 20, fig. 1.

26 Based on graphical analysis of data in Lewis, pp. 323–4.

27 S. Openshaw, 'Processes in urban morphology with special reference to South Shields', unpublished PhD thesis, University of Newcastle upon Tyne, 1974, pp. 51, 54.

28 A further part of the Garscube estate is situated beyond the northern margin of figure 2.12: it remained rural throughout the study period and no transactions were recorded for it. The author is grateful to Mr I. D. B. Fleming of Montgomerie Fleming, Fyfe, Maclean and Co., Mr H. M. Begg of Kerr, Macleod and Macfarlan, C. A., Mr W. Aitken, Factor, Garscube Estates Office, and Mr G. Black, Keeper of the Registers of Scotland, for providing access to information on the three estates selected for study.

29 The main categories of land use defined as institutional were as follows:

educational, medical, military, central and local government, research, recreational (including clubs and public open spaces) and religious (including burial grounds).
30 D. Harvey, 'The urban process under capitalism: a framework for analysis', *International Journal of Urban and Regional Research*, 2 (1978), pp. 106–8.
31 R. G. Rodger, 'Speculative builders and the structure of the Scottish building industry, 1860–1914', *Business History*, 21 (1979), p. 240.
32 Ibid., p. 226.
33 Long, pp. 178–9.
34 Ibid., pp. 173–7.
35 Ibid., pp. 169–73.
36 Ibid., pp. 141–2.

CHAPTER 3   LAND VALUES AND LAND USE

1 For example, C. Steinbrück, *Die Entwickelung der Preise des Städtischen und Ländlichen Immobiliarbesitzes zu Halle (Saale) und im Saalkreise* (Jena, 1901); P. Voight, *Grundrente und Wohnungsfrage in Berlin und seinen Vororten* (Jena, 1901); A. Weber, *Über Bodenrente und Bodenspekulation in der modernen Stadt* (Leipzig, 1904).
2 G. Hallett, *Housing and Land Policies in West Germany and Britain* (London, 1977), p. 91.
3 J. H. von Thünen, *Der Isolierte Staat in Beziehung auf Landwirtschaft und Nationalökonomie* (Rostock, 1826).
4 R. M. Hurd, *Principles of City Land Values* (New York, 1903); R. M. Haig, 'Toward an understanding of the metropolis: II The assignment of activities to areas in urban regions', *Quarterly Journal of Economics*, 40 (1926), pp. 402–34; R. M. Haig, *Regional Survey of New York and its Environs* (New York, 1927); W. Alonso, 'A theory of the urban land market', *Papers and Proceedings of the Regional Science Association*, 6 (1960), pp. 149–57.
5 A. Marshall, *Principles of Economics*, vol. 1 (London, 5th edn, 1907), pp. 440–54.
6 Hurd, p. 13.
7 A. W. Evans, 'The determination of the price of land', *Urban Studies*, 20 (1983), p. 119.
8 W. Alonso, *Location and Land Use: toward a general theory of land rent* (Cambridge, Mass., 1964).
9 A. W. Evans, *The Economics of Residential Location* (London, 1973).
10 Alonso, *Papers and Proceedings of the Regional Science Association*, 6, p. 152.

11 L. Wirth, 'A bibliography of the urban community', in R. E. Park, E. W. Burgess and R. D. McKenzie, *The City* (Chicago, 1925), p. 203.
12 Haig, *Quarterly Journal of Economics*, 40, p. 405, fn. 4.
13 For example, J. A. Quinn, *Human Ecology* (New York, 1950) p. 449.
14 *The Building News*, 17 July 1885, p. 75.
15 M. Ball, *Housing Policy and Economic Power: the political economy of owner occupation* (London, 1983), pp. 112–13.
16 R. Turvey, *The Economics of Real Property* (London, 1957), p. 52.
17 See, for example, R. Drewett, 'Land values and the suburban land market', in P. Hall, H. Gracey, R. Drewett and R. Thomas *The Containment of Urban England*, vol. 2 (London, 1973), p. 217.
18 D. Harvey, *Social Justice and the City* (London, 1973), pp. 187–9.
19 Ibid.
20 Evans, *Urban Studies*, 20, p. 123.
21 J. Springett, 'Landowners and urban development: the Ramsden Estate and nineteenth-century Huddersfield', *Journal of Historical Geography*, 8 (1982), pp. 129–44.
22 Ball, pp. 113–14.
23 W. Isard, *Location and Space Economy: a general theory relating to industrial location, market areas, land use, trade and urban structure* (New York, 1956), pp. 200–6; W. L. Garrison, B. J. L. Berry, D. F. Marble, J. D. Nystuen and R. L. Morrill, *Studies of Highway Development and Geographic Change* (Seattle, Wash., 1959), pp. 62–4.
24 E. S. Mills, 'The value of urban land', in H. S. Perloff (ed.), *The Quality of the Urban Environment* (Baltimore, Md, 1969), p. 234.
25 Harvey, *Social Justice and the City*, p. 189.
26 See, for example, F. M. L. Thompson, *Hampstead: building a borough, 1650–1964* (London, 1974); R. Rodger, 'Rents and ground rents: housing and the land market in nineteenth-century Britain', in J. H. Johnson and C. G. Pooley (eds), *The Structure of Nineteenth Century Cities* (London, 1982), pp. 39–74.
27 D. Keene, 'Spatial order and discrimination in English towns, A.D. 500–1670', unpublished paper presented to the Urban History Group Colloquium on Urban Space and Building Form, London, 21 September 1984, p. 9.
28 *The Builder*, vol. 29, June 3, 1871, p. 420.
29 E. Lichtenberger, *Die Wiener Altstadt: Von der mittelalterlichen Bürgerstadt zur City* (Vienna, 1977), p. 219.
30 H. Hoyt, *One Hundred Years of Land Values in Chicago* (Chicago, 1933).
31 Alonso, *Location and Land Use*, p. 126.
32 P. A. Stone, 'The price of sites for residential building', *Estates Gazette*, 189 (1964), pp. 85–91.
33 J.-J. Granelle, *Espace urbain et prix du sol* (Paris, 1970), pp. 184–6.

34 Ibid., pp. 190–1.
35 H. Böhm, *Bodenmobilität und Bodenpreisgefüge in ihrer Bedeutung für die Siedlungsentwicklung*, Bonner Geographische Abhandlungen, no. 65 (Bonn, 1980), pp. 207–8.
36 G. F. de Gruchy, 'Some land-value relationships in Brisbane's central business district', *Ekistics*, 233 (1975), pp. 268–70.
37 K. Wieand and R. F. Muth, 'A note on the variation of land values with distance from the CBD in St Louis', *Journal of Regional Science*, 12 (1972), pp. 469–73.
38 E. F. Brigham, 'The determinants of residential land values', *Land Economics*, 41 (1965), pp. 325–34.
39 Mills, p. 239.
40 Evans, *The Economics of Residential Location*, pp. 60–1.
41 C. Clark, 'Urban land use here and abroad', *Journal of the Town Planning Institute*, 52 (1966), p. 362.
42 A. H. Hawley, 'Land value patterns in Okayama, Japan, 1940 and 1952', *American Journal of Sociology*, 60 (1955), pp. 487–92.
43 L. Benevolo, *The History of the City* (Cambridge, Mass., 1980), p. 969.
44 Keene, pp. 9–10.
45 Lichtenberger, map volume, map 1.
46 See, for example, H. J. Dyos, *Victorian Suburb: a study of the growth of Camberwell* (Leicester, 1961), p. 51.
47 P. Cowan, 'Hospitals in towns: location and siting', *Architectural Review*, 137 (1965), p. 418.
48 See, for example, Hoyt, pp. 329–37.
49 W. F. Lever, 'Planning standards', in J. Forbes (ed.) *Studies in Social Science and Planning* (Edinburgh, 1974), pp. 30–2.
50 Ibid. For data on the relationship between city size and city-centre land prices in France, see Granelle, p. 206.
51 B. J. L. Berry, 'The economics of land-use intensities in Melbourne, Australia', *Geographical Review*, 64 (1974), pp. 479–97. See also Granelle, p. 226.
52 C. W. Pannell, 'City morphology in T'ai-wan: a variation on a Chinese theme', *Proceedings of the Association of American Geographers*, 5 (1973), pp. 210–16.
53 H. W. Singer, 'An index of urban land rents and house rents in England and Wales 1845–1913', *Econometrica*, 9 (1941), pp. 221–30.
54 Rodger, pp. 55–68.
55 M. T. Daly, *Sydney Boom Sydney Bust: the city and its property market 1850–1981* (Sydney, 1982), p. 148.
56 T. Polensky, *Die Bodenpreise in Stadt und Region München*, Münchner Studien zur Sozial- und Wirtschaftsgeographie, vol. 10 (Kallmünz, 1974), p. 46.

57 W. H. Newman, *The Building Industry and Business Cycles* (Chicago, 1935), p. 18.
58 A. Offer, *Property and Politics 1870–1914: landownership, law, ideology and urban development in England* (Cambridge, 1981), p. 274, 278.
59 See, for example, Greater London Council, *Northern Kensington*, Survey of London, vol. 37 (London, 1973), pp. 13–14; C. M. Allan, 'The genesis of British urban redevelopment with special reference to Glasgow', *Economic History Review*, 18 (1965), p. 607; H. J. Gayler, 'Land speculation and urban development: contrasts in south-east Essex, 1880–1940', *Urban Studies*, 7 (1970), p. 26. Note, however, that M. Gottlieb, *Long Swings in Urban Development* (New York, 1976), pp. 149–55 draws attention to the surprisingly poor synchronism between land prices and development activity in Ohio in the late nineteenth century and early twentieth century, and suggests reasons for this.
60 For example, Turvey, pp. 51–4; Stone, pp. 85–91; Berry, pp. 479–97; R. F. Muth, *Cities and Housing* (Chicago, 1969), esp. pp. 46–69.
61 J. P. Lewis, *Building Cycles and Britain's Growth* (London, 1965), pp. 142–54; M. L. Colean, *American Housing: problems and prospects* (New York, 1944), p. 49.
62 Newman, pp. 17–24.
63 R. F. Muth, 'The demand for non-farm housing', in A. C. Harberger (ed.) *The Demand for Durable Goods* (Chicago, 1960), pp. 29–96.
64 K. Maiwald, 'An index of building costs in the United Kingdom, 1845–1938', *Economic History Review*, 7 (1954), pp. 187–203.
65 Lewis, pp. 316–17.
66 Gottlieb, p. 162.
67 J. W. R. Whitehand, 'Building cycles and the spatial pattern of urban growth', *Transactions of the Institute of British Geographers*, 56 (1972), pp. 39–42.
68 For a full account of this test and the data employed, see ibid.
69 Greater London Council, *Northern Kensington*. For a full account of this test and the data employed, see J. W. R. Whitehand, 'Building activity and intensity of development at the urban fringe: the case of a London suburb in the nineteenth century', *Journal of Historical Geography*, 1 (1975), pp. 211–24.
70 Hoyt, esp. figs 6, 12, 21, 27, 33, 43.
71 J. W. R. Whitehand, 'The building cycle and the urban fringe in Victorian cities: a reply', *Journal of Historical Geography*, 4 (1978), pp. 175–91.
72 T. R. Slater, 'Family, society and the ornamental villa on the fringes of English country towns', *Jounal of Historical Geography*, 4 (1978), pp. 129–44.

CHAPTER 4   INNOVATION AND PLANNING

1   D. H. Aldcroft and H. W. Richardson, *The British Economy, 1870–1939* (London, 1969), pp. 34–44.
2   R. L. Morrill, 'The shape of diffusion in space and time', *Economic Geography*, 46 (1970), p. 266.
3   Bournville Village Trust, *When we Build Again* (London, 1941), p. 9; M. Tomlinson, 'The City of Birmingham: secular architecture', in W. B. Stephens (ed.) *A History of the County of Warwick*, 7 (London, 1964), p. 56.
4   H.-R. Hitchcock, *Architecture: nineteenth and twentieth centuries* (Harmondsworth, Middx, 1958), p. 281; N. Pevsner, *An Outline of European Architecture* (Harmondsworth, Middx, 1963), pp. 394–7.
5   H. J. Dyos and D. H. Aldcroft, *British Transport: an economic survey from the seventeenth century to the twentieth* (Leicester, 1969), pp. 220–2, 336–49; P. Jones, 'Innovation life-span: the urban tramway', *Area*, 10 (1978), pp. 247–9.
6   Bournville Village Trust, pp. 38–9.
7   J. W. R. Whitehand, 'The settlement morphology of London's cocktail belt', *Tijdschrift voor Economische en Sociale Geografie*, 58 (1967), p. 26.
8   Dyos and Aldcroft, pp. 220–2, 336–49.
9   W. Isard, 'A neglected cycle: the transport-building cycle', *Review of Economic Statistics*, 24 (1942), pp. 149–58.
10 J. Schmookler, *Invention and Economic Growth* (Cambridge, Mass., 1966), pp. 131–3.
11 C. A. Forster, *Court Housing in Kingston upon Hull: an example of cyclic processes in the morphological development of nineteenth century bye-law housing*, University of Hull Occasional Papers in Geography, no. 19 (Hull, 1972), pp. 36–51.
12 B. A. Cooper, 'Marks and Spencer: a case of induced diffusion', unpublished BA dissertation, University of Birmingham, 1977, p. 10.
13 J. B. Jeffreys, *Retail Trading in Britain 1850–1950* (Cambridge, 1954), pp. 59–80.
14 M. W. Barley, *The House and Home* (London, 1963), p. 185.
15 J. S. Adams, 'Residential structure of Midwestern cities', *Annals of the Association of American Geographers*, 60 (1970), pp. 54–5.
16 M. R. G. Conzen, *Alnwick, Northumberland: a study in town-plan analysis*, Institute of British Geographers Publication no. 27 (London, 1960), p. 7.
17 Ibid., pp. 8–9.
18 J. P. Lewis, *Building Cycles and Britain's Growth* (London, 1965), pp. 308–12, 314–15, 323–4, 335–6, 351.
19 B. Thomas, *Migration and Economic Growth: a study of Great Britain and the Atlantic economy* (Cambridge, 1973), pp. 207–18.

20 J. W. R. Whitehand, 'The study of variations in the building fabric of town centres: procedural problems and preliminary findings in southern Scotland', *Transactions of the Institute of British Geographers*, NS 4 (1979), pp. 563–4; J. W. R. Whitehand, *Rebuilding Town Centres: developers, architects and styles*, University of Birmingham Department of Geography Occasional Publication, no. 19 (Birmingham, 1984), pp. 15, 20–1.

21 For a discussion of legislation relating to parks and recreation grounds see K. R. Balmer, 'Urban open space planning in England and Wales', unpublished PhD thesis, University of Liverpool, 1972.

22 Adams, p. 54.

23 See, especially, W. Alonso, *Location and Land Use: toward a general theory of land rent* (Cambridge, Mass., 1964), pp. 111–3; A. W. Evans, *The Economics of Residential Location* (London, 1973), pp. 171–87.

24 J.-J. Granelle, *Espace urbain et prix du sol* (Paris, 1970), pp. 163–4.

25 E. Lichtenberger, *Die Wiener Altstadt: Von der mittelalterlichen Bürgerstadt zur City* (Vienna, 1977), pp. 217–9.

26 H. Hoyt, 'Changing patterns of land values', *Land Economics*, 36 (1960), pp. 109–17.

27 M. H. Yeates, 'Some factors affecting the spatial distribution of Chicago land values, 1910–1960', *Economic Geography*, 41 (1965), pp. 57–70.

28 R. J. Johnston, 'Spatial and temporal variations in land and property prices in New Zealand: 1953–1972', *New Zealand Geographer*, 32 (1976), pp. 48–50.

29 T. Polensky, *Die Bodenpreise in Stadt und Region München*, Münchner Studien zur Sozial- und Wirtschaftsgeographie, vol. 10 (Kallmünz, 1974).

30 G. K. Ingram, 'Land in perspective: its role in the structure of cities', in M. Cullen and S. Woolery (eds) *World Congress on Land Policy, 1980: proceedings* (Lexington, Mass., 1982), pp. 112–13.

31 R. Mohan and R. Villamizar, 'The evolution of land values in the context of rapid urban growth: a case study of Bogotá and Cali, Colombia', in M. Cullen and S. Woolery (eds), pp. 217–53.

32 H.-D. Evers, 'Urban landownership, ethnicity and class in southeast Asian cities', *International Journal of Urban and Regional Research*, 8 (1984), p. 483.

33 H. M. Mayer and R. C. Wade, *Chicago: growth of a metropolis* (Chicago, 1969), pp. 132–44.

34 H. Hoyt, *One Hundred Years of Land Values in Chicago* (Chicago, 1933), pp. 174–5.

35 F. A. Randall, *History of the Development of Building Construction in Chicago* (Chicago, 1949), pp. 11–14.

36 G. F. Warren and F. A. Pearson, *World Prices and the Building Industry* (New York, 1937), p. 111.

37 Hoyt, *One Hundred Years of Land Values*, p. 332; Randall, p. 17.

38 R. Johnston and M. Gaskell, 'Building control, building activity and design', unpublished paper presented to the Urban History Group Colloquium on Urban Space and Building Form, London, 21 September 1984.
39 R. Barras, *The Development Cycle in the City of London*, Centre for Environmental Studies Research Series, 36 (London, 1979), pp. 30–1.
40 B. Goodall, 'Some effects of legislation on land values', *Regional Studies*, 4 (1970), p. 17.
41 E. Lichtenberger, 'The nature of European urbanism', *Geoforum*, 4 (1970), pp. 52–3; S.-D. Chang, 'Some observations on the morphology of Chinese walled cities', *Annals of the Association of American Geographers*, 60 (1970), p. 91.
42 H. de la Croix, *Military Considerations in City Planning: fortifications* (New York, 1972), pp. 54–5.
43 Lichtenberger, p. 52.
44 A. E. J. Morris, *History of urban form: before the industrial revolution* (London, 1979), p. 165.
45 M. Williams, 'The parkland towns of Australia and New Zealand', *Geographical Review*, 56 (1966), pp. 67–71.
46 Lichtenberger, p. 52.
47 D. Thomas, 'London's Green Belt: the evolution of an idea', *Geographical Journal*, 129 (1963), p. 14.
48 Ibid., p. 18.
49 Goodall, pp. 15–17; Evans, pp. 254–8.
50 Evans, p. 255.
51 Goodall, pp. 18–21.
52 Lewis, p. 308.
53 R. Smith, 'Multi-dwelling building in Scotland, 1750–1970: a study based on housing in the Clyde valley', in A. Sutcliffe (ed.) *Multi-storey Living* (London, 1974), pp. 207–43; A. Sutcliffe, 'Introduction', in Sutcliffe, p. 13.
54 A. Gomme and D. Walker, *Architecture of Glasgow* (London, 1968), p. 183.
55 Tomlinson, pp. 53–6.
56 E. Gauldie, *Cruel Habitations: a history of working-class housing 1790–1918* (London, 1974), pp. 179–80.

CHAPTER 5 FRINGE BELTS

1 H. Louis, 'Die geographische Gliederung von Gross-Berlin', *Landerkundliche Forschung* Krebs-festschrift, (1936), pp. 146–71.
2 M. R. G. Conzen, *Alnwick, Northumberland: a study in town-plan analysis*,

Institute of British Geographers Publication no. 27 (London, 1960), pp. 58–65.
3   M. R. G. Conzen, 'Zur Morphologie der englischen Stadt im Industriezeitalter', in H. Jäger (ed.) *Probleme des Städtewesens im industriellen Zeitalter* (Cologne, 1978), pp. 18–19.
4   M. R. G. Conzen, 'The plan analysis of an English city centre, in K. Norborg (ed.) *Proceedings of the IGU Symposium in Urban Geography Lund 1960* (Lund, 1962), p. 406.
5   Ibid., esp. pp. 388, 406. See also H. Carter and S. Wheatley, 'Fixation lines and fringe belts, land uses and social areas: nineteenth-century change in the small town', *Transactions of the Institute of British Geographers*, NS 4 (1979), pp. 216–17.
6   M. Williams, 'The parkland towns of Australia and New Zealand', *Geographical Review*, 56 (1966), pp. 67–71.
7   Carter and Wheatley, p. 217.
8   J. W. R. Whitehand, 'Fringe belts: a neglected aspect of urban geography', *Transactions of the Institute of British Geographers*, 41 (1967), pp. 226, 230.
9   Ibid., esp. pp. 228–33.
10 Conzen, in Jäger, p. 21.
11 Ph. Arbos, *Étude de géographie urbaine: Clermont-Ferrand* (Clermont-Ferrand, 1930), pp. 151–2.
12 A. Sutcliffe, 'Review of *The Urban Landscape: historical development and management*', *Journal of Historical Geography*, 9 (1983), pp. 77–9.
13 Conzen, *Alnwick, Northumberland*; Whitehand, *Transactions of the Institute of British Geographers*; M. Barke, 'The changing urban fringe of Falkirk: some morphological implications of urban growth', *Scottish Geographical Magazine*, 90 (1974), pp. 85–97.
14 J. W. R. Whitehand, 'Building cycles and the spatial pattern of urban growth', *Transactions of the Institute of British Geographers*, 56 (1972), pp. 49–53.
15 Conzen, *Alnwick, Northumberland*, p. 81.
16 Whitehand, *Transactions of the Institute of British Geographers*, 41, p. 231.
17 Barke, p. 90.
18 M. P. Conzen, 'Fringe location land uses: relict patterns in Madison, Wisconsin', unpublished paper presented to the Association of American Geographers, West Lakes Division, 19th Annual Meeting, Madison, Wisconsin, 18 October 1968.
19 J. W. R. Whitehand, 'Urban-rent theory, time series and morphogenesis: an example of eclecticism in geographical research', *Area*, 4 (1972), pp. 215–22; J. W. R. Whitehand, 'The changing nature of the urban fringe: a time perspective', in J. H. Johnson (ed.) *Suburban Growth: geographical processes at the edge of the Western city* (London, 1974), pp. 45–9.
20 The seven institutions included one example of each of the following:

children's home, hospital, barracks, botanic gardens, college (later adapted for use by the British Broadcasting Corporation), university, school.
21 If *amount* of investment were substituted for *number* of investments, the relationship would be curvilinear since the size of investments (at constant prices) tended to increase over time.
22 T. R. Slater, 'Family, society and the ornamental villa on the fringes of English country towns', *Journal of Historical Geography*, 4 (1978), pp. 129–44.
23 Carter and Wheatley, pp. 214–38.

CHAPTER 6   RESIDENTIAL GROWTH AND CHANGE

1 E. Gauldie, *Cruel Habitations: a history of working-class housing 1780–1918* (London, 1974), p. 174.
2 D. Cannadine, 'The aristocracy and the towns in the nineteenth century: a case study of the Calthorpes and Birmingham, 1807–1910', unpublished DPhil thesis, University of Oxford, 1975.
3 C. D. Long, *Building Cycles and the Theory of Investment* (Princeton, NJ, 1940), pp. 224–5.
4 M. Abramovitz, *Evidences of Long Swings in Aggregate Construction since the Civil War* (New York, 1964), pp. 206–7.
5 Long, pp. 130, 175–6.
6 R. G. Barrows, 'Beyond the tenement: patterns of American urban housing, 1870–1930', *Journal of Urban History*, 9 (1983), p. 403.
7 R. G. Rodger, 'Scottish urban housebuilding 1870–1914', unpublished PhD thesis, University of Edinburgh, 1976, pp. 84–5; R. G. Rodger, 'Speculative builders and the structure of the Scottish buliding industry, 1860–1914', *Business History*, 21 (1979), p. 241.
8 M. W. Beresford, 'The back-to-back house in Leeds, 1787–1937', in S. D. Chapman (ed.) *The History of Working-class Housing* (Newton Abbot, Devon, 1971), p. 117.
9 B. D. White, *A History of the Corporation of Liverpool 1835–1914* (Liverpool, 1951), p. 204, reproduced in J. H. Treble, 'Liverpool working-class housing, 1805–51', in Chapman, footnote 23, p. 170.
10 Based upon data in A. K. Cairncross, 'The Glasgow building industry (1870–1914)', *The Review of Economic Studies*, 2 (1934), p. 15.
11 See also J. Butt, 'Working-class housing in Glasgow, 1851–1914', in Chapman, footnote 23, p. 72.
12 D. Richmond, *Notes on Municipal Work from November 1896 to November 1899* (Glasgow, n.d.), p. 214.
13 M. A. Jahn, 'Railways and suburban development: outer west London 1850–1900', unpublished PhD thesis, University of London, 1971, p. 124.

14 D. Ward, 'The pre-urban cadaster and the urban pattern of Leeds', *Annals of the Association of American Geographers*, 52 (1962), pp. 150–66.
15 See, for example, G. Rowley, 'Landownership in the spatial growth of towns: a Sheffield example', *East Midland Geographer*, 6 (1975), pp. 200–13; J. Springett, 'Landowners and urban development: the Ramsden Estate and nineteenth-century Huddersfield', *Journal of Historical Geography*, 8 (1982), pp. 129–44.
16 R. G. Rodger, 'The building cycle and the urban fringe in Victorian cities: another comment', *Journal of Historical Geography*, 5 (1979), p. 72.
17 D. Cannadine, 'How much of a mark did aristocratic landowners leave on the Victorian city?', unpublished paper presented to the Annual Conference of the Urban History Group, Swansea, 30–1 March 1979.
18 Ibid.
19 D. Cannadine, 'Victorian cities: how different?', *Social History*, 4 (1977), pp. 468–82.
20 Ibid., p. 471.
21 Ibid., p. 475.
22 Rodger, *Journal of Historical Geography*, pp. 74–5.
23 For an exploration of the theoretical effects of varying degrees of landownership concentration see J. R. Markusen and D. T. Scheffman, 'Ownership concentration and market power in urban land markets', *Review of Economic studies*, 45 (1978), pp. 519–26.
24 Greater London Council, *Northern Kensington*, Survey of London, vol. 37 (London, 1973), pp. 15, 63, 65, 105, 107, 112, 155–8, 197, 209.
25 S. B. Warner, *Streetcar Suburbs: the process of growth in Boston, 1870–1900* (Cambridge, Mass., 1962), pp. 139–40.
26 A. W. Evans, 'Rent and housing in the theory of urban growth', *Journal of Regional Science*, 15 (1975), p. 124; N. Smith, 'Gentrification and uneven development', *Economic Geography*, 58 (1982), p. 147.
27 M. R. G. Conzen, *Alnwick, Northumberland: a study in town-plan analysis*, Institute of British Geographers Publication no. 27 (London, 1960), pp. 92, 94.
28 R. Stewig, 'Bemerkungen zur Entstehung des orientalischen Sackgassengrundrisses am Beispiel der Stadt Istanbul', *Mitteilungen der Österreichischen Geographischen Gesellschaft*, 108 (1966), pp. 25–47.
29 R. J. Johnston, 'An outline of the development of Melbourne's street pattern', *The Australian Geographer*, 10 (1968), p. 454.
30 M. P. Conzen, 'The morphology of nineteenth-century cities in the United States', in W. Borah, J. Hardoy and G. Stelter (eds) *Urbanization in the Americas: the background in comparative perspective* (Ottawa, 1980), p. 136.
31 Ibid.
32 J. Harvey, *The Economics of Real Property* (London, 1981), pp. 73–4.
33 N. Smith, 'Toward a theory of gentrification: a back to the city movement

by capital, not people', *Journal of the American Planning Association*, 45 (1979), pp. 538–48.
34   H. Hoyt, *One Hundred Years of Land Values in Chicago* (Chicago, 1933), pp. 356–8.
35   Cannadine, *Social History*, pp. 480–1.
36   Smith, p. 544.
37   E. Lichtenberger, 'The nature of European urbanism', *Geoforum*, 4 (1970), pp. 45–62.
38   Ibid., p. 54.
39   R. Rodger, 'Rents and ground rents: housing and the land market in nineteenth-century Britain', in J. H. Johnson and C. G. Pooley (eds) *The Structure of Nineteenth Century Cities* (London, 1982), pp. 64–7.
40   S. Muthesius, *The English Terraced House* (New Haven, Conn., 1982), pp. 101–42.
41   Lichtenberger, p. 54.
42   Barrows, p. 403.
43   M. P. Conzen, p. 119; J. E. Vance, *This Scene of Man: the role and structure of the city in the geography of Western civilization* (New York, 1977), pp. 245, 265–9.

CHAPTER 7   COMMERCIAL CORES

1   D. H. Aldcroft and P. Fearon, 'Introduction', in D. H. Aldcroft and P. Fearon (eds) *British Economic Fluctuations 1790–1939* (London, 1972), pp. 33–7; J. Schmookler, *Invention and Economic Growth* (Cambridge, Mass., 1966).
2   B. J. L. Berry, 'The economics of land-use intensities in Melbourne, Australia', *Geographical Review*, 64 (1974), pp. 479–97; H. Hoyt, *One Hundred Years of Land Values in Chicago* (Chicago, 1933), pp. 329–37.
3   J. F. Q. Switzer, 'The life of buildings in an expanding economy', *The Chartered Surveyor*, 96 (1963), pp. 74, 76; W. F. Lean and B. Goodall, *Aspects of Land Economics* (London, 1966), p. 190.
4   Hoyt, p. 337.
5   B. Goodall, *The Economics of Urban Areas* (Oxford, 1972), p. 225; Switzer, p. 74; Lean and Goodall, p. 189.
6   J. Rannells, *The Core of the City: a pilot study of changing land uses in central business districts* (New York, 1956), p. 54; J. D. Buissink and D. J. de Widt, 'Some aspects of the development of the shopping-center of the city of Utrecht (The Netherlands)', in University of Amsterdam, Sociographical Department, *Urban Core and Inner City: proceedings of the international study week Amsterdam 1966* (Leiden, 1967), pp. 324–39.

7 A. Sutcliffe, *The Autumn of Central Paris: the defeat of town planning 1850–1970* (London, 1970), p. 331.
8 L. Améen, *Stadsbebyggelse och domänstruktur: Svensk stadsutveckling i relation till ägoförhallånden och administrativa gränser* (Lund, 1964).
9 M. Blacksell, 'Recent changes in the morphology of West German townscapes', in R. W. Beckinsale and J. M. Houston (eds) *Urbanization and its Problems* (Oxford, 1968), pp. 199–217.
10 M. R. G. Conzen, 'The plan analysis of an English city centre', in K. Norborg (ed.) *Proceedings of the IGU Symposium in Urban Geography Lund 1960* (Lund, 1962), pp. 383–414.
11 Corporation of Glasgow, *Glasgow Central Area* (Glasgow, 1975).
12 C. M. Allan, 'The genesis of British urban redevelopment with special reference to Glasgow', *Economic History Review*, 18 (1965), pp. 598–613.
13 A. K. Cairncross, *Home and Foreign Investment 1870–1913* (Cambridge, 1953), p. 20.
14 A. K. Cairncross, 'The economy of Glasgow', in R. Miller and J. Tivy (eds) *The Glasgow Region: a general survey* (Glasgow, 1958), p. 220.
15 E. Farmer and R. Smith, 'Overspill theory: a metropolitan case study', *Urban Studies*, 12 (1975), pp. 151–68.
16 J. W. R. Whitehand, 'Long-term changes in the form of the city centre: the case of redevelopment', *Geografiska Annaler*, 60B (1978), pp. 79–96, provides a detailed analysis of these data.
17 P. Cowan, 'Studies in the growth, change and ageing of buildings', *Transactions of the Bartlett Society*, 1 (1963), pp. 69–70.
18 C. H. Holden and W. G. Holford, *The City of London: a record of destruction and survival* (London, 1951), p. 173.
19 Hoyt, p. 335.
20 M. van Hulten, 'In search of the urban core of Amsterdam', in University of Amsterdam, Sociographical Department', *Urban Core and Inner City: proceedings of the international study week Amsterdam 1966* (Leiden, 1967), p. 193.
21 R. J. Solomon, 'Procedures in townscape analysis', *Annals of the Association of American Geographers*, 56 (1966), p. 263.
22 Leeds City Planning Department, *Leeds 1981: City of Leeds Development Plan* (Leeds, 1968), cited in M. Bateman, 'The nature and process of urban renewal in the central areas of nine towns of West Yorkshire during the post-war period', unpublished PhD thesis, University of Leeds, 1968, p. 404.
23 Hoyt, p. 335.
24 For a statistical analysis, see Whitehand, pp. 87–8.
25 A. Gomme and D. Walker, *Architecture of Glasgow* (London, 1968), pp. 107–8.
26 J. B. Jefferys, *Retail Trading in Britain 1850–1950* (Cambridge, 1954), pp. 1–39.

27 J. McArthur (Surveyor), *Plan of the City of Glasgow* (1778); D. Smith (Surveyor), *Plan of the City of Glasgow and its Environs* (1828).
28 Available in the Glasgow Room of the Mitchell Library, Glasgow. The provenance of this material is not recorded.
29 Gomme and Walker, pp. 191–230.
30 Cairncross, *Home and Foreign Investment*, p. 20.
31 Cairncross, in Miller and Tivy, p. 220.
32 W. Smith, *An Economic Geography of Great Britain* (London, 1949), pp. 690–2.
33 Jefferys, pp. 59, 69.
34 A. H. Halsey (ed.), *Trends in British Society since 1900: a guide to the changing social structure of Britain* (London, 1972), p. 558.
35 Jefferys, p. 61.
36 Board of Trade, *Census of Distribution and Other Services, 1950*, 1 (London, 1953); Board of Trade, *Report on the Census of Distribution and Other Services, 1961*, supplement (London, 1971).
37 G. Eve & Co., *City of Glasgow: report on the central area* (Glasgow, 1965), pp. 43–4.
38 Ibid., pp. 45–6; Corporation of Glasgow, *Glasgow Central Area*, pp. 69–71.
39 R. Johnston, 'Land use changes in the Melbourne CBD, 1857–1962', in P. N. Troy (ed.) *Urban Redevelopment in Australia* (Canberra, 1967), p. 195.
40 D. Sim, *Change in the City Centre* (Aldershot, Hants, 1982), p. 62.
41 P. Ambrose and B. Colenutt, *The Property Machine* (Harmondsworth, Middx, 1975), p. 21; R. Barras, *The Development Cycle in the City of London*, Centre for Environmental Studies Research Series, 36 (London, 1979), pp. 7–18.
42 I. C. Alexander, *The City Centre* (Nedlands, W. Australia, 1974), p. 139.
43 R. L. Davies, *Marketing Geography* (London, 1976), p. 158.
44 G. C. Cameron and A. W. Evans, 'The British conurbation centres', *Regional Studies*, 7 (1973), p. 47–55.
45 West Midlands County Council, *West Midlands County Structure Plan* (Birmingham, 1980), p. 108.
46 City of Liverpool, *Shopping Trends and Opportunities* (Liverpool, 1980), p. 5.
47 Barras, p. 14.
48 Ibid., p. 34; A. Catalano and R. Barras, *Office Development in Central Manchester*, Centre for Environmental Studies Research Series, 37 (London, 1980), p. 72.
49 Barras, p. 95.
50 Ibid., p. 31.
51 R. L. Davies and D. J. Bennison, *British Town Centre Shopping Schemes* (Reading, 1979), p. 228.

52 Ibid., p. 230.
53 J. Allpass and E. Agergaard, 'The city centre – for whom?' in I. Hammarström and T. Hall (eds) *Growth and Transformation of the Modern City* (Stockholm, 1979), pp. 255–7.
54 F. J. C. Amos, 'Liverpool', in J. Holliday (ed.) *City Centre Redevelopment* (London, 1973), p. 190; K. A. Galley, 'Newcastle upon Tyne', in Holliday, p. 219.
55 Amos, p. 190.
56 Allpass and Agergaard, pp. 233–64.
57 Davies, p. 291.
58 R. L. Davies and D. J. Bennison, 'The planning repercussions of in-town shopping schemes', *Estates Gazette*, 246 (1978), p. 118; Allpass and Agergaard, pp. 233–64.
59 Davies and Bennison, *Estates Gazette*, p. 119.
60 Davies, p. 185.
61 Buissink and de Widt, p. 246.
62 Sim, pp. 30–5.
63 Alexander, p. 152.
64 Department of the Environment, Scottish Development Department, Welsh Office, *Housing and Construction Statistics*, part 1 (London, 1972), p. 62; Department of the Environment, Scottish Development Department, Welsh Office, *Housing and Construction Statistics 1969–1979* (London, 1980), p. 6; Department of the Environment, Scottish Development Department, Welsh Office, *Housing and Construction Statistics 1974–1984* (London, 1985), p. 1.
65 I. A. Thompson, personal communication.
66 G. F. Warren and F. A. Pearson, *World Prices and the Building Industry* (New York, 1937) p. 121; J. P. Lewis, *Building Cycles and Britain's Growth* (London, 1965), pp. 335–40.
67 D. J. Bennison and R. L. Davies, 'The impact of town centre shopping schemes in Britain: their impact on traditional retail environments', *Progress in Planning*, 14 (1980), p. 16.
68 Department of the Environment et al., *Housing and Construction Statistics 1969–1979*, p. 6.
69 Barras, p. 41.
70 Ibid., pp. 30–1; R. Barras, *The Returns from Office Development and Investment*, Centre for Environmental Studies Research Series, 35 (London, 1979), p. 49.
71 Barras, *The Returns from Office Development*, p. 51.
72 Barras, *The Development Cycle*, pp. 32–3.
73 L. S. Bourne, *Private Redevelopment of the Central City*, University of Chicago Department of Geography Research Paper, 112 (Chicago, 1967), p. 175.

74 Whitehand, pp. 92–3.
75 J. M. Luffrum, 'The building fabric of the central areas of small towns in rural England: interurban variations and relationships', *Urban Geography*, 2 (1981), pp. 171–3.
76 P. Cowan, D. Fine, J. Ireland, C. Jordan, D. Mercer and A. Sears, *The Office: a facet of growth* (London, 1969), p. 111.
77 P. Hall, *London 2000* (London, 1963), p. 203.
78 Ambrose and Colenutt, p. 21.
79 D. Atwell, *Cathedrals of the Movies* (London, 1980).
80 G. Törnqvist, *TV-ägandets utveckling i Sverige 1956–65* (Stockholm, 1967), p. 224.
81 Jefferys, p. 59.
82 R. Pringle, *A Guide to Banking in Britain* (London, 1975), p. 26.
83 T. Hägerstrand, 'On the Monte Carlo simulation of diffusion', *Archives Européennes de Sociologie*, 6 (1965), pp. 43–67.
84 H. E. Browning and A. A. Sorrell, 'Cinemas and cinema-going in Great Britain', *Journal of the Royal Statistical Society*, series A, 117 (1954), pp. 137–40.
85 Jefferys, p. 197.
86 J. W. R. Whitehand, 'The study of variations in the building fabric of town centres: procedural problems and preliminary findings in southern Scotland', *Transactions of the Institute of British Geographers*, NS 4 (1979), pp. 559–75; J. M. Luffrum, 'Variations in the building fabric of small towns', *Transactions of the Institute of British Geographers*, NS 5 (1980), pp. 170–3; J. M. Luffrum, 'Economic factors and the physical form of the central areas of small towns', unpublished PhD thesis, University of Birmingham, 1979; Luffrum, *Urban Geography*, pp. 161–77.
87 Luffrum, *Urban Geography*, p. 162.

CHAPTER 8   CONCLUSION

1 N. Smith, *Uneven Development: nature, capital and the production of space* (Oxford, 1984), p. 138.
2 A. J. Lotka, *Elements of Physical Biology* (Baltimore, Md, 1925), p. 304.
3 P. L. Knox, 'The social production of the built environment', *Ekistics*, 49 (1982), esp. pp. 292–4.
4 A. Sutcliffe, 'Why planning history?', *Built Environment*, 7 (1981), p. 66.
5 Ibid.
6 J. K. Wilson, Calthorpe Estates Office, personal communication.
7 J. Underwood, 'Development control: a case study of discretion in action', in S. Barrett and C. Fudge (eds) *Policy and Action: essays in the implementation of public policy* (London, 1981), p. 153.

8 M. R. G. Conzen, 'Historical townscapes in Britain: a problem in applied geography', in J. W. House (ed.) *Northern Geographical Essays in Honour of G. H. J. Daysh* (Newcastle upon Tyne, 1966), pp. 56–78; M. R. G. Conzen, 'Geography and townscape conservation', in H. Uhlig and C. Lienau (eds) *Anglo-German Symposium in Applied Geography, Giessen-Würzburg-München, 1973* (Giessen, 1975), pp. 95–102.

9 M. Schwind, 'Kulturlandschaft als objektivierter Geist', *Deutsche geographische Blätter*, 46 (1951), pp. 5–28.

10 Conzen, in Uhlig and Lienau, p. 101.

11 Ibid., pp. 98–102.

Bibliography

Abramovitz, M. 'The nature and significance of Kuznets cycles', *Economic Development and Cultural Change*, 9 (1961), pp. 225–48.
Abramovitz, M. *Evidences of Long Swings in Aggregate Construction since the Civil War* (New York, 1964).
Adams, J. S. 'Residential structure of Midwestern cities', *Annals of the Association of American Geographers*, 60 (1970), pp. 37–62.
Aldcroft, D. H. and Fearon, P. 'Introduction', in Aldcroft, D. H. and Fearon, P. (eds) *British Economic Fluctuations 1790–1939* (London, 1972), pp. 1–73.
Aldcroft, D. H. and Richardson, H. W. *The British Economy 1870–1939* (London, 1969).
Alexander, I. C. *The City Centre* (Nedlands, W. Australia, 1974).
Allan, C. M. 'The genesis of British urban redevelopment with special reference to Glasgow', *Economic History Review*, 18 (1965), pp. 598–613.
Allpass, J. and Agergaard, E. 'The city centre – for whom?' in Hammarström, I. and Hall, T. (eds) *Growth and Transformation of the Modern City* (Stockholm, 1979), pp. 233–64.
Alonso, W. 'A theory of the urban land market', *Papers and Proceedings of the Regional Science Association*, 6 (1960), pp. 149–57.
Alonso, W. *Location and Land Use: toward a general theory of land rent* (Cambridge, Mass., 1964).
Ambrose, P. and Colenutt, B. *The Property Machine* (Harmondsworth, Middx, 1975).
Améen, L. *Stadsbebyggelse och domänstruktur: Svensk stadsutveckling i relation till ägoförhallånden och administrativa gränser* (Lund, 1964).
Amos, F. J. C. 'Liverpool', in Holliday, J. (ed.) *City Centre Redevelopment* (London, 1973), pp. 175–206.
Arbos, Ph. *Étude de géographie urbaine: Clermont-Ferrand* (Clermont-Ferrand, 1930).
Aspinall, P. J. *The Size Structure of the House-building Industry in Victorian Sheffield*, Centre for Urban and Regional Studies University of Birmingham Working Paper 49 (Birmingham, 1977).

Atwell, D. *Cathedrals of the Movies* (London, 1980).
Ball, M. *Housing Policy and Economic Power: the political economy of owner occupation* (London, 1983).
Balmer, K. R. 'Urban open space planning in England and Wales', unpublished PhD thesis, University of Liverpool, 1972.
Barke, M. 'The changing urban fringe of Falkirk: some morphological implications of urban growth', *Scottish Geographical Magazine*, 90 (1974), pp. 85–97.
Barley, M. W. *The House and Home* (London, 1963).
Barras, R. *The Returns from Office Development and Investment*, Centre for Environmental Studies Research Series, 35 (London, 1979).
Barras, R. *The Development Cycle in the City of London*, Centre for Environmental Studies Research Series, 36 (London, 1979).
Barrows, R. G. 'Beyond the tenement: patterns of American urban housing, 1870–1930', *Journal of Urban History*, 9 (1983), pp. 395–420.
Bastian, R. W. 'The Prairie style house: spatial diffusion of a minor design', *Journal of Cultural Geography*, 1 (1980), pp. 50–65.
Bateman, M. 'The nature and process of urban renewal in the central areas of nine towns of West Yorkshire during the post-war period', unpublished PhD thesis, University of Leeds, 1968.
Benevolo, L. *The History of the City* (Cambridge, Mass., 1980).
Bennison, D. J. and Davies, R. L. 'The impact of town centre shopping schemes in Britain: their impact on traditional retail environments', *Progress in Planning*, 14 (1980), pp. 1–104.
Bentley, J. *Illustrated Handbook of the Bradford City Parks, Recreation Grounds and Open Spaces* (Bradford, 1926).
Beresford, M. W. 'The back-to-back house in Leeds, 1787–1937', in Chapman, S. D. (ed.) *The History of Working-class Housing* (Newton Abbot, Devon, 1971), pp. 93–132.
Berry, B. J. L. 'The economics of land-use intensities in Melbourne, Australia', *Geographical Review*, 64 (1974), pp. 479–97.
Blacksell, M. 'Recent changes in the morphology of West German townscapes', in Beckinsale, R. W. and Houston, J. M. (eds) *Urbanization and its Problems* (Oxford, 1968), pp. 199–217.
Blanchard, R. *Grenoble: étude de géographie urbaine* (Paris, 1912).
Board of Trade, *Census of Distribution and Other Services, 1950*, 1 (London, 1953).
Board of Trade, *Report on the Census of Distribution and Other Services, 1961*, supplement (London, 1971).
Bobek, H. 'Grundfragen der Stadtgeographie', *Geographischer Anzeiger*, 28 (1927), pp. 213–24.
Bobek, H. and Lichtenberger, E. *Wien: Bauliche Gestalt und Entwicklung seit der Mitte des 19. Jahrhunderts* (Graz, 1966).

Böhm, H. *Bodenmobilität und Bodenpreisgefüge in ihrer Bedeutung für die Siedlungsentwicklung*, Bonner Geographische Abhandlungen, 65 (Bonn, 1980).
Bourne, L. S. *Private Redevelopment of the Central City*, University of Chicago Department of Geography Research Paper, 112 (Chicago, 1967).
Bournville Village Trust, *When we Build Again* (London, 1941).
Branston, J. G. 'The development of public open spaces in Leeds during the nineteenth century', unpublished MPhil thesis, University of Leeds, 1972.
Brigham, E. F. 'The determinants of residential land values', *Land Economics*, 41 (1965), pp. 325–34.
Browning, H. E. and Sorrell, A. A. 'Cinemas and cinema-going in Great Britain', *Journal of the Royal Statistical Society*, series A, 117 (1954), pp. 133–65.
Builder, The vol. 29, June 3, 1871.
Buissink, J. D. and Widt, D. J. de 'Some aspects of the development of the shopping-center of the city of Utrecht (The Netherlands)', in University of Amsterdam, Sociographical Department, *Urban Core and Inner City: proceedings of the international study week Amsterdam 1966* (Leiden, 1967), pp. 324–39.
Burgess, E. W. 'The growth of the city', in Park, R. E., Burgess, E. W. and McKenzie, R. D., *The City* (Chicago, 1925), pp. 47–62.
Butlin, N. G. 'Some structural features of Australian capital formation 1861 to 1938/39', *The Economic Record*, 35 (1959), pp. 389–415.
Butt, J. 'Working-class housing in Glasgow, 1851–1914', in Chapman, S. D. (ed.) *The History of Working-class Housing* (Newton Abbot, Devon, 1971), pp. 55–92.
Cairncross, A. K. 'The Glasgow building industry (1870–1914)', *The Review of Economic Studies*, 2 (1934), pp. 1–17.
Cairncross, A. K. *Home and Foreign Investment 1870–1913* (Cambridge, 1953).
Cairncross, A. K. 'The economy of Glasgow', in Miller, R. and Tivy, J. (eds) *The Glasgow Region: a general survey* (Glasgow, 1958), pp. 219–41.
Cameron, G. C. and Evans, A. W. 'The British conurbation centres', *Regional Studies*, 7 (1973), pp. 47–55.
Cannadine, D. 'The aristocracy and the towns in the nineteenth century: a case study of the Calthorpes and Birmingham, 1807–1910', unpublished DPhil thesis, University of Oxford, 1975.
Cannadine, D. 'Victorian cities: how different?', *Social History*, 4 (1977), pp. 457–82.
Cannadine, D. 'How much of a mark did aristocratic landowners leave on the Victorian city?', unpublished paper presented to the Annual Conference of the Urban History Group, Swansea, 30–1 March 1979.
Cannadine, D. *Lords and Landlords: the aristocracy and the towns* (Leicester, 1980).
Carter, H. *The Towns of Wales* (Cardiff, 1965).
Carter, H. and Wheatley, S. 'Fixation lines and fringe belts, land uses and social areas: nineteenth-century change in the small town', *Transactions of the Institute of British Geographers*, NS 4 (1979), pp. 214–38.

172 Bibliography

Catalano, A. and Barras, R. *Office Development in Central Manchester*, Centre for Environmental Studies Research Series, 37 (London, 1980).

Chang, S.-D. 'Some observations on the morphology of Chinese walled cities', *Annals of the Association of American Geographers*, 60 (1970), pp. 63–91.

Chapman, S. D. (ed.) *The History of Working-class Housing* (Newton Abbot, Devon, 1971).

Christaller, W. *Die zentralen Orte in Süddeutschland* (Jena, 1933).

City of Birmingham *Annual Abstract of Statistics*, 1 (1951).

City of Liverpool, *Shopping Trends and Opportunities* (Liverpool, 1980).

City of Manchester Recreational Services Department *Leisure, Pleasure and Recreation* (Manchester, n.d.).

Clark, C. 'Urban land use here and abroad', *Journal of the Town Planning Institute*, 52 (1966), pp. 359–64.

Colby, C. C. 'Centrifugal and centripetal forces in urban geography', *Annals of the Association of American Geographers*, 23 (1933), pp. 1–20.

Colean, M. L. *American Housing: problems and prospects* (New York, 1944).

Conzen, M. P. 'Fringe location land uses: relict patterns in Madison, Wisconsin', unpublished paper presented to the Association of American Geographers, West Lakes Division, 19th Annual Meeting, Madison, Wisconsin, 18 October 1968.

Conzen, M. P. 'The morphology of nineteenth-century cities in the United States', in Borah, W., Hardoy, J. and Stelter, G. (eds) *Urbanization in the Americas: the background in comparative perspective* (Ottawa, 1980).

Conzen, M. R. G. 'Towards a systematic approach in planning science: geoproscopy', *Town Planning Review*, 18 (1938), pp. 1–26.

Conzen, M. R. G. 'Modern settlement', in Isaac, P. C. G. and Allan, R. E. A. (eds) *Scientific Survey of North-eastern England* (Newcastle upon Tyne, 1949), pp. 75–83.

Conzen, M. R. G. 'The growth and character of Whitby', in Daysh, G. H. J. (ed.) *A Survey of Whitby and the Surrounding Area* (Eton, 1958), pp. 49–89.

Conzen, M. R. G. *Alnwick, Northumberland: a study in town-plan analysis*, Institute of British Geographers Publication no. 27 (London, 1960).

Conzen, M. R. G. 'The plan analysis of an English city centre', in Norborg, K. (ed.) *Proceedings of the IGU Symposium in Urban Geography Lund 1960* (Lund, 1962), pp. 383–414.

Conzen, M. R. G. 'Historical townscapes in Britain: a problem in applied geography', in House, J. W. (ed.) *Northern Geographical Essays in Honour of G. H. J. Daysh* (Newcastle upon Tyne, 1966), pp. 56–78.

Conzen, M. R. G. 'Geography and townscape conservation', in Uhlig, H. and Lienau, C. (eds) *Anglo-German Symposium in Applied Geography, Giessen-Würzburg-München, 1973* (Giessen, 1975), pp. 95–102.

Conzen, M. R. G. 'Zur Morphologie der englischen Stadt im Industriezeitalter', in Jäger, H. (ed.) *Probleme des Städtewesens im industriellen Zeitalter* (Cologne, 1978), pp. 1–48.

Cooper, B. A. 'Marks and Spencer: a case of induced "diffusion"', unpublished BA dissertation, University of Birmingham, 1977.
Corporation of the City of Glasgow *Municipal Glasgow: its evolution and enterprises* (Glasgow, 1914).
Corporation of Glasgow, *Glasgow Central Area* (Glasgow, 1975).
Cowan, P. 'Studies in the growth, change and ageing of buildings', *Transactions of the Bartlett Society*, 1 (1963), pp. 69–70.
Cowan, P. 'Hospitals in towns: location and siting', *Architectural Review*, 137 (1965), pp. 417–21.
Cowan, P., Fine, D., Ireland, J., Jordan, C., Mercer, D. and Sears, A. *The Office: a facet of growth* (London, 1969).
Croix, H. de la *Military Considerations in City Planning: fortifications* (New York, 1972).
Daly, M. T. *Sydney Boom Sydney Bust: the city and its property market 1850–1981* (Sydney, 1982).
Davies, R. L. *Marketing Geography* (London, 1976).
Davies, R. L. and Bennison, D. J. 'The planning repercussions of in-town shopping schemes', *Estates Gazette*, 246 (1978), pp. 117–21.
Davies, R. L. and Bennison, D. J. *British Town Centre Shopping Schemes* (Reading, 1979).
Davies, W. K. D. 'The morphology of central places: a case study', *Annals of the Association of American Geographers*, 58 (1968), pp. 91–110.
Dent, R. K. *City of Birmingham: history and description of the public parks, gardens and recreation grounds* (Birmingham, 1916).
Department of the Environment *Housing Statistics: Great Britain*, 20 (1971).
Department of the Environment *Housing and Construction Statistics*, 13 (1975).
Department of the Environment *Housing and Construction Statistics*, 28 (1978).
Department of the Environment, Scottish Development Department, Welsh Office, *Housing and Construction Statistics*, part 1 (London, 1972).
Department of the Environment, Scottish Development Department, Welsh Office, *Housing and Construction Statistics 1969–1979* (London, 1980).
Department of the Environment, Scottish Development Department, Welsh Office, *Housing and Construction Statistics 1974–1984* (London, 1985).
Drewett, R. 'Land values and the suburban land market', in Hall, P., Gracey, H., Drewett, R. and Thomas, R. *The Containment of Urban England*, vol. 2 (London, 1973), pp. 197–245.
Dyos, H. J. *Victorian Suburb: a study of the growth of Camberwell* (Leicester, 1961).
Dyos, H. J. and Aldcroft, D. H. *British Transport: an economic survey from the seventeenth century to the twentieth* (Leicester, 1969).
Ellison, T. *The Cotton Trade of Great Britain* (London, 1886).
Evans, A. W. *The Economics of Residential Location* (London, 1973).
Evans, A. W. 'Rent and housing in the theory of urban growth', *Journal of Regional Science*, 15 (1975), pp. 113–25.

Evans, A. W. 'The determination of the price of land', *Urban Studies*, 20 (1983), pp. 119–29.

Eve, G. & Co. *City of Glasgow: report on the central area* (Glasgow, 1965).

Evers, H.-D. 'Urban landownership, ethnicity and class in southeast Asian cities', *International Journal of Urban and Regional Research*, 8 (1984), pp. 481–96.

Farmer, E. and Smith, R. 'Overspill theory: a metropolitan case study', *Urban Studies*, 12 (1975), pp. 151–68.

Feinstein, C. H. *National Income, Expenditure and Output of the United Kingdom 1855–1965* (Cambridge, 1972).

Flaus, L. 'Les fluctuations de la construction d'habitations urbaines', *Journal de la Société de Statistique de Paris*, 90 (1949), pp. 185–221.

Fleure, H. J. 'Some types of cities in temperate Europe', *Geographical Review*, 10 (1920), pp. 357–74.

Forster, C. A. *Court Housing in Kingston upon Hull: an example of cyclic processes in the morphological development of nineteenth-century bye-law housing*, University of Hull Occasional Papers in Geography, no. 19 (Hull, 1972).

Fritz, J. 'Deutsche Stadtanlagen', *Beilage zum Programm 520 des Lyzeums Strassburg* (Strasbourg, 1894).

Galley, K. A. 'Newcastle upon Tyne', in Holliday, J. (ed.) *City Centre Redevelopment* (London, 1973), pp. 207–33.

Garrison, W. L., Berry, B. J. L., Marble, D. F., Nystuen, J. D. and Morrill, R. L. *Studies of Highway Development and Geographic Change* (Seattle, Wash., 1959).

Gauldie, E. *Cruel Habitations: a history of working-class housing 1780–1918* (London, 1974).

Gayler, H. J. 'Land speculation and urban development: contrasts in south-east Essex, 1880–1940', *Urban Studies*, 7 (1970), pp. 21–36.

Geisler, W. *Danzig: ein siedlungsgeographischer Versuch* (Danzig, 1918).

Geisler, W. *Die deutsche Stadt: ein Beitrag zur Morphologie der Kulturlandschaft*, Forschungen zur deutschen Landes- und Volkskunde, 22 (Stuttgart, 1924).

Gomme, A. and Walker, D. *Architecture of Glasgow* (London, 1968).

Goodall, B. 'Some effects of legislation on land values', *Regional Studies*, 4 (1970), pp. 11–23.

Goodall, B. *The Economics of Urban Areas* (Oxford, 1972).

Gottlieb, M. *Long Swings in Urban Development* (New York, 1976).

Granelle, J.-J. *Espace urbain et prix du sol* (Paris, 1970).

Greater London Council, *Northern Kensington*, Survey of London, vol. 37 (London, 1973).

Grebler, L. 'House-building, the business cycle and state intervention: I', *International Labour Review*, 33 (1936), pp. 337–55.

Gruchy, G. F. de 'Some land-value relationships in Brisbane's central business district', *Ekistics*, 233 (1975), pp. 268–70.

Habakkuk, H. J. 'Fluctuations in house-building in Britain and the United States in the nineteenth century', *Journal of Economic History*, 22 (1962), pp. 198–230.

Hägerstrand, T. 'On the Monte Carlo simulation of diffusion', *Archives Européennes de Sociologie*, 6 (1965), pp. 43–67.

Haig, R. M. 'Toward an understanding of the metropolis: II. The assignment of activities to areas in urban regions', *Quarterly Journal of Economics*, 40 (1926), pp. 402–34.

Haig, R. M. *Regional Survey of New York and its Environs* (New York, 1927).

Halbwachs, M. *Les expropriations et le prix des terrains à Paris (1860–1900)* (Paris, 1909).

Hall, P. *London 2000* (London, 1963).

Hallett, G. *Housing and Land Policies in West Germany and Britain* (London, 1977).

Hallett, G. 'The long-term movement of urban land prices', unpublished paper presented to the Centre for Environmental Studies Urban Economics Conference, Manchester, July 1979.

Halsey, A. H. (ed.) *Trends in British Society since 1900: a guide to the changing social structure of Britain* (London, 1972).

Hammarström, I. 'Urban growth and building fluctuations: Stockholm 1860–1920', in Swedish Council for Building Research *Growth and Transformation of the Modern City* (Stockholm, 1979), pp. 29–47.

Harris, C. D. and Ullman, E. L. 'The nature of cities', *Annals of the American Academy of Political and Social Science*, 242 (1945), pp. 7–17.

Hartke, W. 'Die soziale Differenzierung der Agrarlandschaft im Rhein-Main-Gebiet', *Erdkunde* 7 (1953), pp. 13–22.

Hartke, W. 'Die Sozialbrache als Phänomen der geographischen Differenzierung der Landschaft', *Erdkunde*, 10 (1956), pp. 257–69.

Harvey, D. *Social Justice and the City* (London, 1973).

Harvey, D. 'The urban process under capitalism: a framework for analysis', *International Journal of Urban and Regional Research*, 2 (1978), pp. 101–31.

Harvey, J. *The Economics of Real Property* (London, 1981).

Hassinger, H. *Kunsthistorischer Atlas von Wien*, Österreichische Kunsttopographie 15 (Vienna, 1916).

Hawley, A. H. 'Land value patterns in Okayama, Japan, 1940 and 1952', *American Journal of Sociology*, 60 (1955), pp. 487–92.

Hitchcock, H.-R. *Architecture: nineteenth and twentieth centuries* (Harmondsworth, Middx, 1958).

Holden, C. H. and Holford, W. G. *The City of London: a record of destruction and survival* (London, 1951).

Hoyt, H. *One Hundred Years of Land Values in Chicago* (Chicago, 1933).

Hoyt, H. 'The pattern of movement of residential rental neighborhoods', in *The Structure and Growth of Residential Neighborhoods in American Cities*

(Washington, DC, 1939), pp. 112–22, reprinted in Mayer, H. M. and Kohn, C. F. (eds) *Readings in Urban Geography* (Chicago, 1959), pp. 499–510.

Hoyt, H. 'Changing patterns of land values', *Land Economics*, 36 (1960), pp. 109–17.

Hulten, M. van, 'In search of the urban core of Amsterdam', in University of Amsterdam, Sociographical Department, *Urban Core and Inner City: proceedings of the international study week Amsterdam 1966* (Leiden, 1967), pp. 183–200.

Hunter, R. 'The movements for the inclosure and preservation of open lands', *Journal of the Royal Statistical Society*, 60 (1897), pp. 360–427.

Hurd, R. M. *Principles of City Land Values* (New York, 1903).

Ingram, G. K. 'Land in perspective: its role in the structure of cities', in Cullen, M. and Woolery, S. (eds) *World Congress on Land Policy, 1980: proceedings* (Lexington, Mass., 1982), pp. 103–18.

Isard, W. 'Transport development and building cycles', *Quarterly Journal of Economics*, 57 (1942), pp. 90–112.

Isard, W. 'A neglected cycle: the transport-building cycle', *Review of Economic Statistics*, 24 (1942), pp. 149–58.

Isard, W. *Location and Space Economy: a general theory relating to industrial location, market areas, land use, trade and urban structure* (New York, 1956).

Jackson, P. 'Social geography: the rediscovery of place', *Progress in Human Geography*, 10 (1986), pp. 118–24.

Jahn, M. A. 'Railways and suburban development: outer west London 1850–1900', unpublished PhD thesis, University of London, 1971.

Jakle, J. A. 'Twentieth century revival architecture and the gentry', *Journal of Cultural Geography*, 4 (1983), pp. 28–43.

Jefferys, J. B. *Retail Trading in Britain 1850–1950* (Cambridge, 1954).

Johnston, R. 'Land use changes in the Melbourne CBD, 1857–1962', in Troy, P. N. (ed.) *Urban Redevelopment in Australia* (Canberra, 1967).

Johnston, R. and Gaskell, M. 'Building control, building activity and design', unpublished paper presented to the Urban History Group Colloquium on Urban Space and Building Form, London, 21 September 1984.

Johnston, R. J. 'An outline of the development of Melbourne's street pattern', *The Australian Geographer*, 10 (1968), pp. 453–65.

Johnston, R. J. 'Towards an analytical study of the townscape: the residential building fabric', *Geografiska Annaler*, 51B (1969), pp. 20–32.

Johnston, R. J. 'Spatial and temporal variations in land and property prices in New Zealand: 1953–1972', *New Zealand Geographer*, 32 (1976), pp. 30–55.

Jones, P. 'Innovation life-span: the urban tramway', *Area*, 10 (1978), pp. 247–9.

Keene, D. 'Spatial order and discrimination in English towns, A.D. 500–1670', unpublished paper presented to the Urban History Group Colloquium on Urban Space and Building Form, London, 21 September 1984.

Knox, P. L. 'The social production of the built environment', *Ekistics*, 49 (1982), pp. 291–7.
Krings, W. *Innenstädte in Belgien: Gestalt, Veränderung, Erhaltung* Bonner Geographische Abhandlungen, 68 (Bonn, 1984).
Langford, J. A. *Birmingham: a handbook for residents and visitors* (Birmingham, 1879).
Larkham, P. J. 'Review of *The Past is a Foreign Country*', *IBG Urban Geography Study Group Newsletter*, May (1986), pp. 9–12.
Lean, W. F. and Goodall, B. *Aspects of Land Economics* (London, 1966).
Lee, J. S. 'Recreation in Sheffield: development of public open spaces in the nineteenth century', unpublished MA thesis, University of Sheffield, 1974.
Leeds City Planning Department, *Leeds 1981: City of Leeds Development Plan* (Leeds, 1968).
Leighly, J. B. 'The towns of Mälardalen in Sweden: a study in urban morphology', *University of California Publications in Geography*, 3 (1928), pp. 1–134.
Lever, W. F. 'Planning standards', in Forbes, J. (ed.) *Studies in Social Science and Planning* (Edinburgh, 1974), pp. 9–53.
Lewis, J. P. *Building Cycles and Britain's Growth* (London, 1965).
Lichtenberger, E. 'The nature of European urbanism', *Geoforum*, 4 (1970), pp. 45–62.
Lichtenberger, E. *Die Wiener Altstadt: Von der mittelalterlichen Bürgerstadt zur City* (Vienna, 1977).
Lipsey, R. E. and Preston, D. *Source Book of Statistics Relating to Construction* (New York, 1966).
Long, C. D. *Building Cycles and the Theory of Investment* (Princeton, NJ, 1940).
Lotka, A. J. *Elements of Physical Biology* (Baltimore, Md, 1925).
Louis, H. 'Die geographische Gliederung von Gross-Berlin', *Länderkundliche Forschung* Krebs-festschrift, (1936), pp. 146–71.
Luffrum, J. M. 'Economic factors and the physical form of the central areas of small towns', unpublished PhD thesis, University of Birmingham, 1979.
Luffrum, J. M. 'Variations in the building fabric of small towns', *Transactions of the Institute of British Geographers*', NS 5 (1980), pp. 170–3.
Luffrum, J. M. 'The building fabric of the central areas of small towns in rural England: interurban variations and relationships', *Urban Geography*, 2 (1981), pp. 161–77.
McArthur, J. (Surveyor) *Plan of the City of Glasgow* (1778).
Maiwald, K. 'An index of building costs in the United Kingdom, 1845–1938', *Economic History Review*, 7 (1954), pp. 187–203.
Markusen, J. R. and Scheffman, D. T. 'Ownership concentration and market power in urban land markets', *Review of Economic Studies*, 45 (1978), pp. 519–26.
Marshall, A. *Principles of Economics*, vol. 1 (London, 5th edn, 1907).

Martiny, R. *Die Grundrissgestaltung der deutschen Siedlungen*, Petermanns Mitteilungen, Supplement, 197 (Gotha, 1928).

Mayer, H. M. and Wade, R. C. *Chicago: growth of a metropolis* (Chicago, 1969).

Mills, E. S. 'The value of urban land', in Perloff, H. S. (ed.), *The Quality of the Urban Environment* (Baltimore, Md, 1969), pp. 231–53.

Mitchell, B. R. and Deane, P. *Abstract of British Historical Statistics* (Cambridge, 1962).

Mohan, R. and Villamizar, R. 'The evolution of land values in the context of rapid urban growth: a case study of Bogotá and Cali, Colombia', in Cullen, M. and Woolery, S. (eds) *World Congress on Land Policy, 1980: proceedings* (Lexington, Mass., 1982), p. 217–53.

Möller, I. *Die Entwicklung eines Hamburger Gebietes von der Agrar- zur Groszstadtlandschaft: mit einem Beitrag zue Methode der Städtischen Aufrissanalyse*, Hamburger Geographische Studien, 10 (Hamburg, 1959).

Möller, I. 'Review of *Alnwick, Northumberland: a study in town plan analysis, Petermanns Geographische Mitteilungen*, 108 (1964), pp. 112–13.

Morrill, R. L. 'The shape of diffusion in space and time', *Economic Geography*, 46 (1970), pp. 259–68.

Morris, A. E. J. *History of Urban Form: before the industrial revolution* (London, 1979).

Murphy, R. E. 'Johnstown and York: a comparative study of two industrial cities', *Annals of the Association of American Geographers*, 25 (1935), pp. 175–96.

Muth, R. F. 'The demand for non-farm housing', in Harberger, A. C. (ed.) *The Demand for Durable Goods* (Chicago, 1960), pp. 29–96.

Muth, R. F. *Cities and Housing* (Chicago, 1969).

Muthesius, S. *The English Terraced House* (New Haven, Conn. 1982).

Needleman, L. *The Economics of Housing* (London, 1965).

Newman, W. H. *The Building Industry and Business Cycles* (Chicago, 1935).

Niedercorn, J. H. and Hearle, E. F. R. *Recent Land-use Trends in Forty-eight Large American Cities* RAND Corporation Memorandum RM-3664-FF (Santa Monica, Calif., 1963).

Offer, A. *Property and Politics 1870–1914: landownership, law, ideology and urban development in England* (Cambridge, 1981).

Onions, C. T. (ed.) *The Shorter Oxford English Dictionary* (Oxford, 1950).

Openshaw, S. 'Processes in urban morphology with special reference to South Shields', unpublished PhD thesis, University of Newcastle upon Tyne, 1974.

Pannell, C. W. 'City morphology in T'ai-wan: a variation on a Chinese theme', *Proceedings of the Association of American Geographers*, 5 (1973), pp. 210–16.

Parkes, D. and Thrift, N. *Times, Spaces, and Places: a chronogeographic perspective* (Chichester, Sussex, 1980).

Pevsner, N. *An Outline of European Architecture* (Harmondsworth, Middx, 1963).

Pinchemel, P. 'Geographers and the city: a contribution to the history of urban geography in France', in Patten, J. (ed.) *The Expanding City: essays in honour of Jean Gottmann* (London, 1983), pp. 295–318.
Polensky, T. *Die Bodenpreise in Stadt und Region München*, Münchner Studien zur Sozial- und Wirtschaftsgeographie, vol. 10 (Kallmünz, 1974).
Post Office *Glasgow Directory for 1899–1900* (Glasgow, 1899).
Pringle, R. *A Guide to Banking in Britain* (London, 1975).
Quinn, J. A. *Human Ecology* (New York, 1950).
Randall, F. A. *History of the Development of Building Construction in Chicago* (Chicago, 1949).
Rannells, J. *The Core of the City: a pilot study of changing land uses in central business districts* (New York, 1956).
Ratcliff, R. U. *Urban Land Economics* (New York, 1949).
Richardson, H. W. and Aldcroft, D. H. *Building in the British Economy between the Wars* (London, 1968).
Richmond, D. *Notes on Municipal Work from November 1896 to November 1899* (Glasgow, n.d.).
Rickert, J. E. 'House facades of the northeastern United States; a tool of geographic analysis', *Annals of the Association of American Geographers*, 57 (1967), pp. 211–38.
Rodger, R. 'Rents and ground rents: housing and the land market in nineteenth-century Britain', in Johnson, J. H. and Pooley, C. G. (eds), *The Structure of Nineteenth Century Cities* (London, 1982), pp. 39–74.
Rodger, R. G. 'Scottish urban housebuilding 1870–1914', unpublished PhD thesis, University of Edinburgh, 1976.
Rodger, R. G. 'The building cycle and the urban fringe in Victorian cities: another comment', *Journal of Historical Geography*, 5 (1979), pp. 72–8.
Rodger, R. G. 'Speculative builders and the structure of the Scottish building industry, 1860–1914', *Business History*, 21 (1979), pp. 226–46.
Rowley, G. 'Landownership in the spatial growth of towns: a Sheffield example', *East Midland Geographer*, 6 (1975), pp. 200–13.
Sabelberg, E. *Reginale Stadttypen in Italien*, Erdkundlichen Wissens, Geographische Zeitschrift, Supplement, 66 (Wiesbaden, 1984).
Samuels, I. 'Urban morphology in developed countries', unpublished paper, Joint Centre for Urban Design, Oxford Polytechnic, 1985.
Saul, S. B. 'House building in England 1890–1914', *Economic History Review*, 2nd series, 15 (1962), pp. 119–37.
Schaefer, G. *Kunstgeographische Siedlungslandschaften und Städtebilder: Studien im Gebiet zwischen Strassburg-Bern-Dijon-Freiburg i. Br.* (Basle, 1928).
Scharlau, K. *Siedlung und Landschaft im Knüllgebiet* (Leipzig, 1941).
Schlüter, O. 'Bemerkungen zur Siedlungsgeographie', *Geographische Zeitschrift*, 5 (1899), pp. 65–84.
Schmookler, J. *Invention and Economic Growth* (Cambridge, Mass., 1966).

Bibliography

Schwind, M. 'Kulturlandschaft als objektivierter Geist', *Deutsche geographische Blätter*, 46 (1951), pp. 5–28.

Sheppard, F. H. W. (ed.) *Survey of London*, 40, The Grosvenor Estate and Mayfair, part 2 (London, 1980).

Sim, D. *Change in the City Centre* (Aldershot, Hants, 1982).

Singer, H. W. 'An index of urban land rents and house rents in England and Wales 1845–1913', *Econometrica*, 9 (1941), pp. 221–30.

Slater, T. R. 'Family, society and the ornamental villa on the fringe of English country towns', *Journal of Historical Geography*, 4 (1978), pp. 129–44.

Slater, T. R. 'Medieval new town and port: a plan-analysis of Hedon, east Yorkshire', *Yorkshire Archaeological Journal*, 57 (1985), pp. 23–41.

Smailes, A. E. 'Some reflections on the geographical description and analysis of townscapes', *Transactions of the Institute of British Geographers*, 21 (1955), pp. 99–115.

Smith, D. (Surveyor) *Plan of the City of Glasgow and its Environs* (1828).

Smith, N. 'Toward a theory of gentrification: a back to the city movement by capital, not people', *Journal of the American Planning Association*, 45 (1979), pp. 538–48.

Smith, N. 'Gentrification and uneven development', *Economic Geography*, 58 (1982), pp. 139–55.

Smith, N. *Uneven Development: nature, capital and the production of space* (Oxford, 1984).

Smith, R. 'Multi-dwelling building in Scotland, 1750–1970: a study based on housing in the Clyde valley', in Sutcliffe, A. (ed.) *Multi-storey Living* (London, 1974), pp. 207–43.

Smith, W. *An Economic Geography of Great Britain* (London, 1949).

Solomon, R. J. 'Procedures in townscape analysis', *Annals of the Association of American Geographers*, 56 (1966), pp. 254–68.

Spencer, J. E. 'Changing Chungking: the rebuilding of an old Chinese city', *Geographical Review*, 29 (1939), pp. 46–60.

Spencer, J. E. 'The houses of the Chinese', *Geographical Review*, 37 (1947), pp. 254–73.

Spensley, J. C. 'Urban housing problems', *Journal of the Royal Statistical Society*, 81 (1918), pp. 161–228.

Springett, J. 'Landowners and urban development: the Ramsden Estate and nineteenth-century Huddersfield', *Journal of Historical Geography*, 8 (1982), pp. 129–44.

Steinbrück, C. *Die Entwicklelung der Preise des Städtischen und Ländlichen Immobiliarbesitzes zu Halle (Saale) und im Saalkreise* (Jena, 1901).

Stewig, R. 'Bemerkungen zur Entstehung des orientalischen Sackgassengrundrisses am Beispiel der Stadt Istanbul', *Mitteilungen der Österreichischen Geographischen Gesellschaft*, 108 (1966), pp. 25–47.

Stone, P. A. 'The price of sites for residential building', *Estates Gazette*, 189

(1964), pp. 85–91.
Sutcliffe, A. *The Autumn of Central Paris: the defeat of town planning 1850–1970* (London, 1970).
Sutcliffe, A. 'Introduction', in Sutcliffe, A. (ed.) *Multi-storey Living* (London, 1974), pp. 1–18.
Sutcliffe, A. 'Why planning history?', *Built Environment*, 7 (1981), pp. 65–7.
Sutcliffe, A. 'Review of *The Urban Landscape: historical development and management*', *Journal of Historical Geography*, 9 (1983), pp. 77–9.
Switzer, J. F. Q. 'The life of buildings in an expanding economy', *The Chartered Surveyor*, 96 (1963), pp. 70–7.
Thomas, B. *Migration and Economic Growth: a study of Great Britain and the Atlantic economy* (Cambridge, 1973).
Thomas, D. 'London's Green Belt: the evolution of an idea', *Geographical Journal* 129 (1963), pp. 14–24.
Thompson, F. M. L. *Hampstead: building a borough, 1650–1964* (London, 1974).
Thünen, J. H. von *Der Isolierte Staat in Beziehung auf Landwirtschaft und Nationalökonomie* (Rostock, 1826).
Tomlinson, M. 'The City of Birmingham: secular architecture', in Stephens, W. B. (ed.) *A History of the County of Warwick*, 7 (London, 1964), pp. 43–57.
Törnqvist, G. *TV-ägandets utveckling i Sverige 1956–65* (Stockholm, 1967).
Treble, J. H. 'Liverpool working-class housing, 1801–51', in Chapman, S. D. (ed.) *The History of Working-class Housing* (Newton Abbot, Devon, 1971), pp. 165–220.
Turvey, R. *The Economics of Real Property* (London, 1957).
Underwood, J. 'Development control: a case study of discretion in action', in Barrett, S. and Fudge, C. (eds) *Policy and Action: essays in the implementation of public policy* (London, 1981), pp. 143–61.
Vallis, E. A. 'Urban land and building prices 1892–1969: I', *Estates Gazette*, 222 (1972), pp. 1015–19.
Vance, J. E. *The Scene of Man: the role and structure of the city in the geography of Western civilization* (New York, 1977).
Voight, P. *Grundrente und Wohnungsfrage in Berlin und seinen Vororten* (Jena, 1901).
Ward, D. 'The pre-urban cadaster and the urban pattern of Leeds', *Annals of the Association of American Geographers*, 52 (1962), pp. 150–66.
Warner, S. B. *Streetcar Suburbs: the process of growth in Boston, 1870–1900* (Cambridge, Mass., 1962).
Warren, G. F. and Pearson, F. A. *World Prices and the Building Industry* (New York, 1937).
Weber, A. *Über Bodenrente und Bodenspekulation in der modernen Stadt* (Leipzig, 1904).
West Midlands County Council, *West Midlands County Structure Plan* (Birmingham, 1980).

White, B. D. *A History of the Corporation of Liverpool 1835–1914* (Liverpool, 1951).

Whitehand, J. W. R. 'The settlement morphology of London's cocktail belt', *Tijdschrift voor Economische en Sociale Geografie*, 58 (1967), pp. 20–7.

Whitehand, J. W. R. 'Fringe belts: a neglected aspect of urban geography', *Transactions of the Institute of British Geographers*, 41 (1967), pp. 223–33.

Whitehand, J. W. R. 'Building cycles and the spatial pattern of urban growth', *Transactions of the Institute of British Geographers*, 56 (1972), pp. 39–55.

Whitehand, J. W. R. 'Urban-rent theory, time series and morphogenesis: an example of eclecticism in geographical research', *Area*, 4 (1972), pp. 215–22.

Whitehand, J. W. R. 'The changing nature of the urban fringe: a time perspective', in Johnson, J. H. (ed.) *Suburban Growth: geographical processes at the edge of the Western city* (London, 1974), pp. 31–52.

Whitehand, J. W. R. 'Building activity and intensity of development at the urban fringe: the case of a London suburb in the nineteenth century', *Journal of Historical Geography*, 1 (1975), pp. 211–24.

Whitehand, J. W. R. 'The basis for an historico-geographical theory of urban form', *Transactions of the Institute of British Geographers*, NS 2 (1977), pp. 400–16.

Whitehand, J. W. R. 'Long-term changes in the form of the city centre: the case of redevelopment', *Geografiska Annaler*, 60B (1978), pp. 79–96.

Whitehand, J. W. R. 'The building cycle and the urban fringe in Victorian cities: a reply', *Journal of Historical Geography*, 4 (1978), pp. 175–91.

Whitehand, J. W. R. 'The study of variations in the building fabric of town centres: procedural problems and preliminary findings in southern Scotland', *Transactions of the Institute of British Geographers*, NS 4 (1979), pp. 559–75.

Whitehand, J. W. R. 'Fluctuations in the land-use composition of urban development during the industrial era', *Erdkunde*, 35 (1981), pp. 129–40.

Whitehand, J. W. R. 'Background to the urban morphogenetic tradition', in Whitehand, J. W. R. (ed.) *The Urban Landscape: historical development and management*, Institute of British Geographers Special Publication no. 13 (London, 1981), pp. 1–24.

Whitehand, J. W. R. 'Conzenian ideas: extension and development', in Whitehand, J. W. R. (ed.) *The Urban Landscape: historical development and management*, Institute of British Geographers Special Publication no. 13 (London, 1981), pp. 127–52.

Whitehand, J. W. R. 'Land-use structure, built-form and agents of change', in Davies, R. L. and Champion, A. G. (eds) *The Future for the City Centre*, Institute of British Geographers Special Publication no. 14 (London, 1983), pp. 41–59.

Whitehand, J. W. R. *Rebuilding Town Centres: developers, architects and styles*, University of Birmingham Department of Geography Occasional Publication, no. 19 (Birmingham, 1984).

Whitehand, J. W. R. 'Urban Geography: the city as a place', *Progress in Human Geography*, 9 (1985), pp. 85–98.
Whitehand, J. W. R. 'Taking stock of urban geography', *Area*, 18 (1986), pp. 147–51.
Wieand, K. and Muth, R. F. 'A note on the variation of land values with distance from the CBD in St Louis', *Journal of Regional Science*, 12 (1972), pp. 469–73.
Williams, M. 'The parkland towns of Australia and New Zealand', *Geographical Review* 56 (1966), pp. 67–89.
Wirth, L. 'A bibliography of the urban community', in Park, R. E., Burgess, E. W. and McKenzie, R. D. *The City* (Chicago, 1925), p. 203.
Yeates, M. H. 'Some factors affecting the spatial distribution of Chicago land values, 1910–1960', *Economic Geography*, 41 (1965), pp. 57–70.

Index

Alnwick, Northumberland: a study in town-plan analysis (1960) 6, 65
architecture
  building cycles and 64
  legislation and 61, 62, 70, 132
see also buildings
Australia, building cycles in 17ff

banks 134
bazaars 63
belts
  fringe 76–94: boundary adjustments of 84–5, 143; building cycles and 77–8, 83, 85; capital investment in 89–92, 161n; commercial core and 84; flexibility of development in 103; formation of 77–83; history of concept of 76–8; housebuilding and 85–90; institutional use of 88–93, 161n; land-ownership and development in 102–3; land-uses of 79ff (in Glasgow 45–50, 59, 69, 83, 85–90, 93, 152n; land-values and 43–4); land-values of 68–9 (in Glasgow 69; land-uses and 43–4); modification of 83–93; 142; plot size in 81; redevelopment in 84; rent-theory and 85, 88ff; role of, during change 76; social areas and 94
  green 71–3, 78–9: history of 71–2; land-values and 72–3; modern 72–3; rent theory and 72–3
  parkland 78–9
bid-rent *see under* rent

boundaries
  fringe-belt 84–5, 143
  urban, age of 142
bricks, production of 13
Britain *see* United Kingdom
building cycles *see under* cycles
buildings 2
  age of 89–91
  fabric of, changing 129–30, 134–7, 141: innovation and 60–70, 132–3, 139, 144
  for retailing 115: lifespan of, in commercial core 117–19, 125–7
  users of, changing 141
  see also architecture; cycles, building; housing; legislation, building
burgages 7, 104
  see also plots

capital investment *see* investment, capital
capitalism, and the study of urban morphology 8, 9
car parks, multi-storey 133
CBD *see* cores, commercial
cinemas 114, 122, 123, 133, 134
communications, and townscape changes 123
compulsory purchase legislation 73
Conzen, M. R. G. ix, 2, 5–7, 65, 146
cores, commercial 112–36
  building fabric changes in 129–30
  expansion of 112, 124
  floor-space changes in 114
  fringe-belts and 84

Index 185

functional change in 114–15, 124–5, 127–9
  in Glasgow 115–27, 132
  innovation diffusion and 113, 122ff, 132ff
  in small towns 134–7
  inter-urban variations in 133–7
  land-use of 124, 127–9
  land-value changes in 69
  'neighbourhood effect' and 132, 134
  planning and 115, 132
  plot changes in 113
  population size and 112–13, 133, 134–7
  redevelopment of 113–27: fluctuations in 130–2; transport and 130
  see also offices; retailing
costs, building, and land values 41
credit, and building cycles 16
culture, and urban landscape 138–9, 145–6
cycles
  building 11–26, 141: architectural style and 64; building legislation and 61, 62, 70; building patents and 61, 62, 63; commercial-core 130–2; credit and 16; explanations for 12–16, 26–9; fringe-belt 77–8, 83, 85; house-type and 95–9; in Glasgow 83, 85–90; innovation and 61–70; in retailing 63–4; in United Kingdom 13–15, 17ff; in United States 17ff; land-values and 38–9; morphology and 65–6; office 131–2; parks and 19, 22–5, 67; patents and 61ff; residential areas and 95–9; transport innovation and 61ff, 67–70, 139, 144
  burgage 7, 104
  life: housing needs and 93–4; of landowners, and urban development 59
  planning 141–2
  plot-size 102

density, residential *see under* housing
department stores 63, 122, 134
development, residential 15ff, 95–111
  building cycles and 95–9
  building legislation and 61
  flexibility of 103
  fringe-belts and 85–90
  in Glasgow 45–50, 85–90
  in northern Kensington 52–8, 59
  land-ownership and 99–103
  land-values and 42
  later changes to 104–7
  location of industry and 59
  morphological periods and 65
  plot-size and 51–9
  rent-theory and 42–4, 85
  see also housing; tenements; villas, ornamental
development, urban 11–29
  control of 144
  culture and 138–9, 145–6
  density of 51–8; building innovation and 70; controls of 71–3, 132; green belts and 71–3; in Glasgow 74; in Scotland 74; transport innovations and 74
  flexibility of 103
  fluctuations in 11–26; explanations for 26–9; land values and 38–9; measures of 11
  in Glasgow 45–50, 59, 74
  innovation and 60–70, 139, 144
  landowners' life-cycle and 59
  leases and 143–4
  management of 144–6
  model of 39–44
  in northern Kensington 52–8, 59
  planning and 70–3
  society and 59, 145–6
  unevenness of 141
  see also belts, fringe; cores, commercial; cycles, building; development, residental; retailing
diffusion *see under* innovation

East Anglia, small town centres in 134–7
economics
  building cycles and 12ff
  innovation adoption and 74–5
  urban morphology and 8–9, 10

186 Index

evolution, urban 6

fabric, urban *see* buildings
floor-space
　commercial-core 114
　plot-size and 51ff
fringe, urban *see* belts, fringe

garden cities 74
geography
　cultural 8
　historical 7
Glasgow
　building cycles in 83, 85–90
　commercial core of 115–27, 132
　housebuilding in 45–50, 85–90
　institution-building in 45–50, 59, 88–9
　land transactions in 25–6, 27
　rent theory and 45–50
　retailing development in 121ff
　urban densities in 74
　urban fringe land-use in 45–50, 59, 83, 85–90
gradients, land-value 68–9
green belts *see* belts, green

hierarchy, urban
　building fabric change and 134–7
　commercial core and 133ff
　tenements within the 109–10
history, urban 4, 8–9
housebuilding *see* development, residential
housing
　density of 110: changes in 140, 142; land values and 35, 109–10; parks and 19, 22–5, 67; patents and 61ff
　type of 95–9: building cycles and 95–9; inter-urban variations in 107–10; land ownership and 99–103
　see also development, residential; tenements; villas, ornamental

industry, housing location and 59
innovation 60–75
　adoption of: economic factors and 74–5; population size and 67
　building cycles and 61–70
　commercial cores and 122ff, 132–3, 134–7
　diffusion of 10, 109–11: commercial cores and 113, 122ff, 132ff; urban change and 139–40
　high-rise development and 70
　land-use change and 29
　planning as 70–3, 144
　recreational 67
　technical 132–3
　townscape and 122ff
　transport, and building cycles 61ff, 67–10
　types of 60
　urban development and 60–70, 139, 144
institutions
　building of, in Glasgow 45–50, 59, 88–9
　land-values and 42–4, 143
　rent-theory and 43–4
　space needs of 88–93, 161n
investment, capital
　changes in 142–3
　fringe-belts and 89–92, 161n
　land-use and 12ff, 26–9, 39–44, 140

Kensington, northern
　development of 52–8, 59
　rent theory and 52–8

land-ownership
　fringe-belt development and 102–3
　residential development and 99–103
landscape, urban
　changing composition of 16–26, 140
　classification of 9
　culture and 138–9, 145–6
　fringe-belt 81
　importance of 145–6
　land-values and 34–5
　planning and 141–7
　rates of change in 140ff
　role of, during change 76
　society and 59, 145–6
　see also land-use, urban; morphology, urban; townscape

Index 187

land-use, urban 30–59
  capital investment and 12ff, 26–9, 39–44: rates of change in 140
  change in 16–26, 124, 127–9: explanations for 26–9
  commercial core 124, 127–9: of Glasgow 115–27, 132
  empirical patterns of 34–6
  fringe-belt 43–4, 79ff; of Glasgow 45–50, 59, 69, 83, 85–90, 93, 152n
  land values and 30–59, 69
  maps of 144
  plot size and 51–8
  rent theory and 30–3, 42–4
  urban fringe 43–4: of Glasgow 45–50
  see also development, residential; retailing
land-values, urban 30–59
  building costs and 41
  building cycles and 38–9
  building density and 35, 71, 108ff
  capital-intensive development and 39–44
  commercial core 69
  change through time of 36–9, 68–9
  empirical patterns of 33–4
  fringe-belt 43–4, 68–9
  gradients of 68–9
  green belts and 72–3
  house-building and 42–4
  importance of 138–40
  institution-building and 42–4, 143
  land-use and 30–59, 69
  plot size and 51–8
  in Scotland 109
  theories of 30–3
  transport and 32–3, 67–8
  urban fringe 68–9
  urban landscape and 34–5
  see also rent
leases, and urban renewal rates 143–4
legislation
  building: building density and 71–3, 132; building design and 61, 62, 70, 132; green-belts and 71–3; housebuilding cycles and 61; offices and 124, 131

  compulsory purchase 73
  rent 73
  see also planning
life-cycle
  housing needs and 93–4
  of landowners, and urban development 59
London
  GLC survey of 9
  see also Kensington, northern

maps
  land-use 144
  topographical, morphological limitations of 4
  'Town' 144
  see also plans, large-scale
Marks and Spencer 63–4
model, von Thunen 30ff
monopoly, rent 31–3
morphology, urban 1–10, 148n
  building cycles and 65–6
  evolutionary approach to 6
  justification for 2
  research traditions in 2–10: American 8; British 5–8, 9–10; Central European 3–5, 76–7; Conzenian ix, 2, 5–7, 9–10, 77–8
  see also landscape, urban; townscape

'neighbourhood effect', in central redevelopment 132, 134

offices
  building cycles of 131–2
  growth of 124, 127–8
  legislation and 124, 131
  redevelopment of, in Glasgow 121ff
  space per worker in 132–3

parkland 78–9
parks, and building cycles 19, 22–5, 67
patents, building, and building cycles 61ff
planning 70–5
  commercial core and 115, 132
  cyclical nature of 141–2

as development control 144
fashions in 132
historicity of townscape and 146–7
history of 4, 71
as innovation 70–3, 144
institutions in Glasgow and 45–6
process of 144
see also legislation
plans, large-scale, use of
in studies of land-use 34–5
in studies of urban morphology 4, 6
see also maps, topographical
plots
changes to 113
changes within 104–5
legacy of 142
size of: cyclical variation in 102; floor-space and 51ff; in fringe-belts 81; land use patterns and 51–8
see also burgages
population size
building cycles and 16
building fabric change and 134–7
effect on commercial core of 112–13, 133, 134–7
recreational innovation and 67

recreation, facilities for
building cycles and 19–20, 22–5, 152n
innovation adoption and 67
redevelopment
commercial core 113–27, 130–2, 134: fluctuations in 130–2; in Glasgow 115–27, 132
comprehensive 132, 145
fringe-belt 84
leases and 143–4
office, in Glasgow 121ff
rent
bid- 42–4; *see also* rent, theory of
control of 73
land-use and 30–3, 42–4
monopoly 31–3
residential development and 101
theory of 10, 42–4, 51: applied to Glasgow 45–50; applied to northern Kensington 52–8; fringe belts and 85, 88ff; green belts and 72–3; institutional building and 43–4; land-use and 42–4, 85; limitations of 58–9
see also land-values
retailing
building-cycles and 63–4
building requirements of 115
historical development of 134ff: in Glasgow 121ff; in Scotland 134
recent changes in 127, 128–9, 132
see also stores

Scotland
cinema provision in 134
land transaction records of 25–6
land-values in 109
retailing development in 134
small town centres in 134–7
tenements in 109
urban densities in 74
see also Glasgow
shopping *see* retailing
skyscrapers, distribution of 139
slums, clearance of 144–5
social areas, and fringe-belts 94
society, and urban landscape 145–6
stores
department 63, 122, 134
Marks and Spencer 63–4
multiple 63–4, 122, 123, 128
variety 63, 122, 123, 128, 134
see also retailing
streets, persistence of 140–1

technology, building, and high-rise development 70
tenements 108–10
townscape 2, 6
cultural factors and 138–9, 145–6
importance of 145–6
innovation and 122ff
management of 5, 146–7
see also landscape, urban; morphology, urban
transport
commercial core redevelopment and 130

innovations in: building cycles and 61ff, 67–70, 139, 144; garden cities and 74; urban density and 74
land-values and 32–3, 67–8

United Kingdom
  building cycles in 13–15, 17ff
see also Scotland
United States, building cycles in 17ff
urban development *see* development, urban
urban fabric *see* buildings
'urban fallow' 7
urban morphology *see* morphology, urban
urban rent theory *see under* rent

variety stores 63, 122, 123, 128, 134
villas, ornamental 93–4
von Thunen model 30ff

warehouses 121
Whitby, A Survey of (1958) 5–6

Related Titles: List of IBG Special Publications

1. Land Use and Resource: Studies in Applied Geography (*A memorial to Dudley Stamp*)
2. A Geomorphological Study of Post-Glacial Uplift
   John T. Andrews
3. Slopes: Form and Process
   D. Brunsden
4. Polar Geomorphology
   R. J. Price and D. E. Sugden
5. Social Patterns in Cities
   B. D. Clark and M. B. Gleave
6. Fluvial Processes in Instrumented Watersheds: Studies of Small Watersheds in the British Isles
   K. J. Gregory and D. E. Walling
7. Progress in Geomorphology: Papers in Honour of David L. Linton
   Edited by E. H. Brown and R. S. Waters
8. Inter-regional Migration in Tropical Africa
   I. Masser and W. T. S. Gould with the assistance of A. D. Goddard
9. Agrarian Landscape Terms: A Glossary for Historical Geography
   I. H. Adams
10. Change in the Countryside: Essays on Rural England 1500–1900
    Edited by H. S. A. Fox and R. A. Butlin
11. The Shaping of Southern England
    Edited by David K. C. Jones
12. Social Interaction and Ethnic Segregation
    Edited by Peter Jackson and Susan J. Smith
13. The Urban Landscape: Historical Development and Management (*Papers by M. R. G. Conzen*)
    Edited by J. W. R. Whitehand
14. The Future for the City Centre
    Edited by R. L. Davies and A. G. Champion

15 Redundant Spaces in Cities and Regions? Studies in Industrial Decline and Social Change
    Edited by J. Anderson, S. Duncan and R. Hudson
16 Shorelines and Isostasy
    Edited by D. E. Smith and A. G. Dawson
17 Residential Segregation, the State and Constitutional Conflict in American Urban Areas
    R. J. Johnston
18 River Channels: Environment and Process
    Edited by Keith Richards
19 Technical Change and Industrial Policy
    Edited by Keith Chapman and Graham Humphrys
20 Sea-level Changes
    Edited by Michael J. Tooley and Ian Shennan
21 The Changing Face of Cities: A Study of Development Cycles and Urban Form
    J. W. R. Whitehand
22 Atlas of Drought in Britain
    Edited by J. C. Doornkamp and K. J. Gregory

IN PREPARATION FOR THE IBG

Salt Marshes and Coastal Wetlands
Edited by D. R. Stoddart
Demographic Patterns in the Past
Edited by Richard Smith
Wetlands and Wetland Management
Edited by Michael Williams
Teaching Geography in Higher Education
Alan Jenkins, John R. Gold, Roger Lee, Janice Monk, Judith Riley, Ifan Shepherd, David Unwin